Improving Teacher Evaluation Systems

Making the Most of Multiple Measures

EDITED BY

Jason A. Grissom
Peter Youngs

TEACHERS COLLEGE PRESS
TEACHERS COLLEGE | COLUMBIA UNIVERSITY
NEW YORK AND LONDON

Published by Teachers College Press, 1234 Amsterdam Avenue, New York, NY 10027

Library of Congress Cataloging-in-Publication Data is available at loc.gov

ISBN 978-0-8077-5739-0 (paper)
ISBN 978-0-8077-5740-6 (hardcover)
ISBN 978-0-8077-7450-2 (ebook)

Printed on acid-free paper
Manufactured in the United States of America

23 22 21 20 19 18 17 16 8 7 6 5 4 3 2 1

Contents

CHAPTER 1

Making the Most of Multiple Measures

Jason A. Grissom
Peter Youngs

Teacher evaluation has become serious business. The days of principals hastily completing a teacher evaluation checklist based on one or two short observations and marking everyone *satisfactory* are vanishing in most school districts. Indeed, increased efforts to hold teachers accountable for their performance via multiple measures of their impacts on their students and schools have been among the most important education policy shifts of the last decade. Spurred by the Obama administration's Race to the Top program and its requirements for state waivers from No Child Left Behind, and, in some cases, investment from the Bill and Melinda Gates Foundation and other philanthropies, many states and districts have implemented evaluation systems that combine statistical estimates of teachers' impacts on student achievement (e.g., "value-added" measures) with scores from newly designed rubric-based observation protocols, feedback from student surveys, and other metrics to produce more comprehensive measures of teacher performance than have ever been available before.

The ability to gather more, more rigorous, and more specific information about teacher performance would seem to be an unequivocally positive policy development, given the potential of this information to inform and improve all kinds of school decisions, from how to target supports for teacher development to which teachers should be hired or dismissed to how teachers are compensated. As these systems take hold, though, teachers, administrators, researchers, and policymakers are raising important questions about the measures these systems rely on, what uses of those measures are appropriate or inappropriate, and how new teacher evaluation systems are—and are not—changing teacher practice, school leader decisionmaking, and the culture of schools. In addition, multiple-measures-based teacher evaluation systems have ignited substantial controversy.

Systems to collect, manage, analyze, and report evaluation data cost schools substantial money and time. Value-added measures, which use statistical techniques to calculate teachers' impacts on student achievement growth, have been attacked as biased and misleading. New observation systems have been rolled out in many places with insufficient training for raters and too little attention to ensuring fidelity to instruments and protocols, with some educators raising concerns that they provide information no more useful than what was provided previously. The use of student surveys has been derided by many teachers worried either that students cannot answer them appropriately—a big concern for teachers of younger students—or that they will simply be used as a means for students to get back at teachers they do not like. In sum, many teachers are left feeling that their evaluations do not in fact reflect the quality of the work they do.

Despite the controversy surrounding these data-gathering and evaluation systems and the fact that the changes—positive and negative—they are creating are not well understood, we see continued expansion not only of the systems themselves, but of their use to drive personnel decisions and promote accountability in other domains, such as teacher preparation and principal evaluation. The goal of this volume, therefore, is to take stock of what we have learned about the impacts and challenges of data-intensive teacher evaluation systems from these initial years of development and implementation, and identify challenges for practitioners and researchers in the years ahead. We argue that rigorous teacher evaluation systems have the potential to promote school improvement, but only if the systems are carefully designed and implemented and the data they generate are interpreted and used appropriately. The chapters that follow, penned by scholars and policymakers working at the cutting edge of research and policy in this area, speak to what we know and what remains to be known about evaluation measures themselves, the implementation of evaluation systems, and the use of evaluation data. They also make recommendations for state policymakers and district administrators moving forward with such systems.

The book is loosely organized into two sections. The first section, comprising Chapters 2 through 8, focuses attention on the most important measures of teacher performance currently used by multiple-measures evaluation systems, what their properties are, how they fit together, and the challenges inherent in collecting and interpreting the measures well. The second section—Chapters 9 through 13—turns to the implementation of multiple-measures teacher evaluation systems and what we have learned about the experiences of teachers and principals as they use these new measures, and challenges that school, district, and state administrators face in implementing them. A final chapter pulls together lessons learned and guidelines for practice and policy synthesized from across the two sections.

The first section begins with a chapter by Julie Cohen and Dan Goldhaber that compares the two major components of nearly every multiple-measures-based teacher evaluation system: value-added measures of teacher performance and classroom observation measures. The authors contrast what can be learned from each measure type, what conditions are necessary for the accuracy of each one, and the most important sources of error for each. The authors point out that substantial research on value-added measures has illuminated a variety of concerns about their limitations and biases and may have pushed practitioners to more highly value observation-based measures, when in fact observation instruments face many potential sources of inaccuracy and bias that have not been investigated with the same intensity.

Chapter 3 follows up on issues of accuracy and reliability of teacher observation tools. Drawing on their experiences developing and implementing the Classroom Assessment Scoring System (CLASS) for classroom observations, Robert C. Pianta and Bridget K. Hamre outline a variety of fundamental components that must be in place to facilitate high-quality observation systems at scale that can produce consistent, reliable measures of teacher practice. These include broad components such as a protocol that is grounded in a theory of effective teaching to motivate measurement, as well as features related to the use of that protocol, such as standardization of observation approaches and effective training, certification, and recertification systems for observers. The usefulness of the information gleaned from teacher observations is unlikely to be very high in the absence of such investments.

In Chapter 4, Jason A. Grissom, Susanna Loeb, and Christopher Doss examine whether value-added measures are good proxies for other facets of teachers' contributions to their schools beyond increases in standardized test scores in mathematics and reading. Specifically, they test how well value-added correlates with assessments given by principals in low-stakes interviews of different areas of teachers' job performance. The authors find that value-added tends to correlate well with principals' assessments of a teacher's ability to produce high test performance from students and develop higher-order thinking but weakly or inconsistently with other dimensions, such as building student interpersonal skills or contributing to leadership in the school, suggesting that value-added captures only a relatively narrow range of a teacher's contributions. When asked which teachers they wished to retain, principals named teachers they rated highly on these other performance dimensions but not necessarily those with high value-added scores. The authors conclude that evaluation systems that privilege value-added measures are likely to overlook important contributions to the school that many teachers make and that the multidimensional nature of teachers' work requires a multiple-measures approach to evaluation.

The fifth chapter continues this close look at value-added measures. In this chapter, Sean P. Corcoran discusses the potential pitfalls of using teacher value-added data for teacher evaluation and other high-stakes decisions. He argues that the presumed benefits of value-added scores—their conciseness, their statistical objectivity, the fact that they show variation in teacher effectiveness when other traditional measures often identify everyone as similarly high-performing—are more than outweighed by numerous shortcomings that researchers have begun to catalogue but that policymakers have often been unaware of or discounted. These include numerous sources of bias in the scores, measurement error that produces unstable estimates, and problems with face validity, among others. As a summative measure, they also provide scant guidance to practitioners about what in a teacher's classroom works well or what areas need to be targeted for improvement. The core of Corcoran's argument is that leaders and policymakers should lower their expectations about what can be learned from individual teachers' value-added and avoid giving such measures an outsized role in evaluating job performance.

Chapter 6 focuses on evaluation for a population of teachers in an area given little attention in policy debate and research to this point: special education. Nathan D. Jones considers both value-added and teacher observation measures in the context of special education. He highlights several important features of special education teachers' work that pose particular challenges for evaluation systems geared toward more typical classroom teachers, including that their instruction is often very specific to individual students, with learning objectives distinct from those of general education classrooms. We know little about the properties of student test score–based performance measures for teachers of special education students or about the appropriateness of the most frequently used classroom observation instruments for special education teachers. Jones underscores the need for additional policy discussion and research in this important area.

The seventh chapter turns from value-added and teacher observations to focus on student surveys. Ryan Balch notes that student surveys are potentially useful in systems of teacher feedback and evaluation because they can identify specific areas of focus for teacher improvement and are less resource-intensive than teacher observations while providing potentially similar information. He goes on to synthesize the small literature base on student assessment of teachers and describe a framework for assessing and ensuring the validity of student surveys as measures of teacher practice. He illustrates this framework with the Survey of Teacher Practice that he developed and makes available through My Student Survey, a student survey development and administration company. Balch argues that thoughtfully and carefully constructed student surveys can provide valid and reliable measures of many aspects of teachers' instruction, though student surveys also present important challenges, particularly around building and maintaining teacher buy-in, that districts must address if such measures are to realize their potential for aiding teacher improvement.

Chapter 8 concludes the initial section by reviewing research on edTPA, a teacher performance assessment that is being used widely with preservice candidates. In their chapter, Peter Youngs and Andrea Whittaker first consider ways that classroom observation instruments can be employed to evaluate content-specific instructional practices, as well as some limitations associated with these tools. Next, the authors describe edTPA and review research on edTPA and similar teacher assessments, including evidence related to reliability and validity. Finally, they discuss ways in which edTPA and observation tools represent distinct responses to pressures linked to accountability and explain how edTPA can be used in tandem with observation instruments to evaluate teaching candidates' content-specific instructional practices.

The second section, which begins with Chapter 9, focuses on evaluation system implementation and data use. In this initial chapter, Min Sun, R. Brock Mutcheson, and Jihyun Kim examine how teachers in two rural school systems report using teacher evaluation information for their own instructional improvement. They found this kind of utilization of evaluation information to be more common among early-career teachers on probationary contracts and in schools with more intensive, higher-quality professional development around data use and principals who provided more useful evaluation feedback. Their results suggest that appropriate school supports can push teachers to make use of performance information to increase the effectiveness of their practice.

Chapter 10 turns attention to principals' use of teacher evaluation measures. Timothy A. Drake, Ellen Goldring, and colleagues draw on interview data from principals in six urban school systems that have implemented multiple-measures teacher evaluation systems to examine how the data from those systems are used in teacher dismissal processes. The authors found that rhetoric raising concerns that new teacher evaluation systems are largely about targeting low-performing teachers for dismissal generally is not reflected in principals' experiences with these systems. Instead, evaluation measures for low-performing teachers are used to place teachers on growth or improvement plans to support their growth in areas in which they are weak. Although the documentation associated with teacher growth plans also provides evidence for dismissal proceedings, school and district leaders often view dismissal as a by-product of an unsuccessful attempt to help a teacher improve rather than as a primary goal of the evaluation system.

In Chapter 11, Morgaen L. Donaldson and Casey D. Cobb investigate teachers' and school leaders' experiences with the implementation of Connecticut's new multiple-measures teacher evaluation system. In Connecticut's system, standards-based observations are coupled with student learning objectives, an alternative to value-added models for documenting student learning based on educators' goals. They find that classroom observations were typically welcomed by teachers, who wanted more observations and more feedback to assist them with their instruction, though administrators found them challenging to implement because of time and other capacity constraints. Student learning objectives posed their own capacity challenges, as educators struggled to set appropriate and rigorous learning goals, though the goal-setting process itself was motivating for many teachers. The authors also note that the growing use of student learning objectives in state evaluation systems requires much more research attention than currently is being devoted, particularly to their psychometric properties, which are poorly understood.

In Chapter 12, Gary T. Henry and J. Edward Guthrie outline how principals can incorporate teacher value-added scores into a process for teacher improvement. Drawing on value-added, teacher observation, and student survey data from North Carolina, they demonstrate how correlations between practices—measured by observations and surveys—and value-added in the same year and over time can be used to identify and prioritize specific practices to target for improvement. The system they describe can enable principals to provide evidence-based advice to teachers about the practices that are most likely to lead to improvements in student achievement in their classrooms.

Chapter 13 approaches teacher evaluation implementation issues from the perspective of senior personnel in state education agencies. Venessa A. Keesler and Carla Howe describe efforts by the Michigan Department of Education to support school districts as they enact new teacher evaluation systems. These efforts include providing technical assistance to districts related to the use of classroom observation systems, student learning objectives, and student growth data; supporting the development of interim assessments for use in obtaining information on teacher performance; and maintaining a focus on using evaluation to support teachers' professional development as well as to meet accountability demands. In addition to technical challenges associated with using value-added models, the authors also note that a lack of coherence among state educational policies, along with limited resources in their agency, have affected their ability to support districts as they have implemented new evaluation measures.

In the final chapter, we look across the contributions to this volume and the related literature on multiple-measures teacher evaluation systems to summarize some key implications that can be drawn from this growing body of research. In particular, we conclude that while the information from such systems can be used to improve teacher practice and improve personnel decisions in schools, state and district leaders must think carefully about the design of multiple-measures systems and pay close attention to how they are implemented to realize that potential. As currently put into practice, we worry that measures employed in many school systems have reliability and validity properties that are too questionable to be used for summative evaluation and associated high-stakes decisions. Fortunately, these properties can be improved with attention and resources. Until that time, formative uses of evaluation measures to identify areas for teacher growth that can be addressed through professional development and support may be the highest-value use for much of this information.

With regard to final thoughts in introducing this book, we want to encourage policymakers, administrators, and researchers to continue exploring effective ways to support the process of teaching and the process of teacher evaluation. As the chapters in this book attest, an emphasis on accountability alone is unlikely to result in large-scale improvements in teaching and learning. Instead, schools, districts, and states need to consider how the use of multiple measures of teacher evaluation can be integrated with school-based and external professional development activities. In many schools, teachers' colleagues, instructional coaches, and principals can potentially be very helpful resources in the area of instructional improvement. But this potential will be realized only if and when policymakers place greater emphasis on ways in which teacher evaluation measures can be used for formative purposes to support teacher development.

CHAPTER 2

Observations on Evaluating Teacher Performance

Assessing the Strengths and Weaknesses of Classroom Observations and Value-Added Measures

Julie Cohen
Dan Goldhaber

Teacher evaluation has moved to the forefront of education policy in recent years. This movement has been spurred by research showing differences in the effectiveness of individual teachers to be important predictors of students' test achievement and later life outcomes, evidence that existing evaluation systems do not identify differences between teachers, and recent federal initiatives like the *Race to the Top* and *Teacher Incentive Fund* grant competitions and *No Child Left Behind* waiver requirements.[1] States have responded by revamping existing evaluation systems to incorporate multiple means of assessing teachers, to better recognize the significant differences among them.

New evaluation systems also often tie consequential personnel decisions to summative measures of teacher performance. This in itself engenders controversy, but more controversial is that some states and localities have begun utilizing a direct measure of student growth on standardized tests, often referred to as "value-added," as a component of summative performance evaluation.

The controversy over the use of value-added measures (VAMs) is related to several substantive concerns. Teachers may lack familiarity with VAMs but know they are test-based, and there is disagreement about the extent to which state assessments (or other standardized tests) capture the type of learning many deem important; many doubt, for instance, that tests adequately assess students' conceptual understanding of subjects or ability to engage in complex problem solving (Koretz, 2002; Luna & Turner, 2001; Popham, 2003). There is also doubt that VAMs can separate teachers' contributions to student achievement from other influences (e.g., parents, peers), suggesting that such measures may hold teachers accountable for things outside their control (Rothstein, 2010). Finally, VAMs create a forced distribution of performance, violating traditional school norms around collaboration.

Classroom observations, on the other hand, are used almost universally to judge competence. Analysis of principal survey data from the nationally representative 2011–12 Schools and Staffing Survey shows that more than 99% of untenured teachers and 95% of tenured teachers are evaluated based on a formal classroom observation at least once per year. By contrast, only 40% of principals report using student test achievement as a gauge of teacher performance. Yet these formal observations can vary widely in terms of focus, duration, and frequency. On average, classroom observations last approximately 45 minutes, with untenured teachers observed 3.4 times per year and tenured teachers observed 2.3 times per year. Moreover, the observational tools used in practice are not necessarily consistent across states, districts, or even schools.

Classroom observations have strong face validity because they assess "process," or teaching variables, not student outcomes, which may feel distal from teachers' work. Moreover, VAMs in and of themselves do not illuminate the teaching practice levers contributing to growth in student achievement (Harris, 2009). Yet classroom observations have not generally been an effective means of differentiating teachers: Most ratings based on formal classroom observations suggest teachers are nearly all "highly effective" (Weisberg, Sexton, Mulhern, & Keeling, 2009). This is possible because, unlike VAMs, observation protocols are criterion-referenced measures that do not necessitate a normal distribution of scores.

In this chapter, we compare value-added and classroom observations as means of evaluating teachers. We focus on VAMs given their novelty and controversy and on classroom observations because of their long history as a performance evaluation measure and their current prevalence in evaluation systems. We argue that many of the theoretical and empirical issues, such as sampling error, that arise in the context of performance measurement are common across both measures, but classroom observations also contain other sources of error, such as raters. The reliability and validity of classroom observations have faced less scrutiny than that of value-added measures. Given their ubiquitous use, this form of evaluation merits a good deal more scrutiny.

The chapter proceeds as follows: In the next section, we describe what is measured by VAMs and classroom observations. The third section considers sources of error in both measures. Finally, we offer some concluding thoughts and an agenda for future research.

WHAT IS BEING MEASURED BY VAMS AND CLASSROOM OBSERVATION MEASURES

Assessing teaching, which is complex and multifaceted, is not a straightforward enterprise; there are strengths and weaknesses associated with any means of performance evaluation. The statistical properties of VAMs as a performance metric have been well-explored in the academic literature. Ironically, given their long-term prevalent use, there is considerably less research about the properties of classroom observations as performance assessments.

Both measures share some common sources of error or variability, but they also present unique affordances and constraints (see the summary in Table 2.1). VAMs and classroom observations both attempt to approximate the teacher's contribution to student experiences in classrooms without directly engaging with students. VAMs attempt to assess the broader construct of teacher quality by measuring a student-specific construct, growth in learning or test performance. Value-added estimates of "teacher effects" are culled from a statistical model that attributes a portion of students' test growth to their teachers. The underlying assumption is that the tests used represent a reasonable proxy for a broader domain of interest, academic learning across a school year.

Different tests focus on different content, use different formats, and require differing levels of cognitive demand from students (Grossman, Cohen, Ronfeldt, & Brown, 2014; McCaffrey, 2013; Polikoff & Porter, 2014). Perhaps as a result of these differences in test content, there is a reasonable amount of empirical evidence that VAMs fluctuate based on the content and structure of the student assessment. In particular, a number of studies have found that estimates of teacher effects were statistically different depending on the test used to compute value-added, and the stakes attached to those tests (Cohen, 2015; Corcoran, Jennings, & Beveridge, 2011; Lockwood, McCaffrey, Mariano, & Setodji, 2007; Papay, 2011). This may reflect the fact that different tests address different facets of the broader construct of student learning. Short of administering numerous assessments to students, these differences raise conceptual challenges.

The same issue arises for observational instruments; the construct validity of a protocol rests on the assumption that the practices featured are

Table 2.1. Value-Added Measures and Classroom Observation Measures

	Value-Added Measures	Classroom Observational Measures
What is being measured?	Primarily student constructs: growth in achievement/ learning, which is then attributed to the teacher	Varies somewhat depending on the specific measure used, but all assess the quantity and quality of teaching practices, as well as teacher–student interactions
Distribution of teacher performance	Norm-referenced measures that create a forced distribution of performance	Criterion-referenced measures that do not necessitate a distribution of performance
Information needed for accurate measure	Multiple years of prior student achievement for many students in the classroom	Numbers of lessons and instructional segments within a lesson varies by instrument; in general, multiple lessons of a certain length (e.g., 30 minutes) are needed across a school year
Sources of error	The content of the assessment used to measure achievement, the timing of administration of assessment, the number of students for whom there is longitudinal achievement data, and unobservable variables associated with the assignment of teachers to classrooms of students	The frequency and duration of observations, the scales used to assess "high-quality" practice, the consistency of quality across content areas (e.g., reading, writing, geometry, fractions), and unobservable variables associated with the assignment of teachers to classrooms of students
Reliability of measure	Intertemporal variability, suggesting that teacher effects on student achievement fluctuate somewhat from year to year	Limited direct empirical evidence about intertemporal stability, but lack of variability in these measures suggests high stability
Ways in which measure is or isn't adjusted for context	Some readily measurable factors controlled for in models	Largely not explicitly addressed or controlled for in standardized observation systems
Raters and the objectivity of the measure	Value-added estimates are computed with statistical models, so there are no raters and no scoring issues associated with outside observers	Raters ideally are trained, certified, and calibrated to promote consistent scoring, but bias is hard to completely address and rater error is likely

consequential in term of students' experiences. The measured practices serve as proxies for broader, perhaps less readily measurable constructs such as the instructional or environmental quality of classrooms. Different protocols foreground different practices and stem from different research-based theories about which aspects of teaching are most crucial to assess. Some, such as the *Framework for Teaching* (Danielson, 2013) and the *Classroom Assessment Scoring System* (CLASS; Pianta, Hamre, Haynes, Mintz, & La Paro, 2006), focus on elements of teaching that theoretically apply across content areas, including classroom management and organization and use of materials. Other instruments privilege content-specific aspects of instruction, including the *Mathematical Quality of Instruction* (MQI) instrument (Hill, Kapitula, & Umland, 2011) and the *Protocol for Language Arts Teaching Observation* (PLATO) (Grossman, Loeb, Cohen, & Wyckoff, 2013). There is evidence from the Gates Foundation's Measures of Effective Teaching (MET) project that the composition of practices included in a protocol impacts the degree to which observations predict other measures of quality, including teacher value-added measures. Teacher ratings are fairly consistent across content-generic protocols, but teachers perform differentially on protocols assessing content-specific teaching practices (Kane & Staiger, 2012).

SOURCES OF ERROR

One of the most common critiques of value-added measures is that they are biased, that is, they systematically under- or overstate a teacher's true contribution to student achievement gains (Rothstein, 2010). This bias could arise if, for instance, some teachers are regularly assigned to students for whom it is easier or harder to raise achievement, even after adjustments are made to account for observable differences in the students assigned to the classroom (e.g., their test scores at the beginning of the year, their poverty level). Scholars have reached different conclusions about bias in VAMs; see, for example, Chetty, Friedman, and Rockoff (2014b), Corcoran and Goldhaber (2013), Goldhaber and Chaplin (2015), Kane, McCaffrey, Miller, and Staiger (2013), Kane and Staiger (2008), and Rothstein (2010).

Another concern is that estimated teacher effects on student achievement fluctuate somewhat from year to year, with a number of empirical studies suggesting intertemporal correlations in the .2 to .5 range (Goldhaber & Hansen, 2013; McCaffrey, Sass, Lockwood, & Mihaly, 2009). Vocal opponents of value-added have focused heavily on this instability, suggesting that it makes the measures unsuitable for consequential personnel decisions (Baker et al., 2010; Darling-Hammond, Amrein-Beardsley, Haertel, & Rothstein, 2012). However, this intertemporal fluctuation is not very different from that observed for output-based measures of performance in other professions where work is multifaceted and complex (Brookings Brown Center Task Group on Teacher Quality, 2010). And, not surprisingly, the magnitude of the sampling error (the error associated with the assignment of students to teachers) decreases as the sample of students and/or classes informing the VAM measure increases (Goldhaber & Hansen 2013; McCaffrey et al., 2009).

In contrast to the empirical focus on the bias inherent in value-added measures, there has been comparatively little research focused on the possibility of the same kinds of biases in observational measures. Observational scales could also over- or underestimate the true instructional quality of a classroom. Teachers could be assigned to classrooms in which it is systematically more difficult to engage in the high-quality teaching practices measured on the observation protocols described above. In addition, certain curricula might circumscribe instruction, making it easier or harder to engage in specific practices. As noted, most classroom ratings used by districts suggest that teacher performance is uniformly high; this itself suggests bias given that statistical estimates and common sense suggest a range of teacher quality. The research literature suggests that there is more variation when expert observers conduct observations without high stakes for teachers. This might reflect rater training or cultural barriers in schools that make it difficult for leaders to differentiate among teachers. Regardless of the contributing factors, the lack of differentiation in school-based settings represents a challenge for the utility of classroom observations.

Just as the level of measurement error in VAMs decreases as the number of students informing the measure rises, we might expect measurement error in observations to be influenced by the number or duration of observations. Many observation protocols require that observed lessons be of a certain duration of time, mandate observing multiple instances of instruction, and require those observations to be conducted in multiple "waves" separated by several weeks or months to maximize the likelihood of a more comprehensive and stable estimate of teaching practice (Grossman et al., 2013; Pianta et al., 2006). Generalizability study findings across tools demonstrate a great deal of variability by lesson, segment within a lesson (first 15 minutes vs. last 15 minutes), time of year, and content of instruction (Hill, Charalambous, & Kraft, 2012; Pianta & Hamre, 2009). Some features of "good teaching" might be more stable across instances of instruction (e.g., teachers should have productive, orderly classrooms regardless of what is being taught), but some features (e.g., the quality of the teacher feedback, the amount of classroom discussion) might fluctuate over time. The limited empirical evidence on the topic suggests as much; behavior management is the most stable observational scale across a range of different protocols (Polikoff, 2015).

We know very little about the degree to which observational measures are stable from year to year. Old studies have found year-to-year correlations in discrete teaching practices in the .5 to .7 range, with a great deal of variability across scales for different practices (cf. Brophy, 1979). While these correlations are higher than the value-added year-to-year correlations cited above, they are still lower than some recommend for personnel decisions. Polikoff (2015) finds year-to-year correlations ranging from .4 to .55 for all but one of the observational measures used in the Gates Foundation's Measures of Effective Teaching study, with a great deal of heterogeneity across the individual scales used in each protocol. In addition, most districts' evaluation systems use summative or composite measures of instructional quality, rather than the less stable subscores for specific teaching practices described above. Given the limited variability in these overall measures of teaching, there tends to be far higher levels of intertemporal consistency in observation measures than value-added estimates (Weisberg et al., 2009). In practice, most teachers get consistently high scores across time in consequential evaluations of their teaching.

In sum, while stability is a central part of the argument leveled against value-added measures, those same arguments could also be raised against other measures of quality, including observational measures, especially when such measures actually reflect a distribution in quality. Given the limited data we do have, the argument that VAMs result in inaccurate personnel decisions, both at the top and bottom of the distribution, might also apply to observational measures.

Classroom observation protocols are also associated with a source of potential error that has no real analog in the statistical methods employed in VAMs: the rater. Though observational systems are based on carefully developed scales, they necessitate someone to assess the quality of the teaching practice, and that person inherently brings their own subjective biases to the endeavor. Raters are indeed the largest source of error across multiple generalizability studies (Ho & Kane, 2013; Mashburn, Downer, Rivers, Brackett, & Martinez, 2014). In particular, research has demonstrated that raters struggle to keep multiple dimensions of quality in mind during observations, and that content-specific aspects of instruction are especially cognitively demanding and subject to rater biases (Bell et al., 2014; Park, Chen, & Holtzman, 2014).

To minimize these rater effects, observation protocols need to meet a high standard of reliability, which depends in large part both on how observers are selected and trained and how difficult it is to rate accurately different elements of teaching practice. Some elements are relatively easy to agree on, such as the level of misbehavior in a classroom or the extent to which the teacher makes the purpose of a lesson clear (Gitomer et al., 2014; Grossman et al., 2013). Other elements of instruction, such as the quality of connections the teachers make between the content and students' background knowledge, or the precision of mathematical explanations, might be more difficult to assess consistently.

A necessary first step is a carefully designed system for training and certifying observers, or raters, to use the tools consistently with the theoretical principles underlying the scales. Support documents that include decision rules for scoring and examples of practice at various score points can also help mitigate the potential for rater error. The literature suggests, however, that well-trained raters are insufficient in ensuring accurate measurement (Gitomer et al., 2014; Park et al., 2014). Studies also suggest the need to consistently recalibrate raters, as perceptions of quality can drift away from reliable, rubric-based scoring over time (Wilson & Case, 2000). Moreover, a number of generalizability studies of observation protocols demonstrate the need for multiple raters in developing reliable systems for measuring teaching (Hill et al., 2012; Kane & Staiger, 2012). While employing multiple raters is sensible from a measurement perspective, it represents a costly and logistically challenging proposition for many districts. Here, too, we need a more robust empirical base about how to best select, train, support, and assess raters in high-stakes teacher evaluation contexts.

CONCLUSIONS AND DIRECTIONS FOR FUTURE RESEARCH

Current policies require states to develop comprehensive teacher evaluation systems. Yet while many of the nation's largest districts are already using composite metrics of quality, we are only beginning to develop a body of empirical research about the relationship among these measures. Much of the existing literature base characterizes teacher quality as a monolithic construct. Many issues remain unexplored, particularly about the ways in which a variety of different factors (e.g., grade level, subject area, student and school characteristics, and assessment design) influence the measurement of teaching and learning and/or moderate the relationship between them.

Teaching and student achievement are likely influenced by various contextual factors, including community resources, principal leadership, curricular materials, and technology. Schools are characterized by different cultures, rules, and values, which regulate teaching practices and have been shown to influence the quality of instruction and student learning outcomes (Kraft & Papay, 2014; McLaughlin & Talbert, 2006). So, too, might high-quality instruction vary for specific subpopulations of students, such as English language learners or special education students. Indeed, prior research has demonstrated that the specific school-level environmental features and student demographics influence both teacher value-added (Jackson & Bruegmann, 2009; Ladd, 2011; Loeb, Soland, & Fox, 2014; Master, Loeb, Whitney, & Wyckoff, 2012) and the instructional practices that teachers use (Cohen & Brown, in press).

Unlike growth models, which simply measure student achievement gains between a pretest and a posttest, VAMs explicitly acknowledge and attempt to control for some of these contextual variables that likely impact student performance on standardized assessments, including the characteristics of students in a teacher's classroom (e.g., the percentage of students receiving subsidized lunch, the percentage of African American students, students' prior achievement level) and the school in which a teacher teaches (McCaffrey, Lockwood, Louis, & Hamilton, 2004; Rivkin, Hanushek, & Kain, 2005).

In contrast, classroom observational systems tacitly suggest that "good teaching" looks consistent across school settings and student subpopulations. Most commonly used observation tools do not account for these contextual factors when scoring the quality of teaching practices. It is not yet clear whether these measures in fact isolate the contributions of teacher-specific features of classrooms, or whether teaching is so inherently situated that any teaching practice is contingent upon the students in the classroom. We also know little about the degree to which it is feasible to control for student characteristics in classroom observations, or the benefits or drawbacks of doing so. These are important areas for future research.

To date, little research on the current generation of classroom observation protocols has investigated the stability and generality of teaching relationships. Numerous questions remain, including the following: How stable is instructional quality from year to year? How stable is instructional quality across content areas for elementary teachers, and within subjects for subject specialists (e.g., geometry to algebra, writing to reading)? How can districts best address student characteristics in classroom observations, and to what extent should raters and observational protocols attend to demographic differences of classrooms?

These issues are related to broader questions about comparison groups and which groups represent a sensible counterfactual in assessing teaching quality. Value-added models include numerous assumptions about which groups it makes sense to compare teachers to in terms of impact on student achievement, but we have not determined those same assumptions for observation protocols.

We also need to better understand whether observations or other measures are sensitive to true changes in practice. The question of whether observational protocols are sensitive to real changes in the performance of teachers, as measured by the construct, is vital, since both teachers and policymakers should know that improvements in practice lead to improvements in the measure of the practice of those who improve. For example, we do not know if observational measures detect substantial shifts in teachers' practices following an intensive professional development program, after the advent of a new curriculum, or with a new instructional coach at the school. The literature suggests that teachers' practices change in response to these experiences, but we do not know if their scores on classroom observational measures change correspondingly.

Perhaps most important is a recognition that teacher performance evaluation is fundamentally about making predictions about the future. The theory of action underlying evaluation is that it will be used to inform decisions. These may be low- or high-stakes decisions made by individual teachers or school systems. For instance, teachers may seek out particular types of professional development based on the performance feedback they receive, or school systems may make decisions about which teachers are allowed to continue teaching or their compensation. Regardless of the actions, all are predicated on the idea that the information generated from performance evaluation results in a more effective future workforce. Thus, we need to better understand the extent to which information from a performance measure—any type of measure—leads to actions on the part of teachers or school systems that lead to improvements.

NOTES

The authors wish to thank Carolina Melo and Christopher Tien for their excellent research assistance. All opinions expressed are those of the authors.

1. For evidence on the importance of teachers, see Chetty, Friedman, and Rockoff (2014a) and Rivkin, Hanushek, and Kain (2005).

REFERENCES

Baker, E. L., Barton, P. E., Darling-Hammond, L., Haertel, E., Ladd, H. F., Linn, R. L., . . . Shepard, L. A. (2010). *Problems with the use of student test scores to evaluate teachers* (EPI Briefing Paper 278). Washington, DC: Economic Policy Institute.

Bell, C., Qi, Y., Croft, A., Leusner, D., McCaffrey, D., Gitomer, D., & Pianta, R. (2014). Improving observational score quality: Challenges in observer thinking. In K. Kerr, R. Pianta, & T. Kane (Eds.), *Designing teacher evaluation systems: New guidance from the Measures of Effective Teaching project* (pp. 50–97). San Francisco, CA: Jossey-Bass.

Brookings Brown Center Task Group on Teacher Quality. (2010). *Evaluating teachers: The important role of value-added.* Washington, DC: The Brookings Institution.

Brophy, J. E. (1979). Teacher behavior and its effects. *Journal of Educational Psychology, 71*(6), 733.

Chetty, R., Friedman, J. N., & Rockoff, J. E. (2014a). Measuring the impacts of teachers I: Evaluating bias in teacher value-added estimates. *American Economic Review, 104*(9), 2593–2632.

Chetty, R., Friedman, J. N., & Rockoff, J. E. (2014b). Measuring the impacts of teachers II: Teacher value-added and student outcomes in adulthood. *American Economic Review, 104*(9), 2633–2679.

Cohen, J. (2015). The challenge of identifying high-leverage practices. *Teachers College Record, 117*(7), 1–41.

Cohen, J., & Brown, M. (in press). Teaching quality across school settings. *The New Educator.*

Corcoran, S., & Goldhaber, D. (2013). Value-added and its uses: Where you stand depends on where you sit. *Education Finance and Policy, 8*(3), 418–434.

Corcoran, S. P., Jennings, J. L., & Beveridge, A. A. (2011, March). Teacher effectiveness on high- and low-stakes tests. Paper presented at the Annual Meeting of the Society for Research on Educational Effectiveness, Washington, DC.

Danielson, C. (2013). *The Framework for Teaching Evaluation Instrument.* Princeton, NJ: The Danielson Group.

Darling-Hammond, L., Amrein-Beardsley, A., Haertel, E., & Rothstein, J. (2012). Evaluating teacher evaluation. *Phi Delta Kappan, 93*(6), 8–15.

Gitomer, D., Bell, C., Qi, Y., McCaffrey, D., Hamre, B. K., & Pianta, R. C. (2014). The instructional challenge in improving teaching quality: Lessons from a classroom observation protocol. *Teachers College Record, 116*(6), 1–32.

Goldhaber, D., & Chaplin, D. (2015). Assessing the "Rothstein Falsification Test": Does it really show teacher value-added models are biased? *Journal of Research on Educational Effectiveness*, 8(1), 8–34.

Goldhaber, D., & Hansen, M. (2013). Is it just a bad class? Assessing the long-term stability of estimated teacher performance. *Economica, 80*(319), 589–612.

Grossman, P., Cohen, J., Ronfeldt, M., & Brown, L. (2014). The test matters: The relationship between classroom observation scores and teacher value-added on multiple types of assessment. *Educational Researcher, 43*(6), 293–303.

Grossman, P., Loeb, S., Cohen, J., & Wyckoff, J. (2013). Measure for measure: The relationship between measures of instructional practice in middle school English language arts and teachers' value-added scores. *American Journal of Education, 119*(3), 445–470.

Harris, D. (2009). Teacher value-added: Don't end the search before it starts. *Journal of Policy and Management, 28*(4), 693–699.

Hill, H. C., Charalambous, C. Y., & Kraft, M. A. (2012). When rater reliability is not enough: Teacher observation systems and a case for the generalizability study. *Educational Researcher, 41*(2), 56–64.

Hill, H. C., Kapitula, L., & Umland, K. (2011). A validity argument approach to evaluating teacher value-added scores. *American Educational Research Journal, 48*(3), 794–831.

Ho, A., & Kane, T. (2013). *The reliability of classroom observations by school personnel* (MET project research paper). Seattle, WA: Bill and Melinda Gates Foundation.

Jackson, C. K., & Bruegmann, E. (2009). Teaching students and teaching each other: The importance of peer learning for teachers. *American Economic Journal: Applied Economics, 1*(4), 85–108.

Kane, T. J., McCaffrey, D. F., Miller, T., & Staiger, D. O. (2013). *Have we identified effective teachers? Validating measures of effective teaching using random assignment* (MET project research paper). Seattle, WA: Bill and Melinda Gates Foundation.

Kane, T. J., & Staiger, D. O. (2008). *Estimating teacher impacts on student achievement* (NBER working paper 14607). Cambridge, MA: National Bureau of Economic Research.

Kane, T. J., & Staiger, D. O. (2012). *Gathering feedback for teaching: Combining high-quality observations with student surveys and achievement gains* (MET project research paper). Seattle, WA: Bill and Melinda Gates Foundation.

Koretz, D. (2002). Limitations in the use of achievement tests as measures of educators' productivity. *Journal of Human Resources, 37*(4), 752–777.

Kraft, M. A., & Papay, J. P. (2014). Do supportive professional environments promote teacher development? Explaining heterogeneity in returns to teaching experience. *Educational Evaluation and Policy Analysis, 36*(4), 476–500.

Ladd, H. F. (2011). Teachers' perceptions of their working conditions: How predictive of planned and actual teacher movement? *Educational Evaluation and Policy Analysis, 33*(2), 235–261.

Lockwood, J. R., McCaffrey, D. F., Mariano, L. T., & Setodji, C. (2007). Bayesian methods for scalable multivariate value-added assessment. *Journal of Educational and Behavioral Statistics, 32*(2), 125–150.

Loeb, S., Soland, J., & Fox, L. (2014). Is a good teacher a good teacher for all? Comparing value-added of teachers with their English learners and non-English learners. *Educational Evaluation and Policy Analysis, 36*(4), 399–416.

Luna, C., & Turner, C. L. (2001). The impact of the MCAS: Teachers talk about high-stakes testing. *The English Journal, 91*(1), 79–87.

Mashburn, A. J., Downer, J. T., Rivers, S. E., Brackett, M. A., & Martinez, A. (2014). Improving the power of an efficacy study of a social and emotional learning program: Application of generalizability theory to the measurement of classroom-level outcomes. *Prevention Science, 15*(2), 146–155.

Master, B., Loeb, S., Whitney, C., & Wyckoff, J. (2012). *Different skills: Identifying differentially effective teachers of English language learners* (Working paper no. 68). Washington, DC: National Center for Analysis of Longitudinal Data in Education Research.

McCaffrey, D. F. (2013, June 17). Will teacher value-added scores change when accountability tests change? Stanford, CA: Carnegie Foundation for the Advancement of Teaching. Retrieved from www.carnegieknowledgenetwork.org/briefs/value-added/accountability-tests/

McCaffrey, D. F., Lockwood, J. R., Louis, T. A., & Hamilton, L. (2004). Models for value-added modeling of teacher effects. *Journal of Educational and Behavioral Statistics, 29*(1), 67–101.

McCaffrey, D., Sass, T., Lockwood, J., & Mihaly, K. (2009). The intertemporal variability of teacher effect estimates. *Education Finance and Policy, 4*(4), 572–606.

McLaughlin, M. W., & Talbert, J. E. (2006). *Building school-based teacher learning communities: Professional strategies to improve student achievement.* New York, NY: Teachers College Press.

Papay, J. P. (2011). Different tests, different answers: The stability of value-added estimates across student outcomes. *American Educational Research Journal, 48*(1), 163–193.

Park, Y. S., Chen, J., & Holtzman, S. (2014). Evaluating efforts to minimize rater bias in scoring classroom observations. In K. Kerr, R. Pianta, & T. Kane (Eds.), *Designing teacher evaluation systems: New guidance from the Measures of Effective Teaching project* (pp. 383–414). San Francisco, CA: Jossey-Bass.

Pianta, R. C., & Hamre, B. K. (2009). Conceptualization, measurement, and improvement of classroom processes: Standardized observation can leverage capacity. *Educational Researcher, 38*(2), 109–119.

Pianta, R. C., Hamre, B. K., Haynes, N. J., Mintz, S., & La Paro, K. M. (2006). *CLASS Classroom Assessment Scoring System: Manual Middle Secondary Version Pilot, June 2006.* Charlottesville, VA: University of Virginia.

Polikoff, M. S. (2015). The stability of observational and student survey measures of teaching effectiveness. *American Journal of Education, 121*(2), 183–212.

Polikoff, M. S., & Porter, A. C. (2014). Instructional alignment as a measure of teaching quality. *Educational Evaluation and Policy Analysis, 36*(4), 399–416.

Popham, W. J. (2003). The seductive allure of data. *Educational Leadership, 60*(5), 48–51.

Rivkin, S., Hanushek, E., & Kain, J. (2005). Teachers, schools, and academic achievement. *Econometrica*, *73*(2), 417–458.

Rothstein, J. (2010). Teacher quality in education production: Tracking, decay, and student achievement. *Quarterly Journal of Economics, 125*(1), 175–214.

Weisberg, D., Sexton, S., Mulhern, J., & Keeling, D. (2009). *The widget effect: Our national failure to acknowledge and act on differences in teacher effectiveness.* Chicago, IL: The New Teacher Project.

Wilson, M., & Case, H. (2000). An examination of variation in rater severity over time: A study in rater drift. *Objective Measurement: Theory into Practice*, *5*, 113–133.

CHAPTER 3

Implementing Rigorous Observation of Teachers

Synchronizing Theory with Systems for Implementation and Support

Robert C. Pianta
Bridget K. Hamre

Efforts to develop, implement, and evaluate the use of varying procedures for collecting evidence of teachers' performance and impacts on student learning have been under way for at least a decade, and most states now use some version of a performance evaluation system. These current efforts are an initial phase in what could be a long-term effort and focus for system improvement. It is our view that the interests of teachers and students are best addressed by sustained and systematic engagement in the dialectic that draws together theories of effective teaching and rigorous application of tools and systems intended to document and support effective teaching. Such systematic approaches will lead to the longer-term goal of synchronizing the development of a deeper and stronger knowledge base about effective teaching and applications intended to assess and support teaching in the field.

For the past 15 years, we have been working with a group of colleagues in the broad domain of teacher–student interaction. This work has been anchored in the science and theory of human development, through which proximal processes between individuals (systems of social interactions and relationships and their components and properties) are posited to account for considerable growth in broad areas of development, including cognition, achievement, social relationships, self-regulation, motivation, and identity. This work has resulted in a suite of standardized protocols that describe, define, observe, and form the basis for improving teachers' interactions with students from preschool to high school, each with empirical findings in published peer-reviewed journal articles (authored by members of our team and other investigators). Numerous studies examine matters of psychometrics and measurement properties, conditions of implementation, and questions of effects on student learning and development (see Pianta, 2011, for a summary).

On the applied side of the dialectic, we have a much better understanding now than we did a decade ago of the infrastructure needed to enable rigorous implementation of observations at scale. For example, more than 20,000 observers have been trained to acceptable levels of reliability using the Classroom Assessment Scoring System (CLASS; Pianta, La Paro, & Hamre, 2008). The training, certification, and recertification of observers are fundamental components of the infrastructure needed to sustain implementation of a standardized protocol used with fidelity across time, settings, and purposes. Opportunities to implement at scale have forced us to develop the systems and scaffolds that practitioners need to implement these tools with fidelity and in ways that synchronize with their workflow and roles. As CLASS has been deployed, the obtained empirical results have helped to expand and deepen a theory concerning the nature, developmental course, and role of teacher–student interactions in learning and development (Hafen et al., 2015; Hamre, 2014). Our experiences and the evidence garnered have been helpful in pointing out gaps between instruments being used in research and the supports needed for practitioners to use these tools daily, and the importance of linking theory with application.

TECHNICAL AND PROCEDURAL MATTERS SUPPORTING RIGOROUS APPLICATION OF CLASSROOM OBSERVATIONS

Observations of teachers' interactions with students can be an effective tool in building capacity for teaching and learning (Bill and Melinda Gates Foundation, 2012; Pianta, La Paro, & Hamre, 2008). The use of *standardized* observations, if they reliably and validly measure aspects of teachers' interactions that impact student learning, is a direct and effective mechanism for improving teaching and learning and can also illuminate links between certain inputs to teachers (e.g., professional development experiences) with desired outcomes (e.g., student learning). When using observational tools that are standardized, reliable, and valid, educators can begin to use a common language and lens for teaching. In using a common language and lens, educators know that they are making comparisons across teachers on an even playing field when describing performance across classrooms; by using a valid lens, they know that the behaviors they observe are related to student growth and development (Bill and Melinda Gates Foundation, 2013; Pianta & Hamre, 2009).

Use of standardized, reliable, and valid tools allows for the provision of specific and individualized feedback on defined areas that are consistent across teachers, providing a strong background for interpretation of scores. Using standardized, reliable, and valid tools is far preferable to customized approaches in which every classroom, school, or district adapts an existing tool or develops a new one. Those customizations rarely if ever have the strong technical properties (reliability, validity) present for well-researched tools; inferences and interpretations made using these customized tools often break down quickly.

Available observation systems vary widely in the degree of standardization of protocols, standards, and supports for reliability of scores and validity—particularly as related to associations between observations and student learning. Current systems include observation instruments developed for use in single content areas (e.g., Grossman, Cohen, Ronfeldt, & Brown, 2014; Hill, 2010) and those developed for use across content areas (e.g., Danielson, 2007; Marzano, 2014; Pianta, La Paro, & Hamre, 2008).

Below we briefly discuss important elements in ensuring that these observation systems can be used at scale in ways that will help set the stage for improvements in instruction.

Standardized Procedures for Observation and Scoring

Standardized approaches for using observation systems provide clear instructions for use, both in terms of how to set up and conduct observations as well as how to assign scores. Without standardized directions to follow, observers will make different choices about scheduling and conducting observations, limiting the potential for agreement among observers when making ratings, and thus hampering systemwide applicability (Bill and Melinda Gates Foundation, 2010; Pianta & Hamre, 2009). Importantly, standardization is not the same as reliability or validity; it refers to the rules and procedures for collecting observations and for ensuring consistency and quality control in how information is collected. These rules and procedures include considerations of time of day, qualifications of observers, observation length, and other features that could undermine the quality of data collected and ultimately the inferences drawn from those data.

There are three main components of standardization that users may consider evaluating in an observation instrument: (1) training protocol,

(2) parameters around observation, and (3) scoring directions. With regard to the training protocol, there are several questions to ask, including the following: Are there specific directions for learning to use the instrument? Is there a comprehensive training manual or user's guide? Are there videos or transcripts with gold standard scores available that allow for scoring practice? Are other procedures in place that allow for reliability checks (live, via video, or via transcript) to ensure that their scoring is consistent? Are there guidelines around training to be completed before using the tool (e.g., a reliability test, practice observations)?

Regarding parameters around observation, users are advised to look for direction and standardization in a number of areas. These include length of observations and start and stop times of observations (are there predetermined times, times connected with start and end times of lessons/activities, or some other mechanism for determining when to begin and end?). Direction is also useful around time of day or specific activities to observe, whether observations are announced or unannounced, and other related issues.

With regard to scoring, there should be clear guidelines. Do users score during the observation itself or after the observation? Is there a predefined observe/score interval? How are scores assigned? Is there a rubric that guides users in matching what they observe with specific scores or categories of scores (i.e., high, moderate, low)? Are there examples of the kinds of practices that correspond to different scores?

Reliability Information and Guidelines

Reliability is a key consideration in selecting an observational assessment tool (Bill and Melinda Gates Foundation, 2010; Pianta & Hamre, 2009). Observation measures are not inherently reliable or unreliable. Rather, reliability is determined by the ways in which scores are obtained using any measure. However, measures, and their associated training and supports for observers, do vary in the extent to which they have evidence of being able to support large numbers of observers to make ratings consistently, minimizing the degree of error. Reliability of scores using any measure can be impacted by a wide range of factors (e.g., raters, length of the observation period, training). It is important for users to look for tools with demonstrated ability to produce reliable scores (within a confidence interval acceptable to support the inferences being made) for the same observed behaviors regardless of features of the classroom outside of the scope of the tool and regardless of who is making the ratings.

There are several aspects of reliability, each of which corresponds to the ways in which a specific source of error may undermine a specific inference being made about the meaning of a score. Perhaps the two most relevant when considering classroom observation systems are stability over time and consistency across observers. With regard to stability over time, assuming a goal is to detect consistent and stable patterns of teachers' behaviors, users need to know that constructs being assessed represent a stable characteristic of the teacher across situations in the classroom and are not random occurrences or behaviors that are linked exclusively to the particular moment of observation. If ratings shift notably and unpredictably from one observation cycle or day or week to the next, these ratings may not represent core aspects of teachers' practice. Conversely, if scores are at least moderately consistent across time, they likely represent something stable about the set of skills that teachers bring into the classroom setting, and feedback and support around these behaviors is much more likely to resonate with teachers and to function as useful levers for helping them change their practice. It is advantageous if observational tools provide information on their test–retest reliability, or the extent to which ratings on the tool are consistent across different periods of time (e.g., within a day, across days, across weeks). Recent evidence suggests moderate levels of reliability of most observation measures across time and suggests that obtaining scores that best reflect stable characteristics of teachers will require observations across at least several days (Kane, Kerr, & Pianta, 2014).

With regard to stability across observers, in order for results of observations to be useful and valid, training protocols and provision of scoring directions must be clear enough to produce agreement across observers. If there is very low agreement between two or more observers' ratings of the same observation period, the degree to which the ratings represent the teachers' behavior rather than the observers' subjective interpretations of that behavior or personal preferences is questionable. Conversely, if two independent observers can consistently assign the same ratings to the same patterns of observed behaviors, it is more likely that ratings truly represent attributes of the teacher as defined by the scoring system, as opposed to attributes of the observer, and the system can be deployed using a large number of observers who have been trained. Therefore, users may wish to select systems in which there is documented consensus among trained raters on whether or not or to what extent teachers are engaging in the various behaviors under consideration.

Initial training for new raters typically takes several days (Halle & Vick, 2007). Training raters in large numbers over a short period of time is a significant undertaking (Cash, Pianta, & Suldo, 2014) and requires a highly standardized approach so that calibration across trainers can be assured. Training raters typically involves reviewing the scoring rubrics, providing examples, opportunities to practice scoring followed by discussion and feedback, and an assessment of calibration to scores assigned by expert raters (Johnson, Penny, & Gordon, 2008). Often, training continues until a rater passes the calibration assessment at a predetermined criterion of agreement with expert scores (Moon & Hughes, 2005). Successful training of large numbers of raters quickly and effectively is important for at-scale efforts to operate smoothly. For all of the effort required to coordinate observational assessment in large-scale contexts, and for the impact of decisions resulting from these efforts, establishing a growing cadre of calibrated raters is a crucial first step.

Validity: Associations Between Teachers' Behaviors and Student Learning

Identifying teaching that is *effective* depends on establishing empirical connections between descriptions of teachers' behavior(s) and an array of possible indicators of student learning. Validity is a concept used to capture the many facets of measurement that pertain to the extent to which an instrument measures what it claims to measure. For assessments of teacher effectiveness, one aspect of validity is the degree to which scores or metrics derived from a system used to observe teacher behaviors are associated with the student (or teacher) outcomes about which the observation is designed to provide information or make predictions.

This predictive validity may be one of the most important aspects to consider when selecting and using an observation instrument. Having this evidence supports teacher buy-in to observationally based feedback, and increases confidence of teacher educators and school personnel for establishing observationally based standards and mechanisms for meeting them (Allen, Pianta, Gregory, Mikami, & Lun, 2011; Kane et al., 2014; Pianta & Hamre, 2009; Taylor & Tyler, 2012). Absent credible evidence of predictive validity with regard to an array of student outcomes, users have no such assurances, and care should be taken when considering use either in professional development or accountability frameworks.

LINKING RIGOROUS APPLICATION IN PRACTICE TO THEORIES OF EFFECTIVE TEACHING

There is little question that teachers matter for student achievement (Goe, 2007; Bill and Melinda Gates Foundation 2012), motivation (Wang & Holcombe, 2010), and a range of behavioral and social outcomes (Jones,

Brown, Hoglund, & Aber, 2010). However, most teacher effects studies fail to document the specific teaching behaviors that account for detected impacts on students' outcomes. As a field, our larger aim must be to suggest that *rigorous application* of observational assessments of teacher performance is informed by (and informs) a *theory of effective teaching.*

Efforts to describe effective teaching have led to large numbers of small-scale studies; many attempts at description that lack evidence of validity or standardized tools for data collection (Lemov, 2010); challenges in more systematically discerning and measuring the aspects of teacher behavior that are unique to teaching a certain content area (Grossman et al., 2014; Hill, 2010) or grade level (Pianta et al., 2013); or derivations that are specific to data collection methods such as observation or informant report (Kane et al., 2014; Raudenbush & Jean, 2014). When studies have included various forms of assessing teacher–student interaction, including multiple observation tools (Bill and Melinda Gates Foundation, 2012; Staiger & Rockoff, 2010), or combinations of observation and student report (Kane et al., 2014; Raudenbush & Jean, 2014), the evidence indicates considerable commonality across clusters of behaviors identified as reliably detectable and as salient for student learning (Hamre et al., 2013). These clusters include teachers' social and emotional behaviors toward students, practices related to classroom management, and delivery of instruction (Danielson, 2007; Marzano, 2014). Thus, although operationalized descriptions of the elements of developmentally salient teacher behavior remain fragmented and unstandardized in the sense of a systematic lexicon and lack the precision and structure of a formal classification system, the evidence does suggest possibilities for convergence on common elements.

In a series of theoretical and empirical papers published over the past decade, we, our colleagues, and independent researchers in several countries (e.g., Hafen et al., 2015; Hamre et al., 2013; Hamre, Hatfield, Jamil, & Pianta, 2014; Leyva et al., 2015; Pakarinen et al., 2011; Pianta, Mashburn, Downer, Hamre, & Justice, 2008) have presented and evaluated one such framework of effective teaching, *Teaching Through Interactions* (TTI), operationalized through observation and focusing exclusively on interactions between teachers and students as the proximal process through which teachers influence learning and development.

Research using the CLASS, the observational measure aligned with this framework, has provided partial evidence supporting the three TTI-hypothesized common domains of teacher–child interactions—Emotional Support, Classroom Organization, and Instructional Support—as a theoretically and empirically sound approach to describing teacher–student interactions in classrooms (Hamre et al., 2013). In numerous studies, the three domains of teacher–child interactions (emotional, organizational, instructional) have each been linked to students' social, emotional, regulatory, and cognitive development (see Downer, Sabol, & Hamre, 2010, for review). In general, effect sizes obtained between these ratings of the features of teachers' interactive behaviors and student outcomes such as achievement test scores are modest in magnitude but statistically significant (Burchinal, Vandergrift, Pianta, & Mashburn, 2010; Leyva et al., 2015; Mashburn et al., 2008; Pakarinen et al., 2011), with larger correlations for students with higher risk profiles (Hamre & Pianta, 2005) and for students' motivation (Ferguson with Hirsch, 2014). Similar results have been obtained using different observation measures, such as Danielson's Framework for Teaching (FFT) (Kane et al., 2014). Across measures, the factors or domains tend to be highly correlated, limiting examination of the extent to which individual domains of interactions are associated with specific domains of children's development (Hamre et al., 2013).

Hamre et al. (2014) built on this work by using bifactor modeling to evaluate hypothetically differential predictions of child outcomes by general and domain-specific factors. This study found that children in classrooms with high levels of responsive teaching, a *general* system-level property of teachers' interactions, demonstrated greater gains in cognitive, self-regulatory, and relational functioning. Moreover, there was also support for domain specificity in associations between specific features of teacher–child interaction and child outcomes, with teachers' positive management and cognitive stimulation uniquely predicting self-regulation skills and academic performance, respectively, independent of responsive teaching (Hamre et al., 2014). Several recent replication efforts suggest value to this approach (Downer, Ruzek, Stuhlman, & Hamre, 2014; Hafen et al., 2015).

From a theoretical standpoint, the bifactor modeling results confirm that the multiple facets of teachers' behavior, when observed, are likely to share common underlying features, perhaps reflective of properties of dyadic systems, as has been hypothesized (Pianta, 1999), as well as facets that may be unique to a specific intent, or focus. When factored using conventional techniques of extraction and rotation, the commonalities across features show up as correlations among separate factors that each reveal an intent or focus of teacher behavior. When using bifactor techniques, the common and unique features are more clearly distinguished and show up in differential prediction to outcomes. In each case, approaches to factoring and description of effective teaching help deepen understanding of its form and impact.

IMPROVING QUALITIES OF TEACHER–STUDENT INTERACTION

Perhaps the most important application and test of a theory of effective teaching is whether teachers' behavior will predictably improve as a consequence of exposure to some intervention, and that such improvement will in turn lead to student learning and development. Findings corroborating these links would reinforce not only the theory that describes and identifies effective teaching behavior, but also that a measurement tool used to gather information on these behaviors actually captures information on teacher impact. Over the last decade we have developed and tested a coaching intervention designed to improve student outcomes by explicitly focusing teachers on the nature of their daily interactions with students. The MyTeachingPartner (MTP) coaching program uses the dimensions of the CLASS to operationalize teacher–child interactions for coaches and teachers.

MTP coaching integrates initial workshop-based training, an annotated video library, and personalized online coaching (Allen et al., 2011) and has been evaluated in four randomized controlled studies. The first evaluation, with over 200 prekindergarten teachers, showed that exposure to MTP led to significant improvements in the quality of teachers' interactions with children, increases in children's literacy skills, and decreases in problem behavior (Mashburn, Downer, Hamre, Justice, & Pianta, 2010; Pianta, Mashburn, et al., 2008). A more recent experimental evaluation of MTP with over 400 teachers in 15 preschool program sites reported that exposure to MTP coaching led to significant gains in teacher–child interaction quality and children's self-regulation and expressive language skills (Downer, Pianta, et al., 2014; Pianta et al., 2014). Two separate studies in secondary schools suggest impacts of MTP on student achievement, student engagement, motivation, and teachers' responsiveness to students as compared to a business-as-usual control group (Allen et al., 2011; Allen, Hafen, Gregory, Mikami, & Pianta, in press).

Several other curricular and coaching interventions have shown an impact on both CLASS scores and student learning and development, suggesting the robustness of these methods (Bierman et al., 2008; Piasta et al., 2012). Most of these interventions share common features such as providing teachers with feedback (e.g., information, video, probes for analysis) from a coach, based on that coach's observation of the teachers' actual interactions with students in their classroom. The regularity with which coaching produces changes in features of teacher–student interaction suggests the malleability of interactions and their responsiveness to a range of contextual supports. Malleable features of interaction are not apparently a function of fixed personality traits, but rather properties of a dynamic system of contextual and personal factors.

LEVERAGING MEASUREMENT AND THEORY THROUGH TEACHER PERFORMANCE EVALUATION AND IMPROVEMENT

We conclude with a series of propositions about teachers and teaching: (1) Teachers are the most potent asset the education system provides to foster student learning and development (Sabol, Hong, Pianta, & Burchinal, 2013); (2) qualities of teacher–student interactions that foster student engagement, motivation, thinking, and positive relationships are the reasons why teachers have such effects (Pianta & Allen, 2008); (3) features of teachers' interactions can be observed and measured, and these measures predict student learning (Bill and Melinda Gates Foundation, 2012); (4) effective teaching can be learned, taught, and improved (Allen et al., 2011); and (5) effective teaching is in very short supply and not consistently generated by the very system designed and intended for its production (Hamre, 2014). The key question, at present, is how to leverage existing theory, existing tools, and existing applications to drive improvement in the validity and impact of all.

Unfortunately, teacher performance assessment as typically practiced in the field or in teacher preparation has historically been very unsystematic. With Race to the Top (RTTT) funding, a number of states developed systems to tie data on teacher education graduates to data on K–12 student learning, and many developed multimethod approaches for measuring teachers' performance, including data from observation, state standardized tests, and K–12 student surveys, among others. Missing from this first phase of assessment and uses has been a strong evidence base for the assessments and for their various applications. One could argue that the considerable level of activity in this area has resulted in too little actionable information that translated into real improvements for teachers or for students, leading some to question the utility of the entire effort to assess teacher quality. As policy trends and requirements have forced educators to rethink and redesign their evaluation systems, the need for high-quality and data-driven evidence to guide and drive improvements in these development plans creates a sizable risk that the new systems may not make the significant improvements from the status quo that are needed. We have argued here that one of the reasons for the lack of evidence—for assessments, methods of assessment, uses of assessment, or professional development and training models based on assessment—is a larger lack of capacity in the field pertaining to strong, empirically verifiable theories of effective teaching.

Legislation at the federal, state, and local levels increasingly promotes the formation of teacher evaluation systems that can provide a well-rounded appraisal of a teacher's instruction, including both observational measures of the quality of instruction and quantifiable impacts on students' learning. An effective evaluation and feedback system should provide the basis for making decisions about facets of human capital development such as professional development or merit pay. In creating comprehensive evaluation systems, school districts are tasked with building fair *and* rigorous systems, often from the ground up, that incorporate multiple measures—teacher observational protocol(s), student-report surveys, and teacher value-added scores—often in varying combinations and weights. District leaders face numerous decisions in this work, including determining which of many protocols to use, how best to determine whether their measure(s) of choice corresponds to broader aims to improve student learning, how to determine trigger points for certain contingencies (e.g., supplementary professional development or merit pay), and which of the myriad professional development programs to utilize, among others.

A rigorous approach to gathering, analyzing, and using assessment data should start with a theory of effective teaching that motivates clear statements of what is to be measured and why. It should include what data are to be collected and how they are to be analyzed, decision rules for interpretation and uses of the data, and how the intended and unintended consequences of the overall program of assessment activities will be evaluated and in turn inform theory. The utility of evidence related to effective teaching is predicated on measures, but it is even more dependent on the questions framed, alignment of those questions to theory and data sources, and the quality of analysis. Progress on these questions, as we argue and hopefully illustrate, rests not only on rigorous application of technically strong measures (standardized procedures, technical properties of reliability and validity, supports for high-fidelity implementation) but also with the continued and practice-informed refinement of theory.

REFERENCES

Allen, J. P., Hafen, C. A., Gregory, A. C., Mikami, A. Y., & Pianta, R. (in press). Enhancing secondary school instruction and student achievement: Replication and extension of the My Teaching Partner–Secondary intervention. *Journal of Research on Educational Effectiveness.*

Allen, J. P., Pianta, R. C., Gregory, A., Mikami, A. Y., & Lun, J. (2011). An interaction-based approach to enhancing secondary school instruction and student achievement. *Science, 333*(6045), 1034–1037.

Bierman, K. L., Domitrovich, C. E., Nix, R. L., Gest, S. D., Welsh, J. A., Greenberg, M. T., . . . Gill, S. (2008). Promoting academic and social-emotional school readiness: The Head Start REDI program. *Child Development, 79*, 1802–1817.

Bill and Melinda Gates Foundation. (2010). *Learning about teaching: Initial findings from the Measures of Effective Teaching project* (MET project research paper). Seattle, WA: Author.

Bill and Melinda Gates Foundation. (2012). *Gathering feedback for teaching: Combining high-quality observations with student surveys and achievement gains* (MET project policy and practice brief). Seattle, WA: Author.

Bill and Melinda Gates Foundation. (2013). *Ensuring fair and reliable measures of effective teaching: Culminating findings from the MET project's three-year study.* Seattle, WA: Author.

Burchinal, M., Vandergrift, N., Pianta, R., & Mashburn, A. (2010). Threshold analysis of association between child care quality and child outcomes for low-income children in pre-kindergarten programs. *Early Childhood Research Quarterly, 25*(2), 166–176.

Cash, A. H., Pianta, R. C., & Suldo, S. (2014). The role of scheduling in observing teacher–child interactions. *School Psychology Review, 43*(4), 428–449.

Danielson, C. (2007). *Enhancing professional practice: A framework for teaching* (2nd ed.). Alexandria, VA: Association for Supervision and Curriculum Development.

Downer, J. T., Pianta, R. C., Burchinal, M., Field, S., Hamre, B. K., LoCasale-Crouch, J., . . . Scott-Little, C. (2014). *Coaching and coursework focused on teacher–child interactions during language/literacy instruction: Effects on teacher outcomes and children's classroom engagement.* University of Virginia Working Paper.

Downer, J., Ruzek, E., Stuhlman, M., & Hamre, B. (2014). *Observing teacher–student interactions in upper elementary school with the Classroom Assessment Scoring System (CLASS).* Paper presented at the American Educational Research Association Annual Conference, Philadelphia, PA.

Downer, J., Sabol, T. J., & Hamre, B. K. (2010). Teacher–child interactions in the classroom: Toward a theory of within- and cross-domain links to children's developmental outcomes. *Early Education and Development, 21*, 699–723.

Ferguson, R. F., with Hirsch, E. (2014). How working conditions predict teaching quality and student outcomes. In T. J. Kane, K. A. Kerr, & R. C. Pianta (Eds.), *Designing teaching evaluation systems* (pp. 332–380). San Francisco, CA: Wiley.

Goe, L. (2007). *The link between teacher quality and student outcomes: A research synthesis.* Washington, DC: National Comprehensive Center for Teacher Quality.

Grossman, P., Cohen, J., Ronfeldt, M., & Brown, L. (2014). The test matters: The relationship between classroom observation scores and teacher value-added on multiple types of assessment. *Educational Researcher, 43*(6), 293–303.

Hafen, C. A., Hamre, B. K., Allen, J. P., Bell, C. A., Gitomer, D. H., & Pianta, R. C. (2015). Teaching through interactions in secondary school classrooms: Revisiting the factor structure and practical application of the Classroom Assessment Scoring System—Secondary. *Journal of Early Adolescence, 35*(5–6), 651–680.

Halle, T., & Vick, J. (2007). *Quality in early childhood care and education settings: A compendium of measures.* Washington, DC: Child Trends for the Office of Planning, Research and Evaluation, Administration for Children and Families, U.S. Department of Health and Human Services. Retrieved from www.childtrends.org/Files/Child_Trends-2010_03_10_FR_QualityCompendium.pdf

Hamre, B. K. (2014). Teachers' daily interactions with children: An essential ingredient of effective early childhood programs. *Child Development Perspectives, 8*(4), 223–230.

Hamre, B., Hatfield, B., Jamil, F., & Pianta, R. C. (2014). Evidence for general and domain-specific elements of teacher–child interactions: Associations with preschool children's development. *Child Development, 85*(3), 1257–1274.

Hamre, B. K., & Pianta, R. C. (2005). Can instructional and emotional support in the first grade classroom make a difference for children at risk of school failure? *Child Development, 76*(5), 949–967.

Hamre, B. K., Pianta, R. C., Downer, J. T., DeCoster, J., Mashburn, A. J., Jones, S. M., . . . Hamagami, A. (2013). Teaching through interactions: Testing a developmental framework of teacher effectiveness in over 4,000 classrooms. *Elementary School Journal, 113*(4), 461–487.

Hill, H. C. (2010). The nature and predictors of elementary teachers' mathematical knowledge for teaching. *Journal for Research in Mathematics Education, 41*(5), 513–545.

Johnson, R. L., Penny, J. A., & Gordon, B. (2008). *Assessing performance: Designing, scoring, and validating performance tasks.* New York, NY: Guilford Press.

Jones, S. M., Brown, J. L., Hoglund, W. L. G., & Aber, J. L. (2010). Impacts of an integrated school-based social-emotional learning and literacy intervention on third-grade social-emotional and academic outcomes. *Journal of Consulting and Clinical Psychology, 78,* 829–842.

Kane, T. J., Kerr, K. A., & Pianta, R. C. (Eds.). (2014). *Designing teaching evaluation systems.* San Francisco, CA: Wiley & Sons.

Lemov, D. (2010). *Teach like a champion: 49 techniques that put students on the path to college.* San Francisco, CA: Jossey-Bass.

Leyva, D., Weiland, C., Barata, M., Yoshikawa, H., Snow, C., Treviño, E., & Rolla, A. (2015). Teacher–child interactions in Chile and their associations with prekindergarten outcomes. *Child Development, 86*(3), 781–799.

Marzano, R. (2014). *Marzano Teacher Evaluation Model.* Retrieved from www.marzanoevaluation.com

Mashburn, A. J., Downer, J. T., Hamre, B. K., Justice, L. M., & Pianta, R. C. (2010). Consultation for teachers and children's language and literacy development during pre-kindergarten. *Applied Developmental Science, 14*(4), 179–196.

Mashburn, A., Pianta, R. Hamre, B., Downer, J., Barbarin, O., Bryant, D., . . . Howes, C. (2008). Measures of classroom quality in pre-kindergarten and children's development of academic, language, and social skills. *Child Development, 79*(3), 732–749.

Moon, T. R., & Hughes, K. R. (2005). Training and scoring issues involved in large-scale writing assessments. *Educational Measurement: Issues and Practice, 21*(2), 15–19.

Pakarinen, E., Kiurua, N., Lerkkanenb, M. K., Poikkeusb, A. M., Ahonena, T., & Nurmi, J. E. (2011). Instructional support predicts children's task avoidance in kindergarten. *Early Childhood Research Quarterly, 26*, 376–386.

Pianta, R. C. (1999). *Enhancing relationships between children and teachers.* Washington, DC: American Psychological Association.

Pianta, R. C. (2011). *Teaching children well: New evidence-based approaches to teacher professional development and training.* Washington, DC: Center for American Progress. Retrieved from www.americanprogress.org/issues/2011/11/teaching_children_well.html

Pianta, R. C., & Allen, J. P. (2008). Building capacity for positive youth development in secondary school classrooms: Changing teachers' interactions with students. In M. Shinn & H. Yoshikawa (Eds.), *Toward positive youth development: Transforming schools and community programs* (pp. 21–39). New York, NY: Oxford University Press.

Pianta, R. C., Burchinal, M., Hamre, B., Downer, J., Howes, C., Locasale-Crouch, J., . . . Scott-Little, C. (2013). *Coaching and coursework focused on teacher–child interactions during language/literacy instruction: Effects on children's school readiness skills.* University of Virginia Working Paper.

Pianta, R. C., DeCoster, J., Cabell, S. Q., Burchinal, M., Hamre, B. K., Downer, J. T., & Howes, C. (2014). Dose-response relations between preschool teachers' exposure to components of professional development and increases in quality of their interactions with children. *Early Childhood Research Quarterly, 29*, 499–508.

Pianta, R. C., & Hamre, B. K. (2009). Conceptualization, measurement, and improvement of classroom processes: Standardized observation can leverage capacity. *Educational Researcher, 38*(2), 109–119.

Pianta, R. C., La Paro, K. M., & Hamre, B. K. (2008). *Classroom Assessment Scoring System (CLASS).* Baltimore, MD: Paul H. Brookes.

Pianta, R. C., Mashburn, A., Downer, J., Hamre, B., & Justice, L. (2008). Effects of web-mediated professional development resources on teacher–child interactions in pre-kindergarten classrooms. *Early Childhood Research Quarterly, 23*(4), 431–451.

Piasta, S. B., Justice, L. M., Cabell, S. Q., Wiggins, A. K., Pence Turnbull, K., & Curenton, S. M. (2012). Impact of professional development on preschool teachers' conversational responsivity and children's linguistic productivity and complexity. *Early Childhood Research Quarterly, 27*, 387–400.

Raudenbush, S. W., & Jean, M. (2014). To what extent do student perceptions of classroom quality predict teacher value added? In T. J. Kane, K. A. Kerr, & R. C. Pianta (Eds.), *Designing teaching evaluation systems* (pp. 170–202). San Francisco, CA: Wiley & Sons.

Sabol, T. J., Hong, S. L., Pianta, R. C., & Burchinal, M. R. (2013). Can rating pre-K programs predict children's learning? *Science, 341*(7148), 845–846.

Staiger, D. O., & Rockoff, J. E. (2010). Searching for effective teachers with imperfect information. *The Journal of Economic Perspectives*, *24*(3), 97–117.

Taylor, E. S., & Tyler, J. H. (2012). The effect of evaluation on teacher performance. *American Economic Review, 102*(7), 3628–3651.

Wang, M.-T., & Holcombe, R. (2010). Adolescents' perceptions of school environment, engagement, and academic achievement in middle school. *American Educational Research Journal*, *47*(3), 633–662.

CHAPTER 4

The Multiple Dimensions of Teacher Quality

Does Value-Added Capture Teachers' Nonachievement Contributions to Their Schools?

Jason A. Grissom
Susanna Loeb
Christopher Doss

Already essential to school accountability, student test score growth increasingly factors into decisions about teacher evaluation, compensation, and staffing decisions (Cohen-Vogel, 2011). Critics, however, express concern about whether teacher value-added estimates accurately reflect teachers' job performance (e.g., Harris, 2012). Technical issues aside, teachers can contribute to their schools on multiple dimensions inside and outside the classroom, not all of which may be captured by student test score growth. Moreover, a teacher's performance in different areas of the job need not positively correlate with one another. A teacher who is successful at teaching the kinds of basic skills often assessed in standardized tests need not excel at other aspects of instruction, such as teaching higher-order thinking skills, nor in noninstructional areas, such as helping build a positive school community.

The potential for an effective teacher on one dimension to not necessarily be an effective teacher on other dimensions that hold value for the school leaves open the possibility that evaluation systems focused or exclusively reliant on student growth measures may fail to appropriately differentiate "high" and "low" performers. This chapter illuminates these issues by investigating multiple dimensions of teacher performance and how they compare with one another and with teacher value-added to student test performance. Of course, as just suggested, the absence of a correlation between value-added and a performance dimension is only important if a dimension holds value for the school. We provide some evidence on what dimensions schools value by testing which performance dimensions are associated with whether the principal reports that he or she wishes to continue working with a given teacher.

Our analysis utilizes data from a large set of principal interviews in the Miami-Dade County Public Schools. In these interviews, we asked principals to discuss the roles, strengths, and weaknesses of four of their teachers (identified by the interviewer) and to provide ratings of each teacher's performance along eight dimensions of teacher effectiveness. Four of these dimensions capture job performance related to instruction in their classrooms, such as improving critical thinking, while the remaining four describe performance outside their classrooms, such as building positive colleague relationships. We also asked principals whether they wished to continue working with that teacher next year. Data from the interviews are then linked to administrative records for the specific teachers the principals discussed.

Using these linked data, we investigate two research questions. First, how strongly are the various dimensions of principal-assessed teacher quality associated with teachers' value-added to student test performance in math and reading? Second, do the subjective performance dimensions predict principals' interest in retaining that teacher in the school, and how do these predictions compare to those based on math and reading value-added?

Our analysis underscores the multidimensionality of teacher practice. It also demonstrates the relative values placed on each dimension of that practice by school administrators, an important analysis given the role those administrators play in subjectively evaluating teacher performance. Last, the study provides evidence relevant to the ongoing policy debate about the use of value-added measures to rate teacher effectiveness by assessing the degree to which value-added measures are capable of identifying effective teachers across an array of job performance areas.

MULTIPLE DIMENSIONS OF TEACHER EFFECTIVENESS

The well-established empirical fact that teacher effectiveness is a primary driver of student learning has driven recent policy efforts to measure and reward it. Policy discussion around these measurements and rewards in recent years has centered on teacher value-added (Harris, 2012). The main idea of teacher value-added models is that given enough years of data on the characteristics and performance of a teacher's students, statistical models can identify the average impact on student test score growth associated with a given teacher (McCaffrey, Koretz, Lockwood, & Hamilton, 2004). There is general consensus among researchers that value-added approaches can differentiate effective from ineffective teachers, on average, though measures are imprecise for individual teachers (Hanushek & Rivkin, 2010).

Indeed, among some education policy researchers, *teacher effectiveness* and *teacher performance* have become nearly synonymous with *teacher value-added*. A large and growing number of studies of teachers and their effects operationalize their performance using some variant of the standard value-added model (e.g., Aaronson, Barrow, & Sander, 2007; Rivkin, Hanushek, & Kain, 2005). Even studies questioning the reliability and validity of value-added models for parameterizing teacher effectiveness often focus on statistical and methodological issues rather than on the question of whether contributions to student test score growth capture all relevant aspects of teacher's performance (e.g., Koedel & Betts, 2010; Rothstein, 2010).

Other evidence suggests that the exclusive focus on student test score growth as a measure of teachers' contributions is too narrow. Students' cognitive development is but one dimension of skill growth affecting future outcomes, and test performance is but one dimension of cognitive development. A handful of studies have shown that other attributes are correlated with greater success in the labor market (e.g., Heckman & Rubinstein, 2001; Lindqvist & Vestman, 2011). Few studies, however, measure the effect of teachers on student noncognitive outcomes. Jennings and DiPrete (2010) find that kindergarten teachers can meaningfully affect student noncognitive skills, which in turn correlate with academic outcomes. Jackson (2013) provides evidence that teachers can affect noncognitive dimensions of student outcomes (e.g., motivation, self-restraint), represented by such outcomes as absences and suspensions. These noncognitive outcomes during high school are significant predictors of such postsecondary outcomes as attending college and income at age 25. Importantly, the study also finds that teachers' value-added to learning as measured by student test scores is only weakly related to their contributions to students' noncognitive outcomes. This finding suggests that test-based value-added measures miss key aspects of teacher impacts on students.

The dimensions of teachers' job performance also extend beyond those that directly impact students. Popular evaluation tools, such as Framework for Teaching, rate teachers in part on the basis of nonclassroom outcomes (Danielson, 1996). We are unaware, however, of research investigating the degree to which test-based measures of teacher value-added correlate with execution of professional responsibilities and nonclassroom teacher performance outcomes. The two need not be positively correlated. As with Jackson's (2013) focus on skills that improve students' cognitive and noncognitive outcomes, teachers who excel in teaching students basic skills may not be strong in nonclassroom aspects of the job. Moreover, the accountability pressures teachers face may push them to think of investment in increasing their students' test performance as requiring trade-offs with other aspects of their job performance. In this way, teacher performance dimensions may even be substitutes rather than complements.

In using principal assessments of teachers and linking them to test-score-based effectiveness measures, we add to a small and growing body of literature that tests the degree to which subjective evaluations of teacher skills accurately predict teacher productivity. Several studies have shown that subjective evaluations of teachers by principals are correlated with value-added scores (Grissom & Loeb, 2014; Harris, Ingle, & Rutledge, 2014; Harris & Sass, 2014; Jacob & Lefgren, 2008; Rockoff, Staiger, Kane, & Taylor, 2012). These studies have documented that principals' subjective evaluations can differentiate the highest- and lowest-performing teachers, as measured by value-added, particularly when there are no stakes attached to the principal's ratings (e.g., Jacob & Lefgren, 2008; Rockoff et al., 2012). Low-stakes evaluations tend to show greater variance and higher correlations with value-added metrics than high-stakes personnel evaluation ratings in which principals may face pressures to inflate teachers' scores (Grissom & Loeb, 2014). Yet even in low-stakes settings, correlations between principal ratings of teacher performance and teachers' value-added scores often are low to moderate. Qualitative evidence suggests that principals' performance ratings incorporate their professional judgment about teacher personality, effort, and other factors that may not be captured by value-added (Harris et al., 2014).

DATA AND MEASURES

Our analysis of the relationships among different dimensions of teachers' job performance uses original data we collected in the Miami-Dade County Public Schools (M-DCPS). M-DCPS is the nation's fourth-largest school district, enrolling approximately 350,000 students. Nearly 90% of students in the district are either black or Hispanic, and 60% qualify for free or reduced-price lunches. We combine primary data collected from interviews with administrative data provided to us by the district describing students, teachers, and schools.

Interviews

In the spring of 2012, we conducted structured interviews with 93 principals as part of a larger study of school leadership (see Grissom & Loeb, 2011; Grissom, Loeb, & Master, 2013). The sample of interviewed principals included all high school principals in the district, plus a random sample of elementary and middle school principals. In the interview, we asked principals to discuss the strengths and weaknesses of four specific teachers we identified. Although we did not reveal our choice mechanism to the principals, we chose teachers who were instructors of a tested grade and subject combination for whom we could calculate value-added in math and/or reading. Two random teachers were chosen from below the median of the value-added distribution and two from above the median. Whenever possible, one relatively inexperienced teacher (i.e., less than 5 years) and one experienced teacher (5+ years) was chosen in each group.

For each teacher, principals were asked a series of open- and closed-ended questions, first about their performance in instruction and then about their performance outside the classroom. For instruction, we first asked, "What are this teacher's strengths and weaknesses inside the classroom, that is, in his/her role as an instructor?" We then asked about four specific areas of instruction, asking the principals to rate the teachers on a scale of 1 (very ineffective) to 6 (very effective): (1) getting high standardized test performance from students; (2) developing students' higher-order thinking skills, such as synthesis and evaluation; (3) motivating students to learn; and (4) helping students build strong interpersonal skills. We also asked the principals to rate the teachers' classroom performance overall using the same 1–6 scale.

Next, we asked principals to discuss the teachers' contributions outside the classroom: "I'd like you to think about this teacher's strengths and weaknesses outside his/her own classroom. In other words, I'd like to know about how this teacher contributes (or doesn't contribute) to the school environment beyond his/her role as a classroom instructor. How would you describe these strengths and weaknesses?" We then again asked the principal to rate each teacher on four nonclassroom performance dimensions using a 1–6 scale: (1) building positive interpersonal relationships among the staff at this school; (2) supporting the instructional effectiveness of his/her fellow teachers (e.g., through mentoring or being a resource); (3) helping you and your leadership team manage the school effectively (e.g., by taking on leadership roles or being "someone you can call on"); and (4) building a strong relationship between the school and the community outside the school, including parents. We also asked the principals to rate the teachers' overall performance outside the classroom. As a final question, we asked the principals, "All things considered, to what extent do you hope that you can continue working with this teacher next year?" Principals responded positively for approximately 90% of the teachers.

Principals tended to rate teachers highly across dimensions. Means ranged from 4.1 for building community relationships to 4.7 for motivating students. The two "overall" assessments were also quite high: 4.8 for classroom performance and 4.3 for performance outside the classroom. Standard deviations for all eight dimensions and both overall assessments, however, were 1.1 or higher, pointing to the fact that principals made significant use of the lower ends of the scales.

Administrative Data

The district provided us with three administrative data files: background information for all students in the district, course-level data that link students to each of their teachers in a year, and a staff-level file with information on all district employees. Information on the students includes race and ethnicity, gender, eligibility for free or reduced-price lunch, attendance, suspensions, and test scores from the Florida Comprehensive Assessment Test (FCAT), which is given in reading and math to students in grades 3–10. Staff data include the highest degree earned, years of experience in the district for teachers, years in the job for principals, race, ethnicity, and gender. These data span the 2003–2004 through 2011–2012 school years.

Estimating Teacher Value-Added

We estimate value-added scores for each teacher separately in math and reading. The test scores used to generate the value-added estimates are the scaled scores from the FCAT, standardized by grade and year. We model a student's achievement in math or reading in the current year as a function of the prior year's score in that subject, the prior year's score in the other subject, and a long list of student, classroom, and school characteristics, plus grade effects. Models utilize all data from tested classrooms over the full 9-year grade span and include a teacher-by-year fixed effect to capture teachers' contributions to test scores each year after accounting for other factors in the model. Coefficients on these effects corresponding to the 2011–2012 school year are our primary value-added measures.

In addition to these single-year measures of value-added, we also estimate long-run average value-added for each teacher over all available years of data. This model replaces the teacher-by-year fixed effect with a teacher fixed effect. Coefficients from the fixed-effect terms capture a teacher's covariate-adjusted average effects on all students he or she teaches over the 9-year data span.

Both the single-year and long-run value-added scores include measurement error as well as real differences in achievement gains associated with teachers. We therefore shrink the estimates using the empirical Bayes method to bring imprecise estimates closer to the mean. For further details, see Grissom and Loeb (2014).

The two math measures and the two reading measures are correlated at 0.75 and 0.78, respectively. While reading and math are highly correlated (0.76) for the overall measures, they are less highly correlated in the most recent year (0.48), which is not surprising given the greater measurement error in the single-year predictions. Correlations across subjects are based primarily on scores from elementary teachers because middle and high school teachers less often teach both math and reading.

DOES PRINCIPAL-ASSESSED TEACHER PERFORMANCE CORRELATE WITH VALUE-ADDED?

Our research questions are primarily descriptive in nature and thus employ descriptive methods. To assess the relationship between math and reading value-added and the principals' subjective assessments, we calculate pairwise correlations between the dimensions and the value-added measures. Before turning to the results, we note that in another analysis (Grissom & Loeb, 2014), we show that principals' ratings across dimensions generally are highly correlated. Ratings within category (in-class or outside-class) correlate more highly with each other than with items in the other group. Unsurprisingly, in-class dimensions also correlate highly with principals' assessments of teachers' overall performance within the classroom (the lowest correlation is 0.77), and outside-class dimensions correlate highly with overall performance out of the classroom (the lowest correlation is 0.82).

Table 4.1 provides the correlations between the predictions of each value-added model for the 2011–2012 school year and the teacher performance dimensions. For math and reading, we show the correlations for all schools, then separately for elementary/middle/K–8 schools and high schools. We focus on the single-year value-added measures because they are most similar to the ones employed in most state or district evaluation systems. Although not shown in the table, we also calculated these values for the long-run value-added measures; the values were systematically smaller than those shown in Table 4.1.

Table 4.1. Pairwise Correlations Between Value-Added Measures and Teacher Performance Ratings

	MATHEMATICS VALUE-ADDED (2012)			READING VALUE-ADDED (2012)		
	All Schools ($N \approx 185$)	Elementary/ Middle/K–8 ($N \approx 120$)	High ($N \approx 65$)	All Schools ($N \approx 185$)	Elementary/ Middle/K–8 ($N \approx 100$)	High ($N \approx 85$)
In-Class Dimensions						
Getting High Test Performance	0.41*	0.47*	0.27*	0.28*	0.36*	0.18
Developing Higher-Order Thinking	0.33*	0.37*	0.26*	0.23*	0.32*	0.12
Motivating Students to Learn	0.11	0.17	0.03	0.17*	0.24*	0.08
Building Students' Interpersonal Skills	0.04	0.08	–0.02	0.12	0.19	0.04
Overall In-Class Effectiveness	0.25*	0.29*	0.19	0.25*	0.32*	0.16
Outside-Class Dimensions						
Building Positive Staff Relationships	0.09	–0.03	0.29*	0.08	0.07	0.08
Supporting Other Teachers' Instruction	0.20*	0.11	0.34*	0.18*	0.21*	0.13
Helping Leadership Team to Manage the School	0.12	0.03	0.26*	0.16*	0.17	0.14
Building Relationships with Parents/ Community	0.07	0.00	0.20	0.16*	0.18	0.11
Overall Outside-Class Effectiveness	0.10	0.03	0.22	0.21*	0.26*	0.13

Notes. Asterisks denote correlations statistically significantly different from 0 at the $p < .05$ level. N refers to number of teachers included in each analysis, which varies slightly from item to item.

First, consider the in-class dimensions of quality for which principals rated teachers. Principals' ratings of both teachers' ability to help students produce high standardized test performance and to develop students' higher-order thinking skills, such as synthesis and evaluation, are significantly correlated with value-added scores across subjects and grade levels, with the exception of reading value-added for high schools. The lack of correlation in high school reading may result from multiple teachers affecting students' reading performance in high school, such as teachers of history and science as well as English. In the columns that combine across schools, the rating of the teacher's ability to elicit high test performance is correlated with math value-added at 0.41 and with reading value-added at 0.28; correlations for developing higher-order thinking are 0.33 and 0.23, respectively. In both cases, separating by grade level shows that correlations are stronger for lower grades than for high schools.

Correlations for the other two in-class dimensions—motivating students to learn and helping students build strong interpersonal skills—are smaller. Neither is statistically associated with math value-added, and only student motivation is significantly correlated with reading value-added, and there, not for high schools. Principals' ratings of teachers' overall in-class effectiveness are correlated with math and reading value-added across schools ($r = 0.25$ for both), but this correlation is driven mostly by lower grades. Although positive, neither value-added metric is statistically significantly correlated with the overall in-class effectiveness measure for high schools.

Perhaps unsurprisingly, the outside-class dimensions of teacher performance correlate less strongly with value-added scores than do inside-class dimensions. The most consistently correlated dimension is teachers' effectiveness at supporting their colleagues' instruction, which is the only dimension significantly correlated with both math and reading value-added in the "all schools" columns. None of the other dimensions are correlated with math value-added either overall or for elementary schools, though there are positive and significant correlations for high schools for three of the four dimensions. Reading value-added shows positive and significant correlations across all items except building staff relationships for all schools, though in this case, the correlations appear largely driven by the lower grades rather than by high schools. The overall outside-class effectiveness rating is not significantly correlated with math value-added, though the point estimate is moderate for non-high schools, and also not significantly correlated with reading value-added for high schools, though it is overall and for non-high schools.

Looking across results, two patterns emerge. First, value-added is positively correlated with performance dimensions with the clearest connections to teacher instruction, including test performance, higher-order thinking, and capacity to support colleagues in their teaching. Second, value-added generally cannot be relied on to capture the other dimensions of teacher job performance. Take, for example, high school teachers for whom only reading value-added metrics are available. These measures do not significantly predict *any* of the subjective performance dimensions, suggesting that these teachers' contributions to the school as perceived by the principal generally would be missed by an evaluation that reduces their job performance to a single test-based metric.

DO PERFORMANCE RATINGS AND VALUE-ADDED PREDICT PRINCIPALS' INTEREST IN RETAINING A TEACHER?

Having established that value-added measures tend not to correlate consistently with many aspects of teacher job performance, we next turn to the question of whether principals value these dimensions of teacher performance that are not associated with value-added. We examine whether a principal reports wishing to continue working with the teacher next year under the assumption that principals will report wishing to work with teachers they feel are valuable to the school. Our analysis investigates how the subjective performance dimensions and value-added predict this measure of value.

Specifically, we run logistic regression models for principals' binary responses for whether or not the principal wants to retain the teacher. The models include various combinations of the performance dimensions and value-added measures, plus principal characteristics that might be correlated with principals' responses (e.g., race, gender, highest degree earned). We cluster standard errors at the school level to account for the error correlation arising from the grouping of teachers within schools.

We begin by estimating models that include each teacher performance dimension separately. These results, which we do not tabulate, show that the eight performance dimensions and the two overall ratings are each highly correlated with the likelihood that the principal wishes to retain the teacher. The odds ratio for each performance dimension is above 4, and all are statistically significant at the 0.001 level. Among these dimensions the smallest odds ratio is for building community relationships (odds ratio = 4.1), while the largest is for student motivation (odds ratio = 9.6).

Teachers' value-added scores, however, show a much different pattern. Replacing the performance dimensions with math value-added, column 1 of Table 4.2 shows that there is no evidence of a statistical association with the probability that a principal wishes to keep the teacher in the school next year. Column 2 shows a similar result for reading value-added. Note that neither result is affected by controlling for teacher characteristics or by substituting the long-run measures of value-added for the single-year measure.

Next, we examine the relative association of principal ratings and value-added with principals' assessments of whom they would like to retain. Given the high intercorrelations among the performance ratings, for this analysis we summarize them using the averages of the in-class and outside-class dimensions. The two averages are correlated at 0.75. Column 3 of Table 4.2 shows the results of including these two measures in the model predicting whether the principal wishes to keep a teacher, and, as expected, both are highly positively correlated with desire to retain, with the odds ratio for the average of the in-class dimensions especially large. Column 4 adds math value-added, while column 5 adds reading value-added. The conclusions of the two models are similar: The odds ratios for value-added are attenuated, and the coefficients on the performance dimension averages remain large and statistically different from zero.

An important limitation of the analysis in Table 4.2, of course, is that the common-source bias derived from the fact that the same respondent is providing the dependent and independent variables undoubtedly inflates

Table 4.2. Predicting Whether the Principal Wants to Retain the Teacher

	(1)	(2)	(3)	(4)	(5)
Mathematics Value-Added (2012)	1.18 (0.96)			0.63 (−1.11)	
Reading Value-Added (2012)		1.44 (1.24)			1.02 (0.05)
Average of In-Class Dimensions			10.94*** (3.71)	15.77*** (2.76)	4.01*** (2.68)
Average of Outside-Class Dimensions			3.21*** (2.77)	2.59* (1.92)	9.40** (2.48)
Constant	1.63 (0.68)	3.99* (1.83)	9.30*** (2.66)	12.81** (2.57)	5.43 (1.50)
Observations	155	160	308	154	159
Pseudo R^2	0.07	0.08	0.59	0.66	0.50

Note. Odds ratios shown. Standard errors are clustered by school, with *t*-statistics shown in parentheses. *** $p < 0.01$. ** $p < 0.05$. * $p < 0.1$. All models control for principal characteristics.

the correlations among these variables. Still, it is striking that what principals value as suggested by their decisions about which teachers they would like to keep in their schools reflects their subjective assessments of many performance dimensions that themselves are uncorrelated or inconsistently correlated with value-added. Moreover, the value-added metrics are poor predictors of what principals value in teachers.

DISCUSSION AND CONCLUSIONS

At least according to principals' assessments, dimensions of teacher effectiveness tend to be positively and moderately to strongly correlated with one another (Grissom & Loeb, 2014). In other words, teachers who are strong on one dimension tend to be strong on another; these dimensions are complements to one another rather than substitutes. As we have shown here, it is also the case that value-added scores tend to be relatively good predictors of some aspects of teacher performance, such as the ability to push students to get high test scores.

Yet the strong pattern of interrelationships among teacher performance dimensions and the positive correlation between some dimensions and value-added does *not*, in turn, imply that value-added scores are reliable measures of all facets of teacher job performance. Potentially high-value outcomes, such as success at building students' interpersonal skills, maintaining positive relationships with fellow staff members, or making contributions to school leadership, tend not to correlate well with value-added. This absence of a consistent correlation appears to be important at least from the perspective of principals evaluating which teachers they would like to work with next year. Principals appear to place value on performance indicators not clearly associated with value-added measures and in fact are no more likely to want to retain teachers with higher value-added themselves.

Our results suggest that teacher evaluations that emphasize student test score growth to the exclusion of other outcomes are likely to miss important contributions that "low-value-added" teachers make to their schools. The multidimensional nature of teacher work necessitates evaluation instruments that provide for ratings on a variety of work outcomes. These ratings should be taken seriously as performance indicators in their own right, without regard to their correlations with test score growth. Some analysts take low correlations as evidence that subjective ratings are limited in their capacity to capture performance, when it may be that they capture other important and valuable aspects of teacher work to which test score changes are insensitive.

These findings have implications for research on teacher effectiveness as well. They suggest that studies that reduce teacher effectiveness to value-added measures in fact are measuring only one facet of a construct that has numerous other components worth identifying. How well a teacher motivates a student or builds student interpersonal skills, for example, may well be important for future outcomes beyond greater achievement in math and reading. Education researchers need a more complete understanding of the contributions of teachers to their students and their schools so that means for evaluating those contributions for both research and policy can be developed.

REFERENCES

Aaronson, D., Barrow, L., & Sander, W. (2007). Teachers and student achievement in the Chicago public high schools. *Journal of Labor Economics, 25*(1), 95–135.

Cohen-Vogel, L. (2011). Staffing to the test: Are today's school personnel practices evidence based? *Educational Evaluation and Policy Analysis*, *33*(4), 483–505.

Danielson, C. (1996). *Enhancing professional practice: A framework for teaching.* Alexandria, VA: Association for Supervision and Curriculum Development.

Grissom, J. A., & Loeb, S. (2011). Triangulating principal effectiveness: How perspectives of parents, teachers, and assistant principals identify the central importance of managerial skills. *American Educational Research Journal*, *48*(5), 1091–1123.

Grissom, J. A., & Loeb, S. (2014, March). *Assessing principals' assessments: Subjective evaluations of teacher effectiveness in low- and high-stakes environments.* Presented at the 2014 annual meeting of the Association for Education Finance and Policy, San Antonio, TX.

Grissom, J. A., Loeb, S., & Master, B. (2013). Effective instructional time use for school leaders: Longitudinal evidence from observations of principals. *Educational Researcher, 42*(8), 433–444.

Hanushek, E. A., & Rivkin, S. G. (2010). Generalizations about using value-added measures of teacher quality. *American Economic Review*, *100*(2), 267–271.

Harris, D. N. (2012). *How do value-added indicators compare to other measures of teacher effectiveness?* Stanford, CA: Carnegie Foundation for the Advancement of Teaching.

Harris, D. N., Ingle, W. K., & Rutledge, S. A. (2014). How teacher evaluation methods matter for accountability: A comparative analysis of teacher effectiveness ratings by principals and teacher value-added measures. *American Educational Research Journal*, *51*(1), 73–112.

Harris, D. N., & Sass, T. R. (2014). Skills, productivity and the evaluation of teacher performance. *Economics of Education Review, 40*, 183–204.

Heckman, J. J., & Rubinstein, Y. (2001). The importance of noncognitive skills: Lessons from the GED testing program. *American Economic Review, 91*(2), 145–149.

Jackson, C. K. (2013). *Non-cognitive ability, test scores, and teacher quality: Evidence from 9th grade teachers in North Carolina* (NBER working paper 18624). Cambridge, MA: National Bureau of Economic Research.

Jacob, B. A., & Lefgren, L. (2008). Can principals identify effective teachers? Evidence on subjective performance evaluation in education. *Journal of Labor Economics, 26*(1), 101–136.

Jennings, J. L., & DiPrete, T. A. (2010). Teacher effects on social and behavioral skills in early elementary school. *Sociology of Education, 83*(2), 135–159.

Koedel, C., & Betts, J. (2010). Value added to what? How a ceiling in the testing instrument influences value-added estimation. *Education Finance and Policy, 5*(1), 54–81.

Lindqvist, E., & Vestman, R. (2011). The labor market returns to cognitive and noncognitive ability: Evidence from the Swedish enlistment. *American Economic Journal: Applied Economics, 3*(1), 101–128.

McCaffrey, D. F., Koretz, D., Lockwood, J. R., & Hamilton, L. S. (2004). *Evaluating value-added models for teacher accountability*. Santa Monica, CA: RAND Corporation.

Rivkin, S. G., Hanushek, E. A., & Kain, J. F. (2005). Teachers, schools, and academic achievement. *Econometrica, 73*(2), 417–458.

Rockoff, J. E., Staiger, D. O., Kane, T. J., & Taylor, E. S. (2012). Information and employee evaluation: Evidence from a randomized intervention in public schools. *American Economic Review 102*(7), 3184–3213.

Rothstein, J. (2010). Teacher quality in educational production: Tracking, decay, and student achievement. *Quarterly Journal of Economics, 125*(1), 175–214.

CHAPTER 5

Potential Pitfalls in the Use of Teacher Value-Added Data

Sean P. Corcoran

Value-added measures (VAMs) use historical data on student achievement to assess how a teacher's students performed relative to comparable students in the same grade taught by other teachers in the same state or district. By statistically adjusting for differences across classrooms in student characteristics associated with achievement—such as prior academic performance, socioeconomic background, and special educational needs—value-added measures are designed to isolate the contribution of individual teachers to their students' learning.

The promise that VAMs provide a concise, objective measure of a teacher's classroom performance has led to their rapid adoption into teacher evaluation systems. Their current popularity can be traced to at least three sources. First, there is widespread recognition that the majority of school systems lack a meaningful or rigorous process for evaluating teachers. Formal evaluations often rely on a cursory review by the school principal, provide little constructive feedback, and result in little to no documented variation in teacher job performance (Weisberg, Sexton, Mulhern, & Keeling, 2009). Second, recent large-scale studies have shown that there are significant differences in teacher effectiveness as measured by VAMs, with important consequences for child outcomes (Chetty, Friedman, & Rockoff, 2014b; Hanushek & Rivkin, 2010). Indeed, most educational researchers now agree that teachers are the most important school input affecting student achievement. Third, in an effort to capitalize on this variation and improve educator quality, the Obama administration incentivized states to adopt VAMs as significant criteria in their promotion, compensation, and dismissal. In many states, VAMs are now the cornerstone of teachers' annual performance evaluations, accounting for 50% or more of their overall ratings (Doherty & Jacobs, 2013).

In educational research, value-added measures have contributed much to what we know about the importance and long-run impact of teachers (Chetty et al., 2014b), the effectiveness of different pathways into teaching (Boyd, Grossman, Lankford, Loeb, & Wyckoff, 2006; Harris & Sass, 2011; Kane, Rockoff, & Staiger, 2008), teacher hiring and retention practices (Goldhaber, Gross, & Player, 2011; Loeb, Kalogrides, & Béteille, 2012), and teacher location preferences and turnover (Goldhaber et al., 2011; Hanushek, Kain, & Rivkin, 2004), to name only a few examples. Their significant impact and widespread use in educational research does not, however, imply that VAMs are valid and practically useful measures of individual job performance. In fact, VAMs have a number of properties that inherently limit their utility as performance measures.

In this chapter, I review some of the potential pitfalls and shortcomings associated with VAMs in the evaluation of individual teachers. I divide these shortcomings into five categories, briefly reviewing the evidence on each: (1) errors in attribution (bias), (2) errors in measurement (reliability), (3) sensitivity to the measurement tool, (4) practical utility, and (5) face validity. The upshot is that VAMs are one indicator of a teacher's impact on student learning but are easily influenced by factors outside his or her control. VAMs are imprecise and vary across years and test measures, limiting their validity for high-stakes decisions and their potential for informing professional growth. I argue that education leaders should temper their expectations about what can be learned from VAMs about individual teachers and avoid giving them a preponderant role in evaluating job performance.

ERRORS IN ATTRIBUTION (BIAS)

When VAMs play a significant role in teachers' promotion, retention, compensation, and dismissal, one needs reasonably strong assurance that they reflect true differences in teacher job performance, and not factors outside of the teacher's control, such as neighborhood poverty, school resources, or principal quality. Of course, no measure will be completely immune from these influences, and one might reasonably expect VAMs to vary for idiosyncratic reasons. These idiosyncratic influences—which can affect VAMs positively or negatively—should in theory average out over multiple students and multiple classroom years. However, when external factors cause VAMs to *systematically* over- or underestimate a teacher's impact on student learning, they are considered *biased*.

The question of whether VAMs are biased has been studied extensively by researchers (see Jackson, Rockoff, & Staiger, 2014, for a summary). For example, Rothstein (2010) showed that teachers assigned to students in the future have statistically significant "effects" on current student achievement. Because future teachers cannot have a causal impact on current achievement, this finding suggests that value-added models are failing to account for how students are matched to teachers, and may be biased. In contrast, another study (Chetty, Friedman, & Rockoff, 2014a) found that student achievement increased (or decreased) in predictable ways when a teacher with previously high (or low) value-added transferred into a school, suggesting that VAMs are unbiased predictors of a teacher's future impact. Two experimentally designed studies that randomly assigned teachers to students also found that VAMs calculated under normal conditions were unbiased predictors of value-added under random assignment (Kane & Staiger, 2008; Kane, McCaffrey, Miller, & Staiger, 2013).

On balance, the research to date has not found that VAMs are inordinately biased by external factors. This may be because value-added models sufficiently control for baseline conditions—especially prior achievement—that serve as proxies for these other variables. That said, I see two potential sources of bias that remain a concern for the practical use of VAMs.

First is the issue of distinguishing teacher effects from school effects. When VAMs vary across schools, it is difficult to separate differences in teacher effectiveness from other influences that vary at the school level, such as leadership quality, discipline, supplementary instruction (e.g., subject coaches), parent involvement, and other available resources and services. The effects of school context may be even larger across district boundaries, given the variability across districts in expenditures and socioeconomic composition. If VAMs fail to account for these influences, teacher effects are easily confounded with school or community effects.[1] Some researchers address this possibility by calculating within-school VAMs (via school "fixed effects"), but the fact that true teacher effectiveness is likely to be distributed unevenly across schools makes this approach impractical for real-world evaluation systems (Gordon, Kane, & Staiger, 2006). Consequently, value-added models in practice are inherently limited in their ability to account for differences in school and community contexts.

Second is the challenge of isolating individual effects in a team environment. When students receive instruction from multiple teachers over the course of a day or academic year, as is typical in secondary school, the assumption that achievement gains on a subject test are entirely attributable to that subject's teacher is tenuous. Both conceptually and statistically, it is difficult to separate the contributions of multiple and simultaneous teacher influences on a student's achievement. Moreover, if student outcomes are the product of school-level effort, it is unclear whether performance measurement should be focused on individual impacts. At least one study found that VAMs are influenced by the effectiveness of colleagues within the same school, prima facie evidence that VAMs are affected by school context (Jackson & Bruegmann, 2009).

More evidence is needed on whether and to what extent VAMs are biased, particularly on the two issues raised above. It is important to point out, though, that bias is typically framed as a question of whether, *on average,* VAMs over- or underestimate the effectiveness of teachers serving different populations of students. The answer to this question is not sufficient to say whether *individual* VAM estimates are biased, or whether VAMs are a "good" estimate of relative job performance in a given school year. These are arguably more relevant questions for a real-world teacher evaluation system, and certainly for individual educators. The latter issue—the *reliability* of value-added measures—is discussed in the next section.

ERRORS IN MEASUREMENT (RELIABILITY)

A particularly important shortcoming of VAMs for practice is their imprecision. As described in the introduction, VAMs are estimates based on a model of student achievement. As with any statistical estimate, VAMs have a margin of error, which in practice tends to be large. As an example, I examined the full set of value-added scores reported for more than 12,700 teachers in New York City in 2008–2009 (Corcoran, 2010). Scores were provided as a percentile rank (0–100), along with a margin of error expressing the level of uncertainty in this ranking. Even with as many as 3 years of classroom data, the average NYC teacher had a reported margin of error of about 34 percentile points in math and 44 points in English language arts (ELA). This means that it would not be unusual for a teacher to rank at the 33rd percentile in ELA, for example, but have a margin of error that extends from the 11th percentile to the 55th. While the 33rd percentile may be our *best* estimate of this teacher's relative ELA performance, its margin of error makes it difficult to conclude whether he or she is a highly ineffective or an above-average teacher.

Given their imprecision, it is not surprising that studies have found VAMs to be only moderately stable from year to year, with correlations ranging from 0.3 to 0.5 (e.g., Goldhaber & Hansen, 2013; McCaffrey,

Sass, Lockwood, & Mihaly, 2009). What this means is that a meaningfully large number of teachers can be rated "ineffective" or "highly effective" in one school year while being rated average (or the opposite extreme) in the next. As an example, I examined how VAMs reported for NYC teachers changed from one year to the next (Corcoran, 2010). I first grouped teachers into five bins based on their quintile of value-added in 2007 (from lowest to highest, Q1 to Q5). Then I examined the percentage of teachers in each bin that scored in Q1 to Q5 in the subsequent year. There was clearly considerable movement between categories. For instance, of those who scored in the *lowest* ELA quintile in 2007 (Q1), 32% scored in the top two quintiles (Q4–Q5) in 2008. Similarly, of those who scored in the *highest* mathematics quintile in 2007 (Q5), 12% scored in the bottom two quintiles in 2008. (Generally speaking, VAMs in mathematics have been found to be more stable than those in reading.) It is unlikely that the real job performance of teachers varies so significantly from year to year. Rather, the year-to-year changes observed in NYC were more likely due to other factors, such as sampling error or random variability.

VAMs' imprecision and instability stem from several sources (Loeb & Candelaria, 2012; McCaffrey et al., 2009; Schochet & Chiang, 2013). First, achievement tests themselves are a noisy measure of a student's knowledge and skills in a given domain. On a given test, a student's score could be higher or lower depending on item selection, or whether the student is having a good or bad day. Because VAMs are effectively an adjusted average of a relatively small number of scores (e.g., one classroom of 24 students), they can be sensitive to these variations. Second, there are common classroom- or school-level "shocks" that affect *average* learning and/or test performance. These can include, for example, a cohort with disruptive classmates, an unusually high number of school cancellations due to weather, or poor conditions on the day of the test. As noted earlier, the effects of student- and classroom-level noise can be expected to average out over larger samples of students and multiple classroom years. Such averaging, however, does little to improve the usability of VAMs in the short run, a practical limitation I return to in a later section.

Whether the inherent imprecision of VAMs is problematic for their use in educator evaluation systems is the subject of much debate. On the one hand, an unreliable measure can lead to a large number of Type I and Type II errors (e.g., classifying effective teachers as low-performing, or classifying low-performing teachers as effective, respectively; see Schochet & Chiang, 2013). High error rates can increase job risk, undermine educators' trust in the system, and hamper recruitment into the profession. On the other hand, VAMs have been claimed to be no less stable than quantitative performance measures used in other occupations (e.g.,

Glazerman et al., 2010). Other measures—such as student evaluations and classroom observations—are equally fallible, subject to variability from one year and/or rater to the next. The moderate correlations noted above may also understate their predictive power in the long run, since the correlation between a teacher's single-year VAM and his or her average *career* effectiveness (using multiple years of data) is higher than successive years (Staiger & Kane, 2014). Setting aside the question of how much imprecision is "too much," most researchers agree that the *exclusive* use of VAMs in evaluating, promoting, retaining, or compensating teachers is unwise (Glazerman et al., 2010). Many would also agree that it is inadvisable to base personnel decisions on a single year of classroom data, given the impossibility of distinguishing short-run "shocks" from teacher job performance in a single year. Unfortunately, value-added measures used in practice generally do not make such distinctions (e.g., American Institutes for Research, 2015).

SENSITIVITY TO THE MEASUREMENT TOOL

Often lost in abstract discussions of a teacher's value-added is the fact that, in practice, teacher effectiveness has multiple dimensions, varying across subjects, tests, contexts, and student populations. VAMs can plausibly be generated for as many subject areas and grades for which there are tests. While research finds that VAMs are positively correlated across subjects (in the neighborhood of 0.3 to 0.6), the individual scores can again lead one to different conclusions about a teacher's effectiveness. These differences can occur by chance—in the same way that VAMs vary year to year—or because they reflect true differences in a teacher's skill across subject areas. Absent additional information, it is difficult to know which explanation holds, or whether educators should pay attention to these differences.

Several studies have examined the consistency of VAMs using scores from the *same* subject domain. For example, Lockwood et al. (2007) found that the choice of subscale—that is, the decision to emphasize one set of tested items over another—has a large impact on a teacher's measured effectiveness. Two other studies found a weak-to-moderate correlation between VAMs for the same teacher on different tests of the same subject (Corcoran & Jennings, 2011; Papay, 2011; Sass, 2008). Papay (2011) calculated hypothetical bonuses based on VAMs calculated from two different tests administered to the same students, applying the rules used by a performance pay program in Texas. He found that the use of one test measure over the other affected the bonus of roughly half of all teachers, with the average teacher salary changing by nearly $2,200. He concluded that in this case, the two VAMs were "not sufficiently comparable to rank the same individual teachers as high or low performing" (p. 165).

Another implication of variability across tests is that teachers will rarely be identified as "ineffective" or "highly effective" across all subjects at the same time (e.g., Corcoran & Jennings, 2011). The imprecision in each measure is high enough that the likelihood that a teacher's VAM falls below (or above) a certain threshold on multiple tests is low. Lacking a single dimension of "effectiveness," education leaders must devise decision rules that address differential performance across multiple subjects and tests. Combining VAMs across subjects and tests into a single index is one approach (Lefgren & Sims, 2012), although the resulting measure limits one's ability to learn from differences in performance across subjects and is potentially less transparent to its users than a VAM in a single subject area. The important issues of transparency and practical utility are addressed in the next section.

PRACTICAL UTILITY

By definition, VAMs are *relative* measures: how a teacher's students performed on a test relative to comparable students taught by other teachers. They are typically reported using percentile ranks, points, or performance categories (e.g., "Ineffective," "Developing," "Effective," and "Highly Effective"). There is not, therefore, much more information contained in the rating beyond a broad statement of where the teacher stands relative to others in the state or district teaching similar students. The VAM itself does not offer any information as to *why* a teacher's students performed better or worse than predicted, only that a statistical model determined that they did.

VAMs' imprecision (discussed above) further limits the information they can reliably provide. Because one rarely can make meaningful distinctions between a teacher in, say, the 33rd and 53rd percentiles of value-added, consequential personnel decisions can only be made for teachers with demonstrably very low or very high VAMs *and* an acceptably low level of statistical uncertainty.[2] An evaluation system that meets this conservative—and statistically defensible—standard will ultimately only be meaningful for the most extreme cases, and thus will provide little, if any, feedback to the vast majority of teachers. (Most are effectively told that their performance was statistically indistinguishable from the average.) The distribution of growth ratings in the most recent release of evaluations in New York State is illustrative. Based on their VAMs in ELA and mathematics, most New York teachers were categorized as Effective

(77%) or Developing (10%); only 6% were classified as Ineffective and 8% were Highly Effective (American Institutes for Research, 2015). In the end, a relatively small fraction of teachers are identified as low- (or high-) performing, and the vast majority of teachers will receive no meaningful information about their practice from this score.[3]

Of course, it can be argued that even a modest increase in differentiation in measured performance is an improvement over systems that exhibit little to none (Weisberg et al., 2009). But the above discussion also raises the question of what VAMs add beyond other measures of job performance that could ostensibly be used in their place. If the decision rules applied to VAMs largely identify the most extreme cases (the very best or very worst), it would be surprising if these teachers were not already identifiable by other means. In fact, at least one study has found that principals' subjective evaluations are capable of identifying high- and low- value-added teachers (e.g., Jacob & Lefgren, 2008).

To summarize, aside from broad classifications of relative performance, there is little actionable information contained in VAMs for the average user. Reliable information, moreover, comes with a lag, as annual test results are accumulated and analyzed. Educators who fail to see how their evaluation connects to their day-to-day work may simply choose to ignore it, arguably a lost opportunity for professional growth. Concerns with the face validity of VAM measures are discussed in the next section.

FACE VALIDITY

Despite policymakers' best efforts to design sensible VAM measures, their utility as part of a human capital system ultimately relies on their having face validity and buy-in from their largest constituency: educators themselves. Where researchers may be comfortable with correlations of 0.5 between VAMs in successive years or across tests, teachers who observe high variability in their own value-added score may come to view them as unreliable, especially when they see no apparent connection to variation in their own practice. That VAMs become more precise after several years of classroom teaching is of little benefit to teachers and principals responding to this information in real time.

Face validity also depends on an alignment between stated expectations and performance assessment. Even if it can be demonstrated that VAMs are good predictors of future student outcomes, they are in effect based on the results of a single test. Tests rarely assess more than a fraction of the skills and behaviors teachers are expected to cultivate in their students, and thus are only partially aligned with their job expectations.

If teachers perceive that their performance evaluation depends disproportionately on a single measure that fails to capture the full range of their work, that evaluation loses credibility (and worse, creates perverse incentives to focus solely on that measure).[4]

Perhaps the best way to gauge VAMs' utility as an evaluation tool is to observe how they are used in the field. In a recent study, Goldring and colleagues (2015) conducted hundreds of interviews with principals in six urban school districts who had access to multiple measures of teaching effectiveness, including VAMs. They found that principals tended to privilege observational data over VAMs, citing many of their limitations described here (lack of validity, transparency and actionable information, e.g., and lagged availability). It remains to be seen whether education leaders will make greater use of VAMs as they become more commonly available.

CONCLUDING THOUGHTS

Few would disagree that formal performance evaluation in the teaching profession has been inadequate, and that education leaders could go much further to recognize differences in classroom performance, reward highly effective teachers, and support or remove those not performing at a high level. It is unclear, however, whether evaluations centered on VAMs provide the information educators need to improve classroom performance, foster a culture of continuous professional growth, and increase the quality of the teaching workforce. To accomplish these goals, teachers and school leaders need instructive, actionable information that they can use to make meaningful changes to instructional practice. A statistical prediction that relies on annual tests and multiple years of data to classify teachers into broad performance categories does not, in my view, meet this requirement.

VAMs do, however, have a role to play in modern teacher evaluation systems. There is robust evidence that VAMs are broadly predictive of later student outcomes and thus contain some information about relative effectiveness. There is little harm in using VAMs as an early-warning signal, in triangulation with other measures, to identify teachers whose performance is lagging and who may be good candidates for professional development. VAMs will continue to be useful to researchers validating other, more useful metrics of teaching effectiveness and evaluating the impact of larger policies, programs, and interventions. Unfortunately, the current enthusiasm for VAMs as the predominant metric for evaluating teachers runs the risk of undermining their long-run success. Limiting their role to a supporting one may be a better strategy for genuine, meaningful, and lasting reform.

NOTES

1. The two studies that randomly assigned teachers to students as a test for bias did so within schools, not between them (Kane & Staiger, 2008; Kane et al., 2013).

2. In New York State, teachers' growth ratings are based on both their VAM ("adjusted student growth measure") and its margin of error. This approach requires a minimum degree of confidence that a teacher is above or below average before classifying them as Ineffective or Highly Effective. See American Institutes for Research (2015).

3. An even smaller fraction of teachers were identified as "ineffective" when other measures of teaching effectiveness were included. It is worth pointing out that the thresholds for performance categories are a political decision about what fraction of teachers should be classified as ineffective. Education leaders can change the threshold for failing if they do not believe the percentage of ineffective teachers is high enough. In New York, Governor Andrew Cuomo called for another round of reform to the state's teacher evaluation system in 2015, arguing that too few teachers were being rated ineffective.

4. VAMs also fail to recognize teachers' efforts with all students, since students must have been tested in the current and prior year to contribute to a teacher's VAM estimate. Even if the omission of students with missing data does not bias a teacher's rating, a job evaluation that ignores their work with certain students lacks face validity, and potentially creates incentives to focus their efforts on students who count toward the VAM estimate.

REFERENCES

American Institutes for Research. (2015). *2013–14 growth model for educator evaluation: Technical report prepared for the New York State Education Department.* Washington, DC: Author.

Boyd, D., Grossman, P., Lankford, H., Loeb, S., & Wyckoff, J. (2006). How changes in entry requirements alter the teacher workforce and affect student achievement. *Education Finance and Policy, 1*(2), 176–216.

Chetty, R., Friedman, J. N., & Rockoff, J. E. (2014a). Measuring the impacts of teachers I: Evaluating bias in teacher value-added estimates. *American Economic Review, 104*(9), 2593–2632.

Chetty, R., Friedman, J. N., & Rockoff, J. E. (2014b). Measuring the impacts of teachers II: Teacher value-added and student outcomes in adulthood. *American Economic Review, 104*(9), 2633–2679.

Corcoran, S. P. (2010). *Can teachers be evaluated by their students' test scores? Should they be? The use of value-added measures of teacher effectiveness in policy and practice.* New York, NY: Annenberg Institute for School Reform.

Corcoran, S. P., & Jennings, J. L. (2011). *Teacher effectiveness on high- and low-stakes tests.* Working paper, New York University, New York, NY.

Doherty, K. M., & Jacobs, S. (2013). *Connect the dots: Using evaluations of teacher effectiveness to inform policy and practice.* Washington, DC: National Center for Teacher Quality.

Glazerman, S., Loeb, S., Goldhaber, D., Staiger, D., Raudenbush, S., & Whitehurst, G. (2010). *Evaluating teachers: The important role of value-added.* Washington, DC: The Brookings Institution.

Goldhaber, D., Gross, B., & Player, D. (2011). Teacher career paths, teacher quality, and persistence in the classroom: Are public schools keeping their best? *Journal of Policy Analysis and Management, 30*(1), 57–87.

Goldhaber, D., & Hansen, M. (2013). Is it just a bad class? Assessing the long-term stability of estimated teacher performance. *Economica, 80*(319), 589–612.

Goldring, E., Grissom, J. A., Rubin, M., Neumerski, C. M., Cannata, M., Drake, T., & Schuermann, P. (2015). Make room value added: Principals' human capital decisions and the emergence of teacher observation data. *Educational Researcher, 44*(2), 96–104.

Gordon, R., Kane, T. J., & Staiger, D. O. (2006). *Identifying effective teachers using performance on the job.* Washington, DC: Brookings Institution.

Hanushek, E. A., Kain, J. F., & Rivkin, S. G. (2004). Why public schools lose teachers. *Journal of Human Resources, 39*(2), 326–354.

Hanushek, E. A., & Rivkin, S. G. (2010). Generalizations about using value-added measures of teacher quality. *American Economic Review, 100*(2), 267–271.

Harris, D. N., & Sass, T. R. (2011). Teacher training, teacher quality and student achievement. *Journal of Public Economics, 95*(7–8), 798–812.

Jackson, C. K., & Bruegmann, E. (2009). Teaching students and teaching each other: The importance of peer learning for teachers. *American Economic Journal: Applied Economics, 1*(4), 85–108.

Jackson, C. K., Rockoff, J. E., & Staiger, D. O. (2014). Teacher effects and teacher-related policies. *Annual Review of Economics. 6,* 801–825.

Jacob, B. A., & Lefgren, L. (2008). Can principals identify effective teachers? Evidence on subjective performance evaluation in education. *Journal of Labor Economics, 26*(1), 101–136.

Kane, T. J., McCaffrey, D. F., Miller, T., & Staiger, D. O. (2013). *Have we identified effective teachers? Validating measures of effective teaching using random assignment* (MET project research paper). Seattle, WA: Bill and Melinda Gates Foundation.

Kane, T. J., Rockoff, J. E., & Staiger, D. O. (2008). What does certification tell us about teacher effectiveness? Evidence from New York City. *Economics of Education Review, 27*(6), 615–631.

Kane, T. J., & Staiger, D. O. (2008). *Estimating teacher impacts on student achievement: An experimental evaluation* (Working paper 14607). Cambridge, MA: National Bureau of Economic Research.

Lefgren, L., & Sims, D. (2012). Using subject test scores efficiently to predict teacher value-added. *Educational Evaluation and Policy Analysis*, *34*(1), 109–121.

Lockwood, J. R., McCaffrey, D. F., Hamilton, L. S., Stecher, B. M., Le, V.-N., & Martinez, J. F. (2007). The sensitivity of value-added teacher effect estimates to different mathematics achievement measures. *Journal of Educational Measurement*, *44*(1), 47–67.

Loeb, S., & Candelaria, C. A. (2012). *How stable are value-added estimates across years, subjects, and student groups?* Stanford, CA: Carnegie Foundation for the Advancement of Teaching.

Loeb, S., Kalogrides, D., & Béteille, T. (2012). Effective schools: Teacher hiring, assignment, development, and retention. *Education Finance and Policy*, *7*(3), 269–304.

McCaffrey, D. F., Sass, T. R., Lockwood, J. R., & Mihaly, K. (2009). The intertemporal variability of teacher effect estimates. *Education Finance and Policy*, *4*(4), 572–606.

Papay, J. P. (2011). Different tests, different answers: The stability of teacher value-added estimates across outcome measures. *American Educational Research Journal*, *48*(1), 163–193.

Rothstein, J. (2010). Teacher quality in educational production: Tracking, decay, and student achievement. *Quarterly Journal of Economics*, *125*(1), 175–214.

Sass, T. R. (2008). The stability of value-added measures of teacher quality and implications for teacher compensation policy. Washington, DC: National Center for Analysis of Longitudinal Data in Education Research.

Schochet, P. Z., & Chiang, H. S. (2013). What are error rates for classifying teacher and school performance using value-added models? *Journal of Educational and Behavioral Statistics*, *38*(2), 142–171.

Staiger, D. O., & Kane, T. J. (2014). Making decisions with imprecise performance measures: The relationship between annual student achievement gains and a teacher's career value-added. In T. J. Kane, K. A. Kerr, & R. C. Pianta (Eds.), *Designing teacher evaluation systems: New guidance from the Measures of Effective Teaching project* (pp. 144–169). San Francisco, CA: Jossey-Bass.

Weisberg, D., Sexton, S., Mulhern, S., & Keeling, D. (2009). *The widget effect: Our national failure to acknowledge and act on differences in teacher effectiveness.* Brooklyn, NY: The New Teacher Project.

CHAPTER 6

Special Education Teacher Evaluation

An Examination of Critical Issues and Recommendations for Practice

Nathan D. Jones

With widespread support for teacher evaluation reform from policymakers and other stakeholders, the educational research community has moved quickly to examine how evaluation tools perform in practice. Research efforts in general education are beginning to yield important information about whether and how teacher evaluation instruments, namely value-added scores and observation scores, can be used to make high-stakes decisions about teachers (e.g., Bell et al., 2012; Chetty, Friedman, & Rockoff, 2013; Hill, Charalambous, & Kraft, 2012; Kane & Staiger, 2008). Special education teachers have generally been omitted from large-scale studies, and only a handful of empirical studies have examined the issues raised in the evaluation of such teachers (see, e.g., Buzick & Jones, in press; Semmelroth & Johnson, 2014). Thus, we have little data on whether teacher evaluation measures being used in general education lead to valid, reliable information on special educator effectiveness.

Having common evaluation practices sends the message that special education teachers and general education teachers should be held to the same standards, and such an approach may be warranted. The two groups share many instructional roles and responsibilities, such as providing core academic instruction, aligning their curriculum to the state standards, preparing their students for state assessments, and differentiating instruction to meet students' various needs. At the same time, special education teachers take on numerous roles and responsibilities that general educators do not, and there are critical differences in how instruction is delivered to students with and without disabilities (e.g., Brownell, Ross, Colon, & McCallum, 2005).

This chapter reviews research literature on special education teachers to examine whether existing evaluation practices are likely to lead to valid, reliable information on effective special education teaching. I start by providing an overview of the unique roles and responsibilities of special educators, focusing on those that may present problems for current teacher evaluation practices. These roles and responsibilities then frame my review of existing research. The chapter concludes by discussing implications for teacher evaluation for all teachers moving forward.

THE CONTEXT OF SPECIAL EDUCATION TEACHING

Researchers have named several challenges related to evaluating special educators (Benedict, Thomas, Kimerling, & Leko, 2013; Johnson & Semmelroth, 2014; Jones, Buzick, & Turkan, 2013). Of these, I focus on three that warrant the attention of policymakers. First, special education teaching is both planned and delivered to individual students, often requiring coordinated instruction. Second, special education teaching includes unique instructional goals and professional responsibilities. Third, special education and general education promote differing pedagogical approaches to instruction. Each of these is briefly reviewed before discussing their implications for teacher evaluation.

Special education teaching is both planned and delivered to individual students, often requiring coordinated instruction. The defining characteristic of special education is its focus on individual students. Under the Individuals with Disabilities Education Act (IDEA, 2004), schools are required to develop Individualized Education Programs (IEPs) for all students receiving special education services. The IEP is a road map for how, where, and by whom instruction will be delivered to individual students. Among other things, the IEP includes academic objectives that are tailored to a student's needs and abilities, plans for assessing progress, and supports and modifications to ensure access to the general education curriculum.

As mandated by the IEP, individual students—and not the class—serve as the organizing units of instruction. Stemming from this orientation toward individual students, both general education and special education teachers take on responsibilities in educating students with disabilities (SWDs). Traditionally, special education teachers have either provided services as a co-teacher (i.e., working in a general education classroom to support the general educator or sharing responsibility for providing instruction to the whole class) or pulled students out of general education to provide direct instruction, often referred to as the resource room model. But increasingly, the lines between special education and general education are becoming blurred (Fuchs, Fuchs, & Stecker, 2010; Klingner & Vaughn, 2002). There has been a movement toward a schoolwide model of service delivery for SWDs known as Response to Intervention (RTI). Under RTI, student success depends on full coordination of services across a variety of instructional personnel.

To fully capture the quality of instruction provided to SWDs, we must look at the sum total of services provided, including the quality of each teacher's instruction and how well the two are aligned. Not accounting for this shared instruction could make estimates of a teacher's effectiveness less reliable. For example, special educators' value-added scores may also reveal information about instruction received in general education. Similarly, an observed lesson in special education may provide an incomplete picture of the instruction a student received in the subject, particularly if a special educator is responsible for specific tasks such as basic skills instruction. It is also likely that the validity of effectiveness measures will be limited because they will not reflect the realities of special education instruction. Finally, with instruction in special education and general education becoming increasingly blurred, it will only become more difficult to capture the complex and coordinated instruction provided to SWDs.

Special education teaching includes unique instructional goals and professional responsibilities. Instruction for students with high-incidence disabilities commonly focuses on providing targeted instruction in skills and strategies, with the goal of supporting students' learning in general education; thus, special education teaching is often characterized by the delivery of direct, explicit instruction and a focus on the implementation of research-based interventions (e.g., Cook & Odom, 2013; Vaughn, Gersten, & Chard, 2000). In addition to knowing these evidence-based practices, special education teachers must have specialized knowledge. These teachers must have an understanding of their students' disabilities, including how practices can be delivered in a way that maximizes student engagement and understanding. In addition, per No Child Left Behind (NCLB), effective special educators also must exhibit expertise in their subject area (Brownell et al., 2009).

Special educators also take on a number of responsibilities beyond teaching. It is estimated that they spend only 16% of their school time providing academic instruction (Vannest & Hagan-Burke, 2010). The rest of special educators' time is devoted to a variety of responsibilities required by IDEA. Among others, these activities include developing and implementing IEPs, modifying district curricula to meet their students' needs, developing assessments, and monitoring student progress. To be successful, special educators must also develop effective relationships with multiple stakeholders, including general education teachers, paraprofessionals, and parents. Academic achievement is not the only important outcome for SWDs; positive behavioral, social, adaptive, communication, and transition outcomes are also considered goals for many of these students.

Although these additional responsibilities take up a considerable amount of special educators' time and effort, there are few spaces where they are accounted for in teacher evaluation systems. There may be, for example, an indirect effect of the quality of IEP implementation on a special education teacher's value-added score; that is, if a special education teacher exerts considerable effort in setting academic goals for a student and ensures that both the general education teacher and the special education teacher know what they need to meet these goals, it could increase the amount a student achieves in a given year. Also, it may be possible for special educators' work to be captured in the "Planning" or "Professional Responsibilities" domains of an observation protocol, which would be revealed through a rater's interview with a teacher. However, many states and districts are lessening the burden on local raters by not requiring these domains to be included in teachers' evaluations (Center on Great Teachers & Leaders, n.d.). A handful of evaluation systems evaluate special education teachers based on the timeliness of their IEP completion (e.g., D.C.'s IMPACT system). One threat to special education teachers in current teacher evaluation systems, then, is that the instruments in place do not reflect the totality of their work responsibilities. While general educators are also likely to assume responsibilities not captured by evaluation instruments, these responsibilities typically take up a far smaller proportion of their time.

Special education and general education promote differing pedagogical approaches to instruction. Teacher evaluation brings to the surface longstanding differences in philosophies of teaching between general education and special education. When a district or state adopts a measure of classroom teaching, it also adopts the approach to pedagogy underlying the instrument. For example, Charlotte Danielson's Framework for Teaching (FFT; Danielson, 2013) reflects a constructivist theory of how students learn. From the constructivist perspective, students are more likely to develop an understanding of a concept if they are given opportunities to construct meaning themselves. Under constructivism, the role of learners is to actively explore concepts, questioning their own understanding of ideas and incorporating new experience into existing cognitive structures through reflection and experimentation. The role of the teacher in constructivism is to structure classroom activities that allow students to engage in constructing their own knowledge, and to guide students to question their models of understanding. Constructivist principles are readily apparent in the best practices espoused in fields such as mathematics and science, where there is a strong emphasis on developing student understanding of core concepts and principles through exploration and discovery learning. Constructivism is also apparent in instruction in reading and social studies.

In contrast, special education commonly incorporates behavioral theory into views of effective teaching (Klingner et al., in press). From this perspective, the role of special education teachers is prescriptive; they identify processing deficits and implement interventions designed to help remediate these problems. Embedded in behavioral theory is "explicit instruction," a pedagogical approach that is a hallmark of effective special education teaching (Vaughn et al., 2000; Wanzek, Vaughn, Roberts, & Fletcher, 2011). In explicit instruction, teachers hone in on critical concepts or skills. Instructional sequences involve first providing a rationale for learning a concept or skill, then giving a clear explanation of the concept or skill and modeling it for students. Students then work with the concept or skill under the teacher's guidance until they understand it and can apply it to other contexts. In order for explicit instruction to be effective, it must be cohesive, intensive, interactive, and responsive to student needs (Jones & Brownell, 2014). Further, explicit instruction is commonly the basis of what preservice special education teachers learn during their professional preparation (Brownell, Sindelar, Kiely, & Danielson, 2010).

Admittedly, the two approaches described above are painted in broad strokes. There is considerable heterogeneity within general education regarding views of effective teaching, and there are scholars within special education who align with constructivism (e.g., Trent, Artiles, & Englert, 1998). However, the tension between the two perspectives raises important questions about teacher evaluation. If districts adopt a constructivist observation system such as the FFT, will special education teachers be rated negatively because they teach using what are deemed as "best practices" in special education? Are local raters (i.e., principals or other school or district administrators) familiar enough with special education instruction that they can adapt their scoring practices to fit the needs of their special education teachers? If we assume that the FFT may not be a perfect fit for special educators, would a district have the will or resources to adopt an alternative framework? These are questions that we can test empirically, although existing research on special education teacher evaluation is limited.

RESEARCH ON SPECIAL EDUCATION TEACHER EVALUATION

In this section, I examine how researchers have studied the complex issues raised in the evaluation of special education teachers. Overall, the research is limited, but my review focuses on two measures that are included in almost every evaluation system: student growth measures and observation measures. The question of other kinds of information to include in special educator evaluation is addressed in the final section of the chapter.

Student Growth Measures

Attributing student growth to individual teachers has been a primary goal of teacher evaluation reform, yet research has offered little guidance about how to treat scores from SWDs in student growth measures. A nontrivial proportion of K–12 students receive special education services (13%; National Center for Education Statistics, 2012), and the majority of SWDs (79%) take general state assessments (McCaffrey & Buzick, 2014). However, some have questioned philosophically whether it is appropriate to evaluate special education teachers at the classroom level given their focus on individualized instruction (Council for Exceptional Children, 2012). Researchers have raised a number of measurement concerns related to whether growth data should be used with SWDs (Jones et al., 2013; McCaffrey & Buzick, 2014; Steinbrecher, Selig, Cosbey, & Thorstensen, 2014). A disproportionate number of SWDs score extremely low on state tests; low scores tend to be less reliable and likely tell us less about a student's true growth. Further, a large number of SWDs use accommodations on standardized tests, and there is evidence that some test accommodations affect test performance regardless of whether a student has a disability (Sireci, Scarpati, & Li, 2005). Accommodation use is also likely to be inconsistent across years, and there is evidence that changes in accommodation use can artificially inflate or deflate estimates of student growth (Buzick & Jones, in press).

At the teacher level, the issue of low reliability of scores is likely to affect both general education and special education teachers, although the latter group will be differentially affected given the high concentration of low-performing students with whom they work. Further, because special education classrooms are commonly small by design, their overall scores may be unstable given the limited number of students for whom testing data are available. Finally, given the coordinated nature of instruction to SWDs, it may prove difficult to parse out individual teachers' effects.

Despite these concerns, researchers have failed to quantify the extent of the problem when scores from SWDs are included. And there is no evidence for how these concerns might be mitigated through model specification. In research and practice, approaches to handling these students' test scores vary. There are at least three strategies used to account for SWDs: (1) including scores from SWDs with no disability-specific covariates, (2) including scores from these students with disability-specific covariates, and (3) removing these students when estimating teacher effects. Each of these practices has been adapted in practical and research applications. For example, a number of states explicitly control for students' disability status (e.g., Florida, Louisiana), as do researchers (Chetty et al., 2013; Goldhaber, Gabele, & Walch, 2013). There are trade-offs to each approach. If these students undermine the validity of teachers' test scores, it may be appropriate to drop them out of the model. At the same time, excluding SWDs could have some unintended consequences on teachers' instructional practices; if teachers are no longer held accountable for a subgroup of students, there is little incentive for them to focus their efforts on improving instruction for that group.

One recent study by Buzick and Jones (in press) empirically tested various approaches to treating test scores from SWDs in teacher evaluation models. Drawing on longitudinal data from the population of 4th- and 5th-grade teachers from one state, the authors compared measures of student growth, including value-added models, with a variety of student covariates, including covariates specific to student disability (i.e., disability status and accommodation inconsistency), as well as classroom covariates. Student growth percentiles (SGPs) were also included in the analyses. For each model, comparisons were conducted including and excluding SWDs, and the effects of model specification were tested across three groups of teachers: general education teachers with no SWDs, general education teachers with some SWDs, and special education teachers. The study found that for the majority of teachers, the decision to include or exclude SWDs was of little consequence; most models were correlated at or above 95%. When not accounting for disability covariates, special education teachers and general education teachers with large numbers of SWDs in their classes performed worse, on average, than other teachers. However, these gaps in performance were mitigated through the inclusion of disability-specific covariates. Although we should use caution in overinterpreting findings from one state, the Buzick and Jones study provides practical recommendations for handling data from SWDs.

In another study, Hock and Isenberg (2012) addressed the issue of co-teaching. They focused on situations where instruction is provided by two or more teachers in a given year, with special education serving as one example. Hock and Isenberg tested three methods of accounting for co-teaching: (1) a Partial Credit method in which responsibility for teaching is apportioned based on the proportion of time spent with a given teacher; (2) a Teacher Team method in which a team variable replaces individual teacher variables when teachers share a student; and (3) a Full Roster method in which shared students are duplicated in the analysis, giving each teacher full credit for these students. Of the various approaches, the authors found that the Teacher Team and Full Roster methods were preferable to the Partial Credit method, with the Full Roster method having the additional advantage of retaining individual teacher estimates. The authors also recommend that either of these approaches be coupled with a roster validation system to ensure that student records are accurate.

Finally, while the majority of SWDs participate in state standardized tests, others cannot be included in the calculation of value-added scores. With many states adopting student learning objectives (SLOs) for untested grades and subject areas, it is likely that special education teachers will be required to use SLOs. At this time, there is little evidence supporting the use of SLOs as a reliable measure of teacher effectiveness, and some have raised concerns about their measurement properties, including questions about standardization across schools (Lacireno-Paquet, Morgan, & Mello, 2014). These issues would certainly be relevant in special education, particularly given how much special educators' responsibilities vary across schools. At the same time, SLOs will be a necessary measure for many special education teachers, and they benefit from having high levels of face validity with educators.

Classroom Observations

As in the case of student growth measures, there is virtually no empirical research on whether observation systems developed for use in the evaluation of general education teachers are valid and reliable when used with special educators. However, measuring classroom practice has a long history in special education. In the 1980s, several studies of special education teaching emerged out of the process-product tradition; these studies involved the coding of teaching and classroom interactions in simple, low-inference categories based on teacher and student behaviors. These studies suggested that student achievement was highest in classrooms with teacher-directed instruction where teachers fostered high levels of engagement (see Blanton, Sindelar, & Correa, 2006, for a review). In the 1990s, the process-product tradition fell out of favor given criticism that it did not adequately capture the complexities of classroom teaching (e.g., Englert, Tarrant, & Mariage, 1992).

More recently, there have been multiple studies of classroom reading instruction that focused on ways in which reading instruction fails in special education settings (see Swanson, 2008, for a review). Relevant to teacher evaluation are two studies examining whether teacher preparation routes predict the quality of classroom practice (Nougaret, Scruggs, & Mastropieri, 2005; Sindelar, Daunic, & Rennells, 2004). The study authors used the FFT and PRAXIS III (Dwyer, 1994) respectively to assess differences in candidates from traditional university-based routes and alternative routes offered by districts, finding that traditionally certified teachers outperformed alternatively certified teachers in many important domains. An additional study conducted by Brownell and colleagues (2009) used a reading-specific, special education-specific observation protocol to examine features of special education reading instruction that predicted student academic gains. They found that successful instruction was marked by highly engaging practice, high student interest, intensive and continuous teaching, and effective classroom management.

The studies above have had little to no role in the development of current teacher evaluation practices. However, we are beginning to see research examining whether observations of special education teachers can be implemented in ways that are fair and valid. Jones and Brownell (2014) put forth a formal definition of effective special education teaching and examined this definition side-by-side with the FFT. They found that the language used to describe distinguished performance in the FFT is focused on students' actions, and that these actions may not be feasible or appropriate in special education teachers' classrooms at all times. For example, if a special educator was tasked with providing targeted intervention instruction around phonemic awareness within a 25-minute pullout block and was masterfully fulfilling that goal, he or she would likely receive low scores on several FFT elements.

How might districts proceed in addressing these concerns? At least one state (Idaho) has developed an observation protocol specific to special education teachers. Idaho's Recognizing Effective Special Education Teachers (RESET) tool was developed from core principles of effective special education instruction (Semmelroth & Johnson, 2014). Research on RESET has examined the reliability of the tool when used in practice (Semmelroth & Johnson, 2014). The authors find that the measurement properties of RESET align with previous research on protocols such as FFT: "To achieve acceptable levels of relative reliability and error when evaluating special education teachers, multiple raters and occasions must be used" (p. 139).

Given limited time and resources, districts and states may not adopt separate observation systems for evaluating special educators; we have seen similar resistance to using subject-specific protocols in general education. And as suggested above, schools would benefit from having a common vision of effective teaching, which could be useful for guiding teacher improvement. Therefore, it would be worthwhile to explore ways to improve the accuracy of ratings of special education teachers drawn from observation systems such as the FFT. With many evaluation systems relying on local administrators to conduct classroom observations, the quality of special educator observations could be improved by supporting principals in the scoring process. There is evidence that principals vary greatly in their knowledge about special education instruction, notably co-teaching and inclusive practices (Kamens, Susko, & Elliott, 2013), and that they often have inaccurate pictures of how special educators spend their time (Franz et al., 2008). Thus, it may be useful to provide scoring support to administrators, such as video exemplars tied to specific elements on the FFT and other protocols.

CONCLUSIONS AND PRACTICAL IMPLICATIONS

This chapter began with the question of whether it is appropriate to evaluate general educators and special educators using the same tools. The literature is long on commentary surrounding the challenges of evaluating special educators but short on empirical evidence that can guide policymaking. Perceptions of unfairness may be borne out by data, but we should not assume that this will always hold true. The case of value-added scores is one important example. As Buzick and Jones (in press) document, we can mitigate concerns about including SWDs in VAMs through model specification. Before we go too far down the path of revamping special educator observations, we need evidence related to how the FFT and other protocols, as currently implemented in schools, function with special educators.

While existing practices may not be biased against special educators, it does seem likely that existing evaluation tools may not capture the complexities of their work. In VAM research, studies have examined how to account for nested instruction, but there have been no similar studies in observation research. Moving forward, it will be important to develop measures of coordinated instruction: Measures of teamwork have been developed and validated in fields such as surgery and the military and may serve as a foundation for similar measures in teaching (Brownell, Jones, & Bettini, 2013). Additionally, with much of special educators' work occurring outside of formal instruction, states and districts should consider strategies for capturing special educators' planning and preparation, instructional skills that are also important in general education. The FFT includes domains for (1) Planning and Preparation and (2) Professional Responsibilities, but many districts have dropped these domains given the strain on raters' time. This decision, though sensible, limits the degree to which scores drawn from the FFT actually reflect special educators' teaching.

This chapter argues that there are the potential lessons that policymakers can learn from examining the case of special education teacher evaluation. The same questions raised in this chapter could also apply to general educators. Shared instruction is not limited to special education; general education teachers often coordinate instruction across grades or grade-level teams, and students move in and out of schools. Further, general educators take on many responsibilities not captured in observation protocols and, like special educators, are responsible for nonacademic outcomes such as socioemotional development. Finally, while observation systems have regularly adopted definitions of effective classroom practice based on constructivism, this convergence masks decades-long debates about how best to teach students in subjects such as reading and mathematics. Thus, while limited, the research reviewed in this chapter has implications for general educators and special educators alike.

REFERENCES

Bell, C., Gitomer, D., McCaffrey, D., Hamre, B., Pianta, R., & Qi, Y. (2012). An argument approach to observation protocol validity. *Educational Assessment, 17,* 62–87.

Benedict, A. E., Thomas, R. A., Kimerling, J., & Leko, C. (2013). Trends in teacher evaluation: What every special education teacher should know. *Teaching Exceptional Children, 45,* 60–68.

Blanton, L. P., Sindelar, P. T., & Correa, V. I. (2006). Models and measures of beginning teacher quality. *The Journal of Special Education, 40*(2), 115–127.

Brownell, M. T., Bishop, A. G., Gersten, R., Klingner, J. K., Penfield, R. D., Dimino, J., . . . Sindelar, P. T. (2009). The role of domain expertise in beginning special education teacher quality. *Exceptional Children, 75,* 391–411.

Brownell, M. T., Jones, N. D., & Bettini, E. (2013, October). *Evaluating teacher education programs to improve instruction for students with disabilities.* Paper presented at the Council for Exceptional Children Teacher Education Division Annual Conference, Fort Lauderdale, FL.

Brownell, M., Ross, D. D., Colon, E. P., & McCallum, C. L. (2005). Critical features of special education teacher preparation: A comparison with general teacher education. *Journal of Special Education, 38*, 242–252.

Brownell, M. T., Sindelar, P. T., Kiely, M. T., & Danielson, L. C. (2010). Special education teacher quality and preparation: Exposing foundations, constructing a new model. *Exceptional Children, 76*, 357–377.

Buzick, H. M., & Jones, N. D. (in press). Using test scores from students with disabilities in teacher effectiveness indicators. *Educational Measurement: Issues and Practice.*

Center on Great Teachers & Leaders. (n.d.). Databases on state teacher and principal evaluation policies. Washington, DC: American Institutes for Research. Retrieved from resource.tqsource.org/stateevaldb/

Chetty, R., Friedman, J. N., & Rockoff, J. E. (2013). *Measuring the impacts of teachers II: Teacher value-added and student outcomes in adulthood* (NBER working paper 19424). Cambridge, MA: National Bureau of Economic Research. Retrieved from www.nber.org/papers/w19424

Cook, B. G., & Odom, S. L. (2013). Evidence-based practices and implementation science in special education. *Exceptional Children, 79*, 135–144.

Council for Exceptional Children. (2012). The Council for Exceptional Children's position on special education teacher evaluation. Retrieved from www.cec.sped.org/Policy-and-Advocacy/CEC-Professional-Policies

Danielson, C. (2013). *The framework for teaching evaluation instrument.* Princeton, NJ: The Danielson Group.

Dwyer, C. A. (1994). *Development of the knowledge base for the PRAXIS III: Classroom performance assessments criteria.* Princeton, NJ: Educational Testing Service.

Englert, C., Tarrant, K., & Mariage, T. (1992). Defining and redefining instructional practice in special education: Perspectives on good teaching. *Teacher Education and Special Education, 15*, 62–86.

Franz, D. P., Vannest, K. J., Parker, R. I., Hasbrouck, J. E., Dyer, N., & Davis, J. L. (2008). Time use by special educators and how it is valued. *Journal of School Leadership, 18*(5), 551–576.

Fuchs, D., Fuchs, L. S., & Stecker, P. M. (2010). The "blurring" of special education in a new continuum of general education placements and services. *Exceptional Children, 76*, 301–323.

Goldhaber, D., Gabele, B., & Walch, J. (2013). Does the model matter? Exploring the relationship between different student achievement-based teacher assessments. *Statistics, Politics, and Policy, 1*, 28–39.

Hill, H., Charalambous, C., & Kraft, M. (2012). When rater reliability is not enough: Teacher observation systems and a case for the generalizability study. *Educational Researcher, 41*(2), 56–64.

Hock, H., & Isenberg, E. (2012). *Methods for accounting for co-teaching in value-added models.* Washington, DC: Mathematica Policy Research.

Individuals with Disabilities Education Improvement Act of 2004, Pub. L. No. 108–446. (2004).

Johnson, E., & Semmelroth, C. L. (2014). Special education teacher evaluation: Why it matters, what makes it challenging, and how to address these challenges. *Assessment for Effective Intervention, 39*, 71–82.

Jones, N. D., & Brownell, M. T. (2014). Examining the use of classroom observations in the evaluation of special education teachers. *Assessment for Effective Intervention, 39*(2), 112–124.

Jones, N. D., Buzick, H. M., & Turkan, S. (2013). Including students with disabilities and English language learners in measures of educator effectiveness. *Educational Researcher, 42*(4), 234–241.

Kamens, M. W., Susko, J. P., & Elliott, J. S. (2013). Evaluation and supervision of co-teaching: A study of administrator practices in New Jersey. *NASSP Bulletin, 97*, 166–190.

Kane, T. J., & Staiger, D. O. (2008). *Estimating teacher impacts on student achievement: An experimental evaluation* (NBER working paper 14607). Cambridge, MA: National Bureau of Economic Research. Retrieved from www.nber.org/papers/w14607

Klingner, J. K., Brownell, M. T., Mason, L. H., Sindelar, P. T., Benedict, A. E., Griffin, G. G., . . . Park, Y. (in press). Teaching students with special needs in the new millennium. In D. Gitomer & C. Bell (Eds.), *Handbook for research on teaching.* Washington, DC: American Educational Research Association.

Klingner, J. K., & Vaughn, S. (2002). The changing roles and responsibilities of an LD specialist. *Learning Disability Quarterly, 25*, 19–31.

Lacireno-Paquet, N., Morgan, C., & Mello, D. (2014). *How states use student learning objectives in teacher evaluation systems: A review of state websites.* Washington, DC: U.S. Department of Education, Institute of Education Sciences.

McCaffrey, D., & Buzick, H. (2014). *Is value-added accurate for students with disabilities?* Stanford, CA: Carnegie Foundation for the Advancement of Teaching.

National Center for Education Statistics. (2012). *Digest of Education Statistics, 2011* (NCES 2012-001). Washington, DC: U.S. Department of Education.

Nougaret, A., Scruggs, T., & Mastropieri, M. (2005). Does teacher education produce better special education teachers? *Exceptional Children, 71*, 217–229.

Semmelroth, C. L., & Johnson, E. (2014). Measuring rater reliability on a special education observation tool. *Assessment for Effective Intervention, 39*, 131–145.

Sindelar, P., Daunic, A., & Rennells, M. S. (2004). Comparisons of traditionally and alternatively trained teachers. *Exceptional Children, 12*, 209–223.

Sireci, S. G., Scarpati, S. E., & Li, S. (2005). Test accommodations for students with disabilities: An analysis of the interaction hypothesis. *Review of Educational Research, 75*, 457–490.

Steinbrecher, T. D., Selig, J. P., Cosbey, J., & Thorstensen, B. I. (2014). Evaluating special educator effectiveness: Addressing issues inherent in value-added modeling. *Exceptional Children, 80*, 323–336.

Swanson, E. A. (2008). Observing reading instruction for students with learning disabilities: A synthesis. *Learning Disability Quarterly, 31*, 115–133.

Trent, S. C., Artiles, A. J., & Englert, C. S. (1998). From deficit thinking to social constructivism: A review of theory, research, and practice in special education. *Review of Research in Education, 23*, 277–307.

Vannest, K. J., & Hagan-Burke, S. (2010). Teacher time use in special education. *Remedial and Special Education, 31*, 126–142.

Vaughn, S., Gersten, R., & Chard, D. (2000). The underlying message in LD intervention research: Findings from research syntheses. *Exceptional Children, 67*, 99–114.

Wanzek, J., Vaughn, S., Roberts, G., & Fletcher, J. M. (2011). Efficacy of a reading intervention for middle school students with disabilities. *Exceptional Children, 79*, 73–87.

CHAPTER 7

Using Student Surveys at the Elementary and Secondary Levels

Ryan Balch

Because students have the most contact with teachers and are the most direct consumers of a teacher's work, a growing number of school districts are using student perception survey data for teacher feedback or incorporating student survey measures into teacher evaluation systems. While classroom observations and teacher value-added measures have received extensive attention during the past several years, there has been less focus by researchers on the growing use of student surveys in teacher evaluation. As more districts and states begin to use them for formative or summative teacher evaluation, it is crucial to review what we know from research about student surveys and how they can be used productively with other measures. According to the National Council on Teacher Quality (2013), eight states require student surveys to be incorporated into teachers' evaluations—Alaska, Hawaii, Massachusetts, Kentucky, Utah, Iowa, Georgia and New York—while several others allow for student surveys to be used. Prominent districts that require student surveys as a part of teacher evaluation include Memphis, Pittsburgh, and New York City. Large districts elsewhere are beginning to use student surveys formatively, including the school districts in Dallas, Nashville, and Seattle.

Despite this growing use, concerns remain about the capacity of student surveys to solicit useful and accurate information from students that can identify effective instruction and inform teacher practice. A main goal of this chapter is to address these concerns by describing a validity framework for assessing student surveys.

Proponents of student surveys identify at least three arguments for their use. First, in contrast to value-added measures, student survey measures have the potential to identify specific areas of focus that teachers can work on with instructional leaders to improve, particularly when paired with observation data. This ability to receive feedback can also occur on a more frequent basis, since teachers can administer surveys on their own either online or with the assistance of smartphone applications (see My Student Survey for an example, www.mystudentsurvey.com).

Second, student surveys can provide similar information as observations at a fraction of the cost and time. For example, if one assumes that each teacher in a school building is observed four times per year for 30 minutes, plus 30 minutes for pre- and/or postobservation conferences and time spent writing reports, each teacher requires roughly 5 to 6 hours of time from a supervisor in a given school year. In a 150-school district with 85,000 students and 5,000 teachers, this time can translate into the full-time salary of roughly 40 employees at a total cost (salary plus benefits) of more than $4 million, before even considering the cost of training and licensing fees for specific instruments. With minimal staff requirements and administrative costs of just $1 to $2 per student, student surveys for this hypothetical district would cost about one-third of doing a single observation.

Third, student survey results have research support as a measure of teacher effectiveness. Most empirical investigation of student feedback in teacher evaluation has occurred in higher education. From these studies, student ratings appear to be both reliable and valid measures of instructional quality (Aleamoni, 1999). For example, student ratings of college professors in subsequent years have correlations between .87 and .89, suggesting that they are stable and reliable. Student feedback also shows positive correlations with ratings from colleagues and external observers (Renaud & Murray, 2005).

Although less extensive, research in K–12 settings shows promising results. First, in a study of 1,976 K–12 students in Wyoming, Wilkerson, Manatt, Rogers, and Maughan (2000) compared student ratings to teacher self-ratings, principal ratings, and principal summative evaluations as predictors of student achievement in reading and mathematics. Student ratings strongly predicted achievement in both subjects. Similarly, in a study of 9,765 student surveys, researchers found that student surveys across elementary, middle, and high schools were valid and reliable teacher evaluation measures (Peterson, Wahlquist, & Bone, 2000). This finding aligns with international research from Cyprus, where student surveys of teacher practices were highly correlated with achievement gains in mathematics and Greek language (Kyriakides, 2005). Together these findings "provide convincing evidence that student ratings of teaching are worth considering for inclusion in teacher evaluation systems" (Goe, Bell, & Little, 2008, p. 40).

More recently, an extensive research project, known as the Measures of Effective Teaching (MET) project, investigated the relationship between measures of teaching and value-added estimates of student achievement. The measures included in the study, which took place in seven districts and included more than 3,000 teachers in grades 4 through 8, were prior value-added scores, observational rubrics, and student perceptions (Bill and Melinda Gates Foundation, 2010). Preliminary findings from the project report a significant correlation between a teacher's total score on the student survey and value-added achievement on state tests in both mathematics (.22) and English language arts (.10). These correlations are similar in magnitude to correlations between value-added and observation rubrics that look at general teaching practices such as the Framework for Teaching (Danielson, 1996) and the Classroom Assessment Scoring System (CLASS; Pianta, La Paro, & Hamre, 2008). Also, the MET researchers found that reliability for the student survey measures, calculated as the correlation across different sections taught by the same teacher, was substantially higher than for any of the observation measures (Kane & Staiger, 2012). Overall, the researchers found that teacher evaluation can be enhanced by including multiple measures to differentiate teacher effectiveness, and that incorporating student surveys into overall effectiveness measures could better discriminate between teachers with higher and lower achievement gains.

Given the promise of student surveys, it is important for education researchers and policymakers to have a better understanding of these understudied tools. To this end, I will now discuss a validation framework for the creation of student surveys and outline methods for using students effectively.

A VALIDATION FRAMEWORK FOR STUDENT SURVEY DEVELOPMENT

Establishing true measure validity is an impossible task (Kane, 2006). Instead, one needs to establish a body of evidence that supports the measure's use. As a case study in developing a student survey with multiple sources of evidence, this chapter describes the validation of the Survey of Teacher Practice (STeP), a survey I developed and offer through My Student Survey. The main construct of interest is that of effective teaching practice. Construct validity refers to whether a scale measures the underlying construct that it is intended to measure. Other forms of validity (such as criterion validity) represent evidence that supports construct validity.

Evidence for construct validity comes from content validity, teacher interviews, cognitive interviews with students, convergent validity, and predictive validity. Content validity ensures that a measure has adequate coverage of the content it seeks to measure and will be established by drawing upon effective teaching practices from the literature as well as common observation rubrics. Convergent validity compares scores on a measure to scores on other instruments that intend to measure a similar concept and will be established with measures of academic student engagement and academic self-efficacy. Finally, predictive validity determines whether scores on a measure can predict future scores on measures of similar constructs.

Content Validity

The first question asks whether the survey has adequate coverage of effective teaching practices in an effort to establish content validity. Messick (1989) echoes earlier definitions of content validity in that he claims that it is "founded on relevance between the content of the survey and the representativeness with which it covers the domain" (Messick, 1989, as cited by Porter et al., 2010, p. 142). This step is required to ensure that survey items are exhaustive of potential teacher practices and reflect current knowledge of effective teaching.

The first procedure consisted of identifying overlapping teacher behaviors from various reviews of the research literature on teacher behaviors found to consistently predict student achievement. For instance, all of the reviews highlight a link between providing feedback for students and higher student achievement. Schacter and Thum (2004) note that teachers should provide "frequent, elaborate, and high quality academic feedback" (p. 14). Brophy and Good (1986) discuss "monitoring of students' understanding and providing appropriate feedback" (p. 364). Emmer and Evertson (1981) note that "all student work, including seatwork, homework, and papers, is corrected, errors are discussed, and feedback is promptly provided" (p. 345). Finally, Marzano, Pickering, and Pollock (2001) outline several research-based feedback strategies. When a commonality among the reviews is found, the teacher behavior is then written into a question that allows students to rate the frequency of this behavior. For example, for feedback the item would be, "My teacher gives us helpful comments (or feedback) on our work."

The second procedure involved using common observational rubrics such as the Framework for Teaching (Danielson, 1996) and CLASS for grades K–5 (Pianta, La Paro, & Hamre, 2008). Both of these instruments have been tested for validity by assessing the relationship between teacher scores on the rubric and a teacher's value-added to student achievement. Teacher behaviors identified by the highest levels of these rubrics were transformed into questions appropriate for students to answer. For example, the CLASS rubric includes "Rules and behavior expectations are clearly stated or understood by everyone in the class" and the Danielson Framework lists "Standards of conduct are clear." The resulting survey item was "My teacher explains how we are supposed to behave in class."

Survey item selection was also guided by the question of whether students are able to judge a given teacher behavior. For example, differentiated instruction may be an important teaching practice, but students may not be able to assess whether instruction is differentiated. Items that are not easily observable or that require high degrees of inference are thus eliminated as survey items. Overall, these procedures led to the development of 64 survey questions that all either have a basis in overlapping areas of literature reviews or are grounded in descriptions of teacher behaviors from valid observational rubrics.

Cognitive Interviews

The next source of evidence for construct validity comes from cognitive interviews, which determine whether the objectives for evidence match how the students interpret the actual survey items. Cognitive interviews are helpful in addressing common threats to validity associated with surveys (Desimone & Le Floch, 2004; Porter et al., 2010). To respond accurately, respondents must be able to "comprehend an item, retrieve relevant information, make a judgment based upon the recall of knowledge, and map the answer onto the reporting system" (Desimone & LeFloch, 2004, p. 6). Cognitive interviews allow the researcher to determine which part of the process presents respondents with difficulty and why. Further, in an effort to minimize subject bias for survey items, students were asked to answer questions about teachers in a variety of different academic subjects. Questions that did not apply to certain subjects were revised or eliminated.

In the first round, 10 students were interviewed at a local private high school in Nashville. Instructions and questions that were confusing or questions that were interpreted in ways that did not address the teaching objective were revised on an iterative basis. All revisions were then tested again with a 15-student focus group at a public high school in Atlanta.

These cognitive interviews resulted in adjustments to or elimination of items. For example, in talking through the item, "When working in groups, my teacher has us choose a job, role, or responsibility within the group (recorder, materials person, manager, etc.)," students could not see the applicability in subjects other than science, so this item was dropped.

Concurrent and Predictive Validity

To test both concurrent and predictive validity, a large-scale pilot was conducted in spring 2011 in seven districts as part of Georgia's Race to the

Top initiative. Overall, 12,408 students completed the survey. Concurrent validity was assessed by measuring the relationship between student survey scores and academic student engagement and academic self-efficacy, both of which were collected at the same time as the rest of the student survey, while predictive validity was tested by correlating student survey scores with teachers' value-added to student achievement.

Academic engagement refers to student reports of their interest in learning. The measures for the current investigation were developed and tested by the Consortium on Chicago School Research (CCSR) with more than 100,000 demographically diverse elementary and high school students in the Chicago Public Schools. The 4-point Likert scale ranges from *Strongly Agree* to *Strongly Disagree* and includes six questions, such as "The topics we are studying are interesting and challenging" and "I am usually bored with this class." Individual reliability as tested by the survey developers for these items is 0.65 (Fredricks & McColskey, 2011).

Academic efficacy refers to student perceptions of their competence to do their classwork. Measures were developed as part of the Patterns for Adaptive Learning Scales (PALS) survey at the University of Michigan. The scales, tested in nine Midwestern districts, are based on research showing that an emphasis on mastery rather than performance is related to more adaptive patterns of learning (Midgley et al., 2000). The five-question scale, which includes items such as "I'm certain I can master the skills taught in class this year" and "I can do even the hardest work in this class if I try," uses a five-point Likert rating, and the authors report a Cronbach alpha score of .78.

Teacher value-added looks at the relationship of student surveys to estimates of a teacher's value-added scores to provide evidence for criterion validity, as gains in student achievement are arguably the most common metric for performance in education. Given the alignment of behaviors on the survey to those that have previously demonstrated a relationship to student achievement, one would expect that a greater frequency of these behaviors would be associated with larger gains in achievement.

To calculate value-added scores for teachers, a standard model adapted from the MET project is employed. This model estimates current-year student achievement scores as a function of last year's scores, student characteristics (e.g., subsidized lunch status, race), classroom mean demographic characteristics, and a grade fixed effect. Residuals from this model are taken as the teacher value-added measure.

Relationship to Outcome Measures

Correlations between teachers' total scores from the student survey and both academic engagement and academic self-efficacy were quite high.

Overall, the correlation with academic engagement was 0.72, and the correlation with self-efficacy was 0.64, with minimal differences by school level. The interpretation is that students with teachers who adopt the practices asked about by the survey are more engaged in the class and report a greater level of confidence in the subject. As these behaviors are the outcome of effective teaching practice, a strong correlation with a convergent measure provides evidence for construct validity.

Correlations with value-added were lower (see Table 7.1), though this attenuation is not surprising given research on the error in value-added calculations (Guarino, Reckase, & Wooldridge, 2011; McCaffrey, Lockwood, Koretz, & Hamilton, 2003). Findings from the MET project show a .38 correlation in mathematics between value-added for the same teacher in different sections, and a .40 correlation with value-added from the prior year. For English language arts, the correlation among different sections is .18 and the correlation with the prior year is .20. Correlations in my sample were in the range of 0.16 to 0.30 overall across subjects. As value-added is a measure of gains in student achievement attributed to the teacher, the fact that student surveys are predictive of value-added establishes evidence for construct validity.

In summary, the validation framework established multiple sources of evidence for construct validity, including content validity, cognitive interviews, convergent validity, and predictive validity. The validation framework can be applied to customized surveys for districts and states in order to both improve the survey and provide support for the use of the final survey in an evaluation context.

CHALLENGES OF USING STUDENT SURVEYS

The primary challenge in adopting student surveys comes from developing buy-in and engagement from teachers. Placing a value on student voice

Table 7.1. Correlation Between Survey Total and Value-Added Scores in Mathematics, English Language Arts (ELA), Science, and Social Studies

	Mathematics	ELA	Science	Social Studies
Overall	.1632* (N = 110)	.1773* (N = 86)	.2059* (N = 72)	.3043** (N = 75)
Middle School	0.0225 (N = 54)	.2204* (N = 49)	0.2921 (N = 26)	.2713* (N = 37)
High School	.2634* (N = 56)	0.1286 (N = 37)	0.2248 (N = 46)	.3460** (N = 38)

* $p < .10$. ** $p < .05$. *N* denotes sample size for each analysis.

upsets the normal hierarchy within schools and therefore requires a culture shift for teachers to gain comfort with students providing feedback. In some circumstances, resistance to this shift can lead to teachers' being less receptive to results and the instructional adjustments suggested by feedback reports. There are, however, several methods by which policymakers can increase the engagement in student surveys. These include being transparent with survey items, providing high-quality feedback reports, and utilizing screening procedures to eliminate invalid surveys.

The first method of fostering a sense of engagement involves transparency of survey items, which allows teachers to recognize that the behaviors asked about in the survey are familiar teaching practices. Because the STeP survey was derived from research-based practices and common observation rubrics, the behaviors are generally ones that teachers have previously encountered. To aid with transparency, districts and/or states implementing surveys should provide easy access to survey items for teachers, administrators, parents, and other stakeholders through public websites affiliated with the district.

Second, user-friendly feedback reports allow teachers to take advantage of the instructional benefits of student surveys. Reports should be easy for teachers to navigate but also facilitate change in instruction. To help build teacher engagement, feedback reports should contain the following features:

1. Inclusion of overall and scale results *as well as* item-level information
2. Identification of areas of strength and areas of focus using comparison methods
3. The ability to track results over time
4. The ability to provide principals with information about high-scoring teachers in the building on each item/instructional practice to serve as examples for other teachers

An example feedback report that incorporates these principles can be viewed at mystudentsurvey.com/reports/sample/.

The final method for building engagement comes from identifying and eliminating invalid surveys. Previous studies have indicated that invalid surveys exist for roughly 5 to 8% of surveys (Balch, 2012). However, the perception of teachers is often greater than the reality and therefore needs to be addressed for teachers to place credibility in the results. Teachers are specifically worried about the student in the classroom who has "an ax to grind" and will use the survey as an opportunity for retribution.

To address these issues, systems should employ screening procedures to identify invalid responses. The presence of these safeguards can have a dramatic impact on teacher comfort with student survey and confidence in the results. Current research is under way on the best method for incorporating screening procedures, varying from outlier removal to minimum time spent on surveys, with the goal of strengthening the relationship between student surveys and achievement (Balch & Robinson-Cimpian, 2014).

TWO CASE STUDIES IN STUDENT SURVEY DEVELOPMENT

From an organizational perspective, there are several possible benefits of developing a customized student survey. This customization allows for student surveys to reflect local teaching standards and allows for feedback to be provided by local stakeholders. Here I outline two cases of organizations that created surveys using the previously described validation framework. The first comes from work with the New York State United Teachers (NYSUT), and the second comes from work with Metro Nashville Public Schools (MNPS). Though the validation process used in both contexts was similar, the differing motivations for each project provide examples of the various advantages of customized survey development.

Initially, NYSUT was seeking to develop a student survey that was aligned to the NYSUT Teaching Practice Rubric. Since the state required teachers to have student surveys as a part of their evaluation, union representatives wanted to ensure that there was a state-approved option available that aligned to their values in teaching practice reflected in the rubric. Survey items were adapted or developed to align with the instructional components of the Teaching Practice Rubric. Following the creation of the initial survey, items were tested in focus groups with 68 teachers in five different districts. Teachers were asked about difficult items, items that should be eliminated, and items that might be challenging for certain subjects. The survey was revised in response to this teacher feedback, and an updated version was then tested with students. Cognitive interviews took place in eight NYSUT schools. Overall, 49 interviews were conducted. To ensure a fair and adequate coverage of all grades, 4 to 5 students were chosen from each grade. The final stage used data from a pilot to establish convergent validity with teacher scores from the NYSUT teaching practice rubric. The overall correlation between the two measures for the 161 teachers who participated was .24, with scores consistent across the five participating districts.

In the other case, My Student Survey was contracted by MNPS to develop an in-house student survey that aligned with the Tennessee Educator Acceleration Model rubric. MNPS was interested in developing a student survey for three primary reasons. First, MNPS wanted to have greater control over survey length and item content. Second, MNPS was interested in having a survey that reflected feedback and input from a variety of stakeholders, including teachers, union representatives, parents, and administrators. They wanted to ensure that the survey addressed the needs of each of these groups, with the additional benefit of increasing buy-in and engagement for the final product. Third, MNPS was looking to develop an instrument that was internally owned in order for student survey administration to be financially sustainable. Because student voice is an important part of the strategic plan for MNPS, being able to continue to include this element for years in the future was an important consideration. The validation process was similar to the one described above and used initial alignment work, teacher focus groups, student interviews, and pilot data to establish construct validity.

FURTHER RESEARCH

The use of student surveys as a measure of teacher evaluation is still in the very early stages. Thus, there are several unanswered questions regarding the use of student surveys whose answers will aid policymakers in decisions regarding their use in measuring teacher effectiveness. Two primary concerns are addressed below.

First, some critics argue that students are incapable of providing accurate feedback, particularly when the responses are part of a high-stakes evaluation of a teacher (Rothstein, 2010). Researchers might address this concern by randomly providing students with different instructions—one that says that their feedback is part of the teacher's yearly evaluation that determines whether the teacher's contract is renewed, and one that says the results are simply for feedback—and assessing whether responses differ between the two. Results could also be compared with principal evaluations and value-added assessments.

Other possible investigations include a more detailed investigation of how teachers incorporate feedback from student surveys. Teachers appear to appreciate feedback reports, but a more systematic study could analyze whether the suggestions for improvement were actually implemented and whether this had an impact on student achievement. Further, it would be possible to incorporate coaching in similar ways as previous studies of coaching using feedback for principals (Bickman, Goldring, Andrade, Breda, & Goff, 2012).

CONCLUSION

Student surveys offer an alternative option for systems seeking to design a multiple-measure evaluation system. Student surveys have a growing base of research supporting their use, and they offer certain advantages of lower cost and the ability to inform professional development. Districts and states seeking to develop their own surveys would benefit from following an established validation framework and by engaging in a targeted effort to build teacher engagement and buy-in.

REFERENCES

Aleamoni, L. (1999). Student ratings myths versus research facts from 1924 to 1998. *Journal of Personnel Evaluation in Education, 13*(2), 153–166.

Balch, R. T. (2012). *The validation of a student survey on teacher practice* (Doctoral dissertation). Retrieved from Dissertations and Theses at Vanderbilt University (1266431696).

Balch, R., & Robinson-Cimpian, J. (2014). *Toward improving measures of teacher effectiveness: Identifying invalid responses in student surveys of teacher practice.* Presented at the annual meeting of the Association of Public Policy and Management, Albuquerque, NM.

Bickman, L., Goldring, E., Andrade, A., Breda, C., & Goff, P. (2012, March). *Improving principal leadership through feedback and coaching.* Presented at the annual meeting of the Society for Research on Educational Effectiveness, Washington, DC.

Bill and Melinda Gates Foundation. (2010). *Learning about teaching: Initial findings from the Measures of Effective Teaching Project* (MET project research paper). Seattle, WA: Author.

Brophy, J., & Good, T. (1986). Teacher behavior and student achievement. In M. Wittrock (Ed.), *Handbook of research on teaching* (pp. 340–370). New York, NY: Macmillan.

Danielson, C. (1996). *Enhancing professional practice: A framework for teaching.* Alexandria, VA: Association for Supervision and Curriculum Development.

Desimone, L. M., & Le Floch, K. C. (2004). Are we asking the right questions? Using cognitive interviews to improve surveys in education research. *Education Evaluation and Policy Analysis, 26*(1), 1–22.

Emmer, E., & Evertson, C. (1981). Synthesis of research on classroom management. *Educational Leadership, 38*(4), 342–347.

Fredricks, J., & McColskey, W. (2011). *Measuring student engagement in upper elementary through high school: A description of 21 instruments.* Washington, DC: Institute for Education Sciences.

Goe, L., Bell, C., & Little, O. (2008). *Approaches to evaluating teacher effectiveness: A research synthesis.* Washington, DC: National Comprehensive Center on Teacher Quality.

Guarino, C., Reckase, M., & Wooldridge, J. (2011). *Can value-added measures of teacher performance be trusted?* East Lansing, MI: Education Policy Center at Michigan State University.

Kane, M. (2006). Validation. In R. Brennan (Ed.), *Educational measurement* (pp. 17–64). Washington, DC: American Council on Education.

Kane, T., & Staiger, D. (2012). *Gathering feedback for teaching: Combining high-quality observations with student surveys and achievement gains* (MET project research paper). Seattle, WA: Bill & Melinda Gates Foundation.

Kyriakides, L. (2005). Drawing from teacher effectiveness research and research into teacher interpersonal behaviour to establish a teacher evaluation system: A study on the use of student ratings to evaluate teacher behaviour. *Journal of Classroom Interaction, 40*(2), 44–66.

Marzano, R., Pickering, D., & Pollock, J. (2001). *Classroom instruction that works: Research-based strategies for increasing student achievement.* Alexandria, VA: Association for Supervision and Curriculum Development.

McCaffrey, D., Lockwood, J. R., Koretz, D., & Hamilton, L. (2003). *Evaluating value-added models for teacher accountability.* Santa Monica, CA: RAND.

Messick, S. (1989). Validity. In R. Linn (Ed.), *Educational measurement* (3rd ed., pp. 13–104). New York, NY: American Council on Education/Macmillan.

Midgley, C., Maehr, M. L., Hruda, L., Anderman, E. M., Anderman, L., Freeman, K.E., . . . Urdan, T. (2000). *Manual for the Patterns of Adaptive Learning Scales (PALS).* Ann Arbor, MI: University of Michigan.

National Council on Teacher Quality. (2013). State of the States 2013: Connect the Dots: Using Evaluations of Teacher Effectiveness to Inform Policy and Practice. Washington, DC: Author.

Peterson, K., Wahlquist, C., & Bone, K. (2000). Student surveys for school teacher evaluation. *Journal of Personnel Evaluation in Education, 14*(2), 135–153.

Pianta, R. C., La Paro, K. M., & Hamre., B. K. (2008). *Classroom Assessment Scoring System (CLASS): Pre-K.* Baltimore, MD: Paul H. Brookes.

Porter, A., Polikoff, M., Goldring, E., Murphy, J., Elliott, S., & May, H. (2010). Developing a psychometrically sound assessment of school leadership: The VAL-ED as a case study. *Educational Administration Quarterly, 46*(2), 135–173.

Renaud, R., & Murray, H. (2005). Factorial validity of student ratings of instruction. *Research in Higher Education, 46*(8), 929–953.

Rothstein, J. (2010). *Review of learning about teaching.* Boulder, CO: Great Lakes Center for Education Research and Practice.

Schacter, J., & Thum, Y. (2004). Paying for high and low-quality teaching. *Economics of Education Review, 23*(4), 411–430.

Wilkerson, D., Manatt, R., Rogers, M. A., & Maughan, R. (2000). Validation of student, principal, and self-ratings in 360 Feedback for Teacher Evaluation. *Journal of Personnel Evaluation in Education, 14*(2), 179–192.

CHAPTER 8

The Role of edTPA in Assessing Content-Specific Instructional Practices

Peter Youngs
Andrea Whittaker

The Common Core State Standards (CCSS) and other recent state-developed standards call for elementary and secondary teachers to enact ambitious instruction—that is, helping students develop strong conceptual knowledge and engage in disciplinary practices (Lampert et al., 2013; Newmann & Associates, 1996)—to improve educational outcomes for all students. Research indicates that ambitious instruction is associated with student achievement in reading, writing, and mathematics (Guthrie et al., 2004; Harris, Graham, & Mason, 2006; National Mathematics Advisory Panel, 2008). At the same time, ensuring that all teachers can enact such instruction will require significant, large-scale changes in teacher preparation and assessment.

During the past decade, there have been several efforts to create new approaches to teacher assessment and implement them in teacher education programs and at the school district and state levels. These new approaches include generic and content-specific observation instruments as well as content-specific teaching portfolios. While these assessments are all designed to support teachers in developing ambitious instruction and to hold them accountable for teaching effectively, observation instruments and teaching portfolios represent distinct responses to the accountability imperative and are typically used at different stages in the professional teaching continuum. Further, there have been few efforts to explore how these distinct approaches can potentially be used in conjunction with one another with preservice teaching candidates.

In this chapter, we outline ways in which generic and content-specific observation instruments used in teacher evaluation systems with practicing teachers can support implementation of the Common Core and other rigorous state-developed standards while also considering some limitations inherent in these tools. These instruments include the Classroom Assessment Scoring System (CLASS), the Framework for Teaching (FFT), the Protocol for Language Arts Teaching Observation (PLATO), and the Mathematical Quality of Instruction (MQI) instrument. We then describe edTPA, a content-specific portfolio assessment currently used with teaching candidates in a growing number of states, and review empirical research on edTPA and similar teacher assessments. Finally, we explicate ways in which edTPA and observation instruments represent different responses to accountability pressures and describe how edTPA and similar teacher assessments can be used in combination with observation tools in evaluating teaching candidates' content-specific instructional practices, including those associated with the Common Core.

CLASS AND THE FRAMEWORK FOR TEACHING

During the past decade, virtually all school districts and states in the United States have adopted or modified generic classroom observation instruments for use in evaluating teachers and supporting their professional growth. Two of the most widely used tools are CLASS (Pianta & Hamre, 2009) and the FFT (Danielson, 2013). CLASS addresses the domains of instructional supports, classroom organization, and emotional supports, while the FFT focuses on four domains: planning and preparation, classroom management, teaching for student learning, and professionalism (CLASS is described in more detail in Chapter 3 of this volume). For both instruments, trained evaluators assess teachers in all domains; classroom observations for CLASS address all three CLASS domains while observations for the FFT focus on classroom management and instruction. In most districts that use CLASS or the FFT, teachers are observed at least four to six times per school year.

There are several reasons why school districts and states have implemented CLASS, the FFT, or similar observation instruments. First, CLASS and the FFT are generic with regard to grade level and subject area; thus, the same instrument (i.e., CLASS or the FFT) can be used in grades Pre-K–12. This means that districts can train principals and other evaluators to use a single observation tool (as opposed to training them to employ multiple tools). Second, there is evidence that CLASS and the FFT can be validly and reliably used for summative teacher evaluation

(Bell et al., 2012; Bill and Melinda Gates Foundation, 2012; Kane, Taylor, Tyler, & Wooten, 2010; Pianta & Hamre, 2009, this volume; Taylor & Tyler, 2012). Third, to some extent, CLASS and the FFT assess teachers' ability to promote students' conceptual learning. In particular, the CLASS domain of instructional supports focuses on concept development, while the FFT domain of instruction addresses the teacher's use of questioning and discussion techniques (Danielson, 2013; Pianta & Hamre, 2009). Finally, there is evidence that teachers' performances on CLASS and FFT are associated with student achievement gains (Bill and Melinda Gates Foundation, 2012; Kane et al., 2010; Pianta & Hamre, this volume; Taylor & Tyler, 2012).

Despite the promise of CLASS, the FFT, and similar generic observation instruments, such tools have some limitations in light of the CCSS's call for ambitious instruction in English language arts (ELA) and mathematics. First, these generic instruments assume that the same types of knowledge and instructional practices are suitable for teaching vastly different grade levels and subjects, such as early elementary reading and pre-calculus or biology. To some extent this is true, but there are significant differences in the skills and expertise needed to teach reading to 1st-graders and those required to engage adolescents in mathematical problem solving or scientific investigation (Hill & Grossman, 2013).

Second, CLASS and the FFT assume that evaluators can adequately assess instruction regardless of whether they have knowledge or teaching experience in the subject area being assessed. But many argue that attempts to improve teaching require breaking down or decomposing broad practices (e.g., differentiating instruction, leading discussion, formatively assessing learning) into more detailed and content-specific practices on which teachers can focus (Boerst, Sleep, Ball, & Bass, 2011; Grossman et al., 2009; Kucan et al., 2011). Therefore, evaluators must have sufficient content knowledge to assess and provide feedback on these types of more specific practices. Given that CLASS and FFT raters often do not have strong knowledge of the content areas they are observing, there are limitations to the extent to which these raters (and, thus, these instruments) can reliably assess the extent to which a particular teacher is promoting conceptual learning in a specific content area.

PLATO AND THE MQI

In recent years, several researchers have created content-specific observation tools to complement the use of more generic instruments. Two prominent content-specific tools are PLATO and the MQI. Originally developed for use in ELA classrooms, PLATO is a standardized observation tool (Grossman, Loeb, Cohen, & Wyckoff, 2013) that has been proven valid and reliable at predicting elementary reading and mathematics achievement (Bill and Melinda Gates Foundation, 2012; Cohen, 2015). It focuses on rigorous content and intellectually challenging tasks, the centrality of classroom discourse in developing understanding of content and disciplinary skills, and teachers' role in providing instructional scaffolding to help students succeed. Like PLATO, the MQI is a standardized observation instrument that measures how explanations, representations, precise language, and generalizations are developed in a lesson, and also the disciplinary integrity of the mathematics presented to students, including the degree to which teacher errors occur during the lesson. The MQI has been proven valid and reliable at predicting elementary mathematics achievement (Hill, Kapitula, & Umland, 2011).

PLATO and the MQI address the two limitations of the generic observation tools described above. First, they both focus on content-specific teaching knowledge and skills that teachers need to enact ambitious instructional practices and help students learn rigorous content and develop conceptual understanding associated with the Common Core. Second, PLATO and the MQI both require evaluators to have sufficient content expertise in order to assess and provide feedback to teachers on detailed, content-specific practices. Thus, these instruments have greater potential than CLASS or the FFT to evaluate the degree to which a given teacher is promoting conceptual learning in ELA or mathematics.

At the same time, as observation tools, PLATO and the MQI also have some limitations. For one, each of these instruments focuses on individual lessons as opposed to units of instruction. Thus, even when evaluators observe the same teacher on multiple occasions, they are unable to make inferences about a given teacher's learning objectives, instructional tasks, and assessments across lessons within the same unit. Second, neither PLATO nor the MQI focuses on teachers' use of summative assessments at the end of units or their ability to analyze data on student learning from such assessments.

ANTECEDENTS TO EDTPA

edTPA is a content-specific portfolio assessment used with preservice teaching candidates that addresses many shortcomings of classroom observation instruments and for which there is a growing body of evidence related to validity and reliability. In this section, we describe two antecedents to edTPA: the BEST portfolios and the PACT assessments. The next section introduces edTPA and explains how it builds on these earlier teacher performance assessments.

From 1995 to 2005 under the leadership of Raymond Pecheone, the Connecticut State Department of Education developed and implemented a set of content-specific assessments known as the Beginning Educator Support and Training (BEST) portfolios. The BEST portfolios were developed in 10 certification areas and modeled on the National Board for Professional Teaching Standards (NBPTS) assessments. As of the early 2000s, teachers in virtually all content areas in the state completed the BEST portfolio process in their 2nd year of teaching (Youngs, Pogodzinski, & Low, 2010). Similar to the NBPTS assessments, teachers completing BEST were required to develop several entries that were integrated around a unit of instruction. These entries included a description of their teaching context, a set of lesson plans for an instructional unit, two video recordings of instruction during the unit, samples of student work, and teacher commentaries on their planning, instruction, and assessment of student progress (Pecheone & Stansbury, 1996). In contrast to the NBPTS assessments, the BEST portfolios did not include a written exam or teacher commentary on their professionalism outside of the classroom.

A study by Wilson, Hallam, Pecheone, and Moss (2014) examined the relationship between Connecticut elementary teachers' performance on the BEST portfolio and their students' reading achievement as measured by the Degrees of Reading Power (DRP test). This study drew on data over a 4-year period from 110 2nd-year teachers in grades 3–6 in two urban Connecticut districts as well as their students; the DRP was administered in the fall and spring during each year for which there was BEST portfolio data. Using hierarchical linear modeling (HLM), the researchers reported that a one-unit change in a teacher's portfolio score was associated with a 2.2 change in DRP units for their students, or approximately 46% of a year's average change—that is, about 4 months of instruction (Wilson et al., 2014).

In the early 2000s, a group of universities in California created Performance Assessment for California Teachers (PACT) in response to a 1998 law (CA Senate Bill 2042) that required teacher preparation programs to use a summative performance assessment to evaluate their preservice candidates (Sato, 2014). The effort to develop the PACT assessments was led by Pecheone and a team of teacher educators and researchers at Stanford University and several University of California and California State University institutions. The PACT assessments were similar to the BEST portfolios in that they were content-specific and focused on the application of subject-specific pedagogical knowledge, and they required candidates to complete a series of entries integrated around a unit of instruction (Pecheone & Chung, 2006). The main difference was that the

PACT assessments focused on preservice candidates' instruction during student teaching while the BEST portfolios were completed by teachers in their 2nd year of full-time teaching. In addition, along with providing artifacts of teaching similar to those required by BEST, candidates completing PACT had to write reflective commentaries about their instruction. The 2007 PACT Technical Report (Pecheone & Chung, 2007) summarized a series of studies undertaken in 2003–2004 to provide evidence related to the validity, reliability, and fairness of the PACT assessments.

EDTPA

The Stanford Center for Assessment, Learning, and Equity (SCALE) and the American Association of Colleges of Teacher Education (AACTE) led the development of edTPA over a multiyear period during the first decade of the 21st century. Much like the PACT assessments and the BEST portfolios, edTPA is a content-specific assessment focused on a short unit of instruction that is designed to evaluate teaching candidates' ability to plan instruction, enact lessons and engage students in learning, and assess student learning. In particular, for edTPA, candidates complete several entries integrated around a short unit. These include a description of their teaching context, a set of lesson plans for the unit, one or two video recordings of instruction during the unit, samples of student work, and commentaries on their planning, instruction, and assessment of student learning.

As of 2014–2015, there were 27 edTPA assessments in fields ranging from early childhood to secondary education and in numerous subjects including English/language arts, history/social studies, mathematics, science, world languages, visual arts, and performing arts. edTPA is aligned with the Interstate Teacher Assessment and Support Consortium (InTASC) standards, the CCSS in ELA and mathematics, and specialized professional association standards (National Governors Association Center for Best Practices & Council of Chief State School Officers, 2010a, 2010b; Pecheone, Shear, Whittaker, & Darling-Hammond, 2013; Youngs, 2013). The rubrics for edTPA clearly distinguish among five performance levels and feature evaluative criteria and detailed definitions that articulate practice at each of the performance levels.

The conception of teaching underlying edTPA emphasizes teachers' ability to help students acquire foundational and procedural knowledge, engage in higher-level thinking and analytical writing, develop conceptual understanding, and investigate and solve problems (Darling-Hammond, Newton, & Wei, 2012). Each completed edTPA assessment reveals information about the teaching candidate's instructional unit, the appropriateness of their instructional decisions based on their knowledge of students' backgrounds and prior academic learning, and the range of pedagogical strategies they use effectively. In addition, each edTPA assessment provides information about the quality of the candidates' assignments, their skill in assessing student learning and providing feedback, and their ability to analyze their teaching and make changes based on evidence of student learning. Further, edTPA "requires the teach[ing] candidate to describe the context of teaching and how their instructional planning and decisions are justified for that context and for the particular students in his or her classroom" (Sato, 2014, p. 429).

As of early 2015, 12 states had enacted policies requiring a state-approved performance assessment as part of teacher preparation program completion or for state licensure and/or state program accreditation/review. In these states, edTPA had been approved as a performance assessment for these purposes (SCALE, 2014). As of early 2015, several additional states were considering enacting similar policies.

EMPIRICAL RESEARCH ON EDTPA

The *2013 edTPA Field Test: Summary Report* (Pecheone et al., 2013) described results from a 2012–2013 field test with over 3,500 teaching candidates. In particular, the report described evidence related to content validity, construct validity, test reliability, interrater reliability, and fairness/bias within a technical framework of psychometric practice and principles guided by the Standards for Educational and Psychological Testing (AERA, APA, & NCME, 1999). In terms of content validity, a committee of more than 100 educators rated the significance, alignment, and representativeness of the skills and knowledge associated with each edTPA rubric in relation to national teaching and content standards, and a second committee rated the importance of edTPA outcomes for the work of teaching. After two rounds of content validation and job-analysis activities, all edTPA tasks (i.e., planning, instruction, and assessment) and task components were rated above 4 on a 5-point scale in terms of importance, alignment, and representativeness (Pecheone et al., 2013).

With regard to construct validity, Pecheone and colleagues used factor analysis to examine (1) whether there was empirical support for using one score, summed across all 15 edTPA rubrics, to represent a candidate's performance; and (2) whether the pattern of scores across the edTPA rubrics supports the theory underlying the development of the edTPA tasks and rubrics. The researchers reported that for the first factor analysis, "all factor loadings (were) positive and of moderate to large magnitude. These results support the use of a single total score (reflecting overall teaching effectiveness). The second factor analysis demonstrated that the hypothesized task structure (planning, instruction, and assessment) of the edTPA is supported by the patterns of candidates' scores" (Pecheone et al., 2013, p. 23).

During the 2012–2013 edTPA field test, about 10% of all edTPA submissions were randomly selected to be assessed by a second, independent evaluator. Pecheone and colleagues investigated agreement between evaluators by calculating the rate at which they assigned the same score to a candidate's performance on the edTPA or scores within 1 point of each other. They reported adjacent agreement rates on the 15 edTPA rubrics that ranged from 0.83 to 0.96 with an average rate of adjacent agreement of 0.92; this means that pairs of evaluators assigned scores within 1 point of each other 92% of the time (Pecheone et al., 2013).

In terms of fairness, Pecheone and colleagues examined differences in edTPA scores by gender, race/ethnicity, and primary language. They reported no significant differences between females and males or between English speakers and candidates whose primary language was not English. With regard to race/ethnicity, they found small differences among subgroups and cautioned that the comparisons were based on unequal samples. More specifically, the average edTPA scores were 42.7 for White candidates (n = 3,005), 45.0 for Asian candidates (n = 145), 42.3 for Hispanic candidates (n = 143), and 39.7 for Black (non-Hispanic) candidates (n = 83). The researchers also noted that "there was greater variation in scores within subgroups than there was variation across subgroups" (Pecheone et al., 2013, p. 22).

In sum, the *2013 edTPA Field Test: Summary Report* provides evidence related to validity, reliability, and fairness/bias for edTPA. In contrast to the observation tools described earlier in this chapter, though, the evidence base for the validity and reliability of edTPA is still under development. In the years ahead, it will be important to see if future edTPA operational summary reports provide additional evidence that edTPA can be validly and reliably used in making high-stakes decisions regarding initial teacher licensure. In addition, there is a need for independent researchers to examine edTPA's predictive and consequential validity, particularly as it is implemented more widely. For example, it would be useful for researchers to explore whether candidates' edTPA scores predict (1) their ratings on PLATO or the MQI as 1st- and 2nd-year teachers and/or (2) their impact on student achievement in reading and mathematics during their first years of teaching.

COMPARING AND COMBINING EDTPA WITH CLASSROOM OBSERVATION INSTRUMENTS

In this section, we explicate how edTPA and classroom observation instruments represent distinct responses to accountability pressures and describe ways that these two approaches could be used in conjunction with each other. edTPA is different from commonly used observation instruments in that it is employed during preservice teacher education and serves as a performance screen for entry into full-time teaching. In contrast, the observation tools discussed above are often used as performance screens after teachers earn their initial license and begin working as full-time teachers of record. Both edTPA and observation instruments enable raters to quantify and, therefore, compare the relative quality of teaching practice at distinct points in the professional continuum, but they do so in different ways.

edTPA concentrates on the application of content-specific teaching knowledge and skills; this is similar to PLATO and the MQI, but different from CLASS and the FFT. For one example, for the elementary literacy edTPA, teaching candidates must organize their portfolio around helping students develop an essential strategy for comprehending or composing text, and skills aligned with that strategy (SCALE, 2012a). For a second example, for the secondary science edTPA, candidates must organize their portfolios around supporting students' use of scientific concepts and application of scientific practices through inquiry (SCALE, 2012b). In addition, edTPA raters must have expertise in the same content area as those they are assessing. By focusing on content-specific knowledge and skills and requiring raters to have content-specific expertise, edTPA addresses a potential shortcoming of generic observation tools such as CLASS and the FFT: their de-emphasis on subject matter and candidates' ability to apply subject-specific teaching knowledge (Porter, Youngs, & Odden, 2001).

Unlike most observation instruments, edTPA requires candidates to submit a series of entries integrated around a short unit of instruction. By requiring candidates to complete a series of lesson plans for a unit of instruction, edTPA is able to assess their ability to plan multiple tasks across several lessons within the same unit and multiple means of assessing students (Pecheone & Stansbury, 1996). In contrast, CLASS, the FFT, PLATO, and the MQI provide information about teachers' ability to plan tasks and strategies for assessing students across a series of unrelated lessons. Thus, edTPA could be used in conjunction with these observation tools during preservice preparation to provide detailed information about candidates' ability to plan, teach, and assess across multiple lessons integrated around a unit of instruction.

Another difference between edTPA and most observation instruments has to do with how they address student assessment. For edTPA, candidates must include an assessment they used to evaluate their Pre-K–12 students' knowledge and skills during the focal unit, student work samples, an analysis of student learning during the unit, and plans for modifying their future instruction. In particular, candidates are required to identify quantitative and qualitative patterns of learning among their students, to use three work samples to illustrate patterns in learning across the class, and to submit feedback that they provided to the three students. In contrast, CLASS, the FFT, PLATO, and the MQI address Pre-K–12 student assessment in much more limited ways. Given the strong relationship between teachers' use of formative assessment and student learning (Black & Wiliam, 1998; Hattie & Timperley, 2007), this is another area where edTPA could be utilized in tandem with observation tools in evaluating teaching candidates.

It is important to note that for edTPA, candidates select one to two video-recorded clips of their instruction, and in most fields, additional video clips can be used as evidence of teacher feedback, students' academic language use, and/or student learning. In comparison, CLASS, the FFT, and PLATO focus on live observations and enable raters to see what the teacher and all of the students are doing and to evaluate the teacher's behavioral management skills with regard to the entire class over the course of a full lesson. Therefore, edTPA may provide less information than classroom observation instruments about a candidate's ability to establish a productive learning environment and manage student behavior (Porter et al., 2001). In addition, edTPA allows candidates to choose examples of their instruction as evidence of edTPA assessment requirements, while the observations conducted for CLASS, the FFT, PLATO, and the MQI are more likely to represent the breadth of teachers' instructional practice. For these reasons, it is important to supplement use of edTPA with classroom observations.

IMPLICATIONS FOR USE OF EDTPA WITH TEACHING CANDIDATES

In conclusion, edTPA has strong potential to contribute to a robust system of multiple measures for use in evaluating teaching candidates' content-specific knowledge and skills. It would be valuable to combine edTPA with classroom observation instruments in teacher preparation and licensure decisions given the fact that such tools provide ongoing information about candidates' ability to create an effective classroom learning environment and to address issues related to student behavior. At the same time, edTPA provides more information than observation instruments about candidates' ability to plan and teach lessons and assess student learning across a unit of instruction. In addition, edTPA provides more detailed information about candidates' content-specific knowledge and skills than CLASS, the FFT, and other generic observation tools. Given the emphasis in the Common Core State Standards, the Next Generation Science Standards, and other recent state-developed standards on ambitious instruction, teacher preparation programs and states should consider using edTPA to evaluate candidates' content-specific knowledge and skills.

Despite edTPA's strong potential, we conclude with two caveats. First, edTPA is specifically designed for use with teaching candidates or practicing teachers who have provisional teaching licenses. In other words, it is not designed for school districts or charter management organizations (CMOs) to use in summatively evaluating practicing teachers with standard licenses. While districts and CMOs may find it useful to incorporate aspects of edTPA (e.g., a series of lesson plans integrated around a unit, analyses of student work) into their summative evaluations, edTPA should not be used in annual evaluations of practicing teachers. Second, while researchers from SCALE have examined the use of edTPA in making initial teacher licensure decisions and provided evidence related to its content validity, construct validity, reliability, and fairness (Pecheone et al., 2013), it will also be important for independent researchers to continue to investigate predictive and consequential validity for edTPA in coming years, especially as more states adopt or consider adopting edTPA for use in licensure decisions.

REFERENCES

American Educational Research Association (AERA), American Psychological Association (APA), & National Council on Measurement and Education (NCME). (1999). *Standards for educational and psychological testing.* Washington, DC: Author.

Bell, C. A., Gitomer, D. H., McCaffrey, D. F., Hamre, B. K., Pianta, R. C., & Qi, Y. (2012). An argument approach to observation protocol validity. *Educational Assessment, 17*(2–3), 62–87.

Bill and Melinda Gates Foundation. (2012). *Gathering feedback for teaching: Combining high-quality observations with student surveys and achievement gains* (MET project research paper). Seattle, WA: Author.

Black, P., & Wiliam, D. (1998). Assessment and classroom learning. *Assessment in Education, 5*(1), 7–72.

Boerst, T. A., Sleep, L., Ball, D. L., & Bass, H. (2011). Preparing teachers to lead mathematics discussions. *Teachers College Record, 113*(12), 2844–2877.

Cohen, J. (2015). The challenge of identifying high-leverage practices. *Teachers College Record, 117*(7), 1–41.

National Governors Association Center for Best Practices & Council of Chief State School Officers. (2010a). *Common Core State Standards for English language arts & literacy in history/social studies, science, and technical subjects*. Retrieved from www.corestandards.org/ELA-Literacy/

National Governors Association Center for Best Practices & Council of Chief State School Officers. (2010b). *Common Core State Standards for mathematics*. Retrieved from www.corestandards.org/Math/

Danielson, C. (2013). *The framework for teaching evaluation instrument*. Princeton, NJ: The Danielson Group.

Darling-Hammond, L., Newton, S. P., & Wei, R. C. (2012). *Developing and assessing beginning teacher effectiveness: The potential of performance assessments*. Stanford, CA: Stanford Center for Opportunity Policy in Education and Stanford Center for Assessment, Learning, and Equity.

Grossman, P., Compton, C., Igra, D., Ronfeldt, M., Shahan, E., & Williamson, P. W. (2009). Teaching practice: A cross-professional perspective. *Teachers College Record, 111*(9), 2055–2100.

Grossman, P., Loeb, S., Cohen, J., & Wyckoff, J. (2013). Measure for measure: The relationship between measures of instructional practice in middle school English language arts and teachers' value-added scores. *American Journal of Education, 119*(3), 445–470.

Guthrie, J. T., Wigfield, A., Barbosa, P., Perencevich, K. C., Taboada, A., Davis, M. H., . . . Tonks, S. (2004). Increasing reading comprehension and engagement through concept-oriented reading instruction. *Journal of Educational Psychology, 96*(3), 403–423.

Harris, K. R., Graham, S., & Mason, L. H. (2006). Improving the writing, knowledge, and motivation of struggling young writers: Effects of self-regulated strategy development with and without peer support. *American Educational Research Journal, 43*(2), 295–340.

Hattie, J., & Timperley, H. (2007). The power of feedback. *Review of Educational Research, 77*(1), 81–112.

Hill, H. C., & Grossman, P. (2013). Learning from teacher observations: Challenges and opportunities posed by new teacher evaluation systems. *Harvard Educational Review, 83*(2), 371–384.

Hill, H. C., Kapitula, L., & Umland, K. (2011). A validity argument approach to evaluating teacher value-added scores. *American Educational Research Journal, 48*(3), 794–831.

Kane, T. J., Taylor, E. S., Tyler, J. H., & Wooten, A. L. (2010). Identifying effective classroom practices using student achievement data. *Journal of Human Resources, 46*(3), 587–613.

Kucan, L., Palincsar, A. S., Busse, T., Heisey, N., Klingelhofer, R., Rimbey, M., & Schutz, K. (2011). Applying the Grossman et al. theoretical framework: The case of reading. *Teachers College Record, 113*(12), 2897–2921.

Lampert, M., Franke, M. L., Kazemi, E., Ghousseini, H., Turrou, A. C., Beasley, H., . . . Crowe, K. (2013). Keeping it complex: Using rehearsals to support novice teacher learning. *Journal of Teacher Education, 64*(3), 226–243.

National Mathematics Advisory Panel. (2008). *Foundations for success: The final report of the National Mathematics Advisory Panel.* Washington, DC: U.S. Department of Education.

Newmann, F. M., & Associates. (1996). *Authentic achievement: Restructuring schools for intellectual quality.* San Francisco, CA: Jossey-Bass.

Pecheone, R. L., & Chung, R. R. (2006). Evidence in teacher education: The Performance Assessment for California Teachers (PACT). *Journal of Teacher Education, 57*(1), 22–36.

Pecheone, R. L., & Chung, R. R. (2007). *PACT Technical Report: Summary of validity and reliability studies for the 2003–04 pilot year.* Stanford, CA: Performance Assessment for California Teachers Consortium.

Pecheone, R. L., Shear, B., Whittaker, A., & Darling-Hammond, L. (2013). *2013 edTPA field test: Summary report.* Stanford, CA: Stanford Center for Assessment, Learning, and Equity.

Pecheone, R. L., & Stansbury, K. (1996). Connecting teacher assessment and school reform. *The Elementary School Journal, 97*(2), 163–177.

Pianta, R. C., & Hamre, B. K. (2009). Conceptualization, measurement, and improvement of classroom processes: Standardized observation can leverage capacity. *Educational Researcher, 38*(2), 109–119.

Porter, A. C., Youngs, P., & Odden, A. (2001). Advances in teacher assessment and their uses. In V. Richardson (Ed.), *Handbook of research on teaching* (4th ed., pp. 259–297). New York, NY: Macmillan.

Sato, M. (2014). What is the underlying conception of teaching of the edTPA? *Journal of Teacher Education, 65*(5), 421–434.

SCALE. (2012a). *edTPA Elementary Education Assessment Handbook.* Stanford, CA: Author.

SCALE. (2012b). *edTPA Secondary Science Assessment Handbook.* Stanford, CA: Author.

SCALE. (2014). *edTPA Support and Assessment: State Policies and Educator Preparation Program (EPP) Implementation Support Dashboard.* Stanford, CA: Author.

Taylor, E. S., & Tyler, J. H. (2012). The effect of evaluation on teacher performance. *American Economic Review, 102*(7), 3628–3651.

Wilson, M., Hallam, P. J., Pecheone, R., & Moss, P. (2014). Evaluating the validity of portfolio assessments for licensure decisions. *Education Policy Analysis Archives, 22*(6). Retrieved from epaa.asu.edu/ojs/article/view/955

Youngs, P. (2013). *Using teacher evaluation reform and professional development to support Common Core assessments.* Washington, DC: Center for American Progress.

Youngs, P., Pogodzinski, B., & Low, M. (2010). The role of formative assessments in new teacher induction. In M. Kennedy (Ed.), *Teacher assessment and teacher quality: A handbook* (pp. 165–199). San Francisco, CA: Jossey-Bass.

CHAPTER 9

Teachers' Use of Evaluation for Instructional Improvement and School Supports for Such Use

Min Sun
R. Brock Mutcheson
Jihyun Kim

As states and districts reinvent teacher evaluation systems to provide better measures of teacher performance, their utilization of information to improve instruction has become key to improving student learning outcomes. One popular use is to inform human resources decisions regarding hiring, firing, promoting, and compensating teachers (Chingos & West, 2011; Rockoff, Staiger, Kane, & Taylor, 2012). Another important mechanism, discussed much less in the research literature, involves how teachers themselves use information about their past performance to improve instruction.

Conventional teacher evaluation systems have been criticized for not promoting individual teacher development (In Search of, 2012; Toch, 2008). The lack of information on the status of an individual's teaching and what constitutes effective teaching are often identified as main barriers to improvement (Stiggins & Bridgeford, 1985; Taylor & Tyler, 2012). To overcome these issues, newly designed teacher evaluation systems commonly use multiple measures of teacher performance that focus on classroom instruction and are closely linked to student learning outcomes. These new approaches, if effective, have the potential to promote teacher improvement in several ways. First, teachers have opportunities to reflect on their practices when they collect evidence to demonstrate their own effectiveness in promoting students' learning. Second, links between evaluation and professional development can potentially make evaluation practices more constructive. Third, most new evaluation procedures include feedback from principals, peers, students, and parents.

In this chapter, we discuss teachers' reports on the use of teacher evaluation to improve their instruction and what types of school supports aid in this process. We conducted descriptive analyses of survey data that were collected in two rural school districts in southwest Virginia during the 2012–2013 and 2013–2014 school years, following the state of Virginia's receipt of a waiver from requirements of the No Child Left Behind Act in 2012 and moves to revamp teacher evaluation. Our analyses aimed to address the following questions: Which types of teachers are more likely to use evaluation for improvement? What types of school supports are related to teachers' use of evaluation for improvement? And how does the relationship between school supports and teachers' use vary for different types of teachers?

Anticipating our key findings, early-career teachers who were on annual contracts, on average, were more likely to use evaluation to improve their instruction than teachers who were on continuing contracts. Teachers in the top and bottom quartiles with regard to their evaluation ratings were significantly more likely to use performance information for improvement than teachers in the middle of the distribution. Moreover, among a variety of potentially effective school supports for teachers' use of evaluation for improvement (e.g., professional development, principal feedback, and collegial supports), the usefulness of principals' feedback particularly mattered to early-career teachers.

The remainder of this chapter is organized as follows: We first present the key components of the evaluation policy in the two districts. Next, we develop conjectures regarding how the policy may influence instruction and the role of school supports. We then describe the sample and measures. Last, we present the analytic strategies for testing these conjectures, summarize our main findings, and discuss their policy implications.

TEACHER EVALUATION POLICIES IN TWO VIRGINIA DISTRICTS

Virginia issued the *Guidelines for Uniform Performance Standards and Evaluation Criteria for Teachers* on July 1, 2012, which marked a significant overhaul of conventional evaluation criteria. The guidelines called for 40% of teacher evaluation to be based on the standard of *student academic progress*. Each of the other six standards is weighted 10% in teachers' total evaluation scores: *professional knowledge, instructional planning, instructional delivery, assessment for and of learning, learning environment,* and *professionalism*. For each standard, teacher performance is rated on a 4-point scale from "exemplary" to "unacceptable." The annual summative evaluation separates teacher performance into four groups: those whose performance consistently exceeds expectations on all standards ("exemplary"), those who meet the standards ("proficient"), those who have an opportunity for improvement ("developing"), and those who do not meet expectations ("unacceptable").

The evaluation procedures, instruments, and materials adopted by the two districts (pseudonyms: District 1 and District 2) in this study were essentially consistent with the state guidelines and recommendations. The districts collected evidence on teachers' performance from three sources. First, teachers underwent classroom observations and walkthroughs conducted by administrators or peers. Probationary teachers (similar to pretenured teachers) were observed at least three times per year. Teachers employed under a continuing contract (similar to tenured teachers) were observed at least once per year. Second, teachers were asked to set up learning goals for students and to document the extent to which students had achieved these goals by the end of the semester or school year. Third, the districts conducted student surveys. At the end of each semester, teachers were asked to provide a summary of the survey data that described their strengths and areas in need of improvement as well as their own reflections.

In both school districts, teachers on annual contracts received a summative evaluation during each of their probationary years (i.e., pretenure), and these teachers also went through a midyear interim review featuring systematic feedback prior to the summative review. However, the evaluation procedures for teachers on continuing contracts (i.e., with tenure) differed. District 1 teachers received a summative evaluation every year, while their counterparts in District 2 received a summative evaluation every 3 years. These attributes of evaluation policies and the variation between districts and for different teachers had important implications for the conceptual framing of this study and our data analyses.

CONCEPTUAL FRAMING

How Do Teachers Use Performance Information?

The use of performance measures based on explicit and uniformly defined criteria and metrics has long been a fundamental component of both public- and private-sector personnel incentive systems (Heinrich & Marschke, 2010). One of the most popular concepts for understanding performance measurement systems is "principal-agent theory" (e.g.,

Eisenhardt, 1989). This theory is based on the assertion that the principal (e.g., the employer) cannot observe the true effects of agents (e.g., employees); rather, only agents themselves know their true effort and performance. To address this asymmetric information, the employer can align the incentives for employees with the organization's goals. For example, aligning measures of teachers' performance closely with students' learning is expected to motivate teachers' efforts and in turn contribute to schools' organizational values. Moreover, performance management, such as the increase in incentives via performance accountability, is more effective if principals and agents engage in interactive dialogues that support more effective use of performance information and organizational learning (Moynihan, 2008).

This conception of using performance information to initiate changes is congruent with a recent study of teacher performance evaluation in the Cincinnati Public Schools. Taylor and Tyler (2012) studied a sample of mid-career elementary and middle school teachers, all of whom were evaluated in a yearlong program based largely on classroom observation between the 2003–2004 and 2009–2010 school years. Their analyses showed that teachers were more effective at raising student achievement during the school year when they were being evaluated than they were previously, and even more effective in the years after evaluation, particularly in mathematics. Yet this study failed to identify how teachers used performance information or the factors that supported their use of such information.

In this chapter, we hypothesize three potential processes of teacher improvement in the two districts. First, learning about the seven professional teaching standards and documenting their performance may have helped teachers reflect on their instruction. During the process of collecting student survey data and documenting students' academic progress, teachers were asked to analyze these data to identify personal strengths and weaknesses and ways to improve their instruction. Second, the links between evaluation and professional development (or individual assistance programs) may have made the evaluation practices more constructive and effective. After being informed of their strengths and weaknesses, teachers could make more intelligent decisions in terms of selecting professional development programs that catered to their development needs. The link between teachers' needs identified by evaluation and professional development potentially strengthened teachers' learning from evaluation.

Last, learning to teach is situated in social contexts through interactions with others and through one's own practices in classroom settings (Putnam & Borko, 2000). The following situations provide rich learning opportunities for teachers: observing others and being observed by others in actual classrooms, referring to one's own practices in group discussions, and integrating what is learned outside of classrooms into one's own practices. The uniform professional standards and evaluation criteria may have facilitated teachers' interactions with their administrators and peers by giving them a common "language" to use in discussing instruction. They likely felt that such discussions were useful because they were based on evidence from observing their classroom practices.

We further hypothesize that the use of evaluation for instructional improvement may vary by individuals. For instance, studies have shown that teachers make steep gains in effectiveness early in their careers (Boyd, Grossman, Lankford, Loeb, & Wyckoff, 2008; Harris & Sass, 2011; Papay & Kraft, 2013; Rockoff, 2004; Wiswall, 2013), in general, because probationary teachers often show more interest in learning and improvement and because there is often a learning curve when starting the teaching career. Moreover, they face more risks of losing their jobs due to a bad evaluation than teachers who have continuing contracts; therefore, they may be more motivated to improve. We also expect variations by teachers' prior ratings. Teachers who received low ratings in a prior year may have an incentive to improve, while teachers who were rated at the top may be motivated to become better and stay at the top. In comparison, teachers in the middle of the distribution may have the least incentive to change, because they are not directly threatened by the negative consequences of losing their jobs or being assigned to special assistance, or by the positive consequences of receiving a bonus or recognition.

What Types of School Supports Are Related to Teachers' Use of Evaluation for Improvement?

Next, we describe three types of school supports that seem related to teachers' use of evaluation for improvement. First, professional development programs can help teachers understand the goals and procedures of teacher evaluation and see the evaluation process as a means of improving their practices. These programs should also develop teachers' capacity to collect measures of their effects on students' growth and use these measures to adjust their instructional practices (Lachat & Smith, 2005; Supovitz, 2006).

Second, principals and other observers should provide timely feedback as close to the time when the observation happens as possible (Goe, 2013). It should also be specific and tied to aspects of effective teaching. Useful feedback often focuses on evidence about an individual teacher's pedagogy, curriculum and materials, and ways the teacher can improve his or her practices and student learning outcomes. Furthermore, the tone of the conversations between principals and a teacher should be constructive by inviting the teacher to share his or her thoughts, with a goal of developing a common understanding about high-quality teaching.

Last, teachers' use of evaluation data may also be influenced by their colleagues (Sun, Penuel, Frank, Gallagher, & Youngs, 2013). We hypothesize that collegial interactions will generate a larger effect on teachers if they address specific details from the teacher evaluation process. Moreover, teachers benefit from help with general instructional issues, including knowledge about differentiating instruction, using data to adjust their teaching, and classroom management skills. In the following sections, we use empirical data to assess these conjectures about the effects of supports on teachers' use of evaluation for improvement.

SAMPLE AND MEASURES

Sample

The two participating school districts included 17 elementary and secondary schools: 3 high schools, 3 middle schools, and 11 elementary schools. These two districts were 30 miles apart and located in rural areas or small towns. They served students with similar demographic characteristics (predominantly White) and poverty status. In 2013–2014, District 1 had all of its schools accredited by the state based its performance on the 2012–2013 state standardized tests, while 9% of District 2 schools received accreditation with warning because these schools did not meet the state benchmark in mathematics. For federal accountability measures, 16.7% of the schools in District 1 and 36.4% of the schools in District 2 did not meet the Annual Measurable Objectives (AMO) for all subjects. In our later analyses, we used school fixed effects to control for variation in school performance and, consequently, variation in the accountability pressures experienced by different schools.

In this chapter, besides using district administrative data on personnel backgrounds and evaluation ratings, we primarily drew on data from a teacher survey administered in fall 2014 to learn about teachers' practices and the implementation of teacher evaluation policy in 2013–2014. Survey response rates were about 72% in District 1 and 58% in District 2. District 1 had a total of approximately 254 full-time equivalent teachers (FTE), while District 2 had about 387 FTE teachers. There were no differences in the percentage of White teachers or in average prior ratings between respondents and nonrespondents in either district. However, probationary teachers were significantly more likely to respond to the survey in both school districts. This sample with overrepresentation of probationary teachers allows us to sufficiently capture probationary teachers' responses to the new evaluation system, given that only 11% of the teachers in District 1 and only 16% in District 2 were probationary.

Measures

We drew on teacher survey data to assess teachers' use of evaluation for improvement and how school supports were associated with this use in the 2013–2014 school year. For composite variables (e.g., *teachers' use of evaluation for performance improvement*, *collegial support for general instruction* and *for evaluation implementation*, and *usefulness of principal feedback*), we ran exploratory factor analysis to explore the latent constructs of the survey items relevant to these composite variables. Survey items were on a 4-point scale of 0 = not at all, 1 = some extent, 2 = moderate extent, and 3 = great extent. We considered item loadings of at least 0.4 necessary for inclusion in a factor and eigenvalue > 1 to be considered as a factor. Each factor had high internal consistency (Cronbach's $\alpha > 0.85$ and eigenvalue = 5.36).

Teachers' use of evaluation for performance improvement is the standardized mean of teachers' responses to four items. These included, for example, "The information collected about my teaching in the 2012–13 evaluation really helped me to know my strengths and weaknesses" and "My professional development programs were more informative because their selection was based on my evaluation results in 2012–13."

Collegial support for general instruction is the sum of teachers' responses to seven items about the extent to which each of several aspects of instruction was discussed between the teacher and her or his colleagues. These included, for example, "How the lesson relates to the curriculum and the sequence of learning for the class," "Knowledge of students and differentiated instruction," "What changes I could make if I were to re-teach the lesson," and "Alternative strategies of delivering the content to my students."

Collegial support for evaluation implementation is the sum of teachers' responses to seven items about the extent to which each of several aspects of teacher evaluation was discussed between a teacher and her or his colleagues. These included, for example, "The multiple measures of teaching," "How to document student progress using formative assessments," "How to use data on student academic progress to adjust my teaching," and "Communicating my teaching and student performance with my principal."

Usefulness of principal feedback is a mean of 11 items about teachers' perceptions of principal feedback during postobservation conferences and the end-of-year summative evaluation conference. These included, for example, "How the lesson related to the curriculum and the sequence of learning for the class," "My knowledge of my students and differentiating instruction," "Most discussions were constructive and I can directly use the feedback to improve my instruction," and "Overall, the conferencing helped to develop a common understanding about high-quality teaching between me and my principal."

Frequency of principal feedback is measured as the number of times a teacher reported that her/his principal conducted informal visits to her/his classrooms (e.g., walkthroughs), formal observations, postobservation conferences, and/or summative evaluation conferences. We then summed the frequencies across these different types of interactions between a teacher and her/his principal.

Professional development is indicated by both the frequency and the usefulness of professional development programs that help teachers implement teacher evaluation policy and use data to improve instruction. Teachers reported the frequency by the number of hours of professional development they participated in during 2013–2014 and the usefulness on a 4-point scale.

VARIATIONS IN THE USE OF EVALUATION FOR IMPROVEMENT AMONG TEACHERS

Employment Status

The variable *teachers' use of evaluation for improvement* was regressed on a dummy variable for whether the teacher was on either a probationary or continuing contract, controlling for teachers' gender, subject areas (1 = high-stakes subjects, e.g., reading, mathematics, and science; 0 = otherwise), advanced degree (1 = master's or higher; 0 = otherwise), and race (1 = White; 0 = otherwise). We used school fixed effects to account for variation in accountability pressure due to school performance on state standardized tests, variation in school-level implementation of teacher evaluation, and variation in school contexts and practices. Examining residuals from the regression, probationary teachers were about 0.3 standard deviation higher than the expected use of evaluation for improvement (p = 0.06), while teachers on continuing contracts were about 0.045 standard deviation below the expected use ($p = 0.46$). Probationary teachers' estimated use was significantly higher than the use of teachers on continuing contracts at the 95% confidence level ($F = 4.24$, $p = 0.04$).

Prior Ratings

We separated teachers based on prior performance ratings in the 2012–2013 school year into four groups: prior ratings in the first quartile (0–25%, low performers), prior ratings in the second quartile (26%–50%, mid-low performers), prior ratings in the third quartile (51%–75%, mid-high performers), and prior ratings in the fourth quartile (76%–100%, high performers). The variable *teachers' use of evaluation for improvement* was regressed on the dummy variables for these four groups, controlling for teachers' employment status, gender, subject area, race, advanced degree, and school fixed effects.

Teachers who were at the bottom and the top of the distribution of prior ratings were more likely to report using evaluation for improvement. In particular, high-performing teachers' estimated use was about 0.29 standard deviation above the expected use, which is significant at a 90% confidence level ($p = 0.07$). In contrast, teachers in the middle of the distribution reported about 0.2 standard deviation lower than the expected use. Moreover, the difference of use information between top performers and middle performers was significant ($F = 6.18$, $p = 0.01$ for mid-low performers; and $F = 5.41$, $p = 0.02$ for mid-high performers).

School Supports for Teachers' Use of Evaluation for Improvement

Next, we regressed teachers' use of evaluation for improvement on several types of school supports, controlling for teacher covariates and school fixed effects. When estimating the effects of principal feedback, we replaced school fixed effects with school covariates, because school fixed effects would have absorbed all of the variation in principal leadership. We first estimated the main effects of these supports, and then added interaction effects between the school support variables and teacher subgroups by their employment status and prior ratings. These interaction terms enabled us to assess the heterogeneous effects of these school supports. The first column in Table 9.1 includes only main effect estimates, the second column includes estimates of effects of interactions with being a probationary teacher, and the last three columns include interaction effects with teachers' prior performance ratings.

Professional development programs with both intensity and quality positively influenced the likelihood that teachers reported using evaluation for improvement ($\beta = 0.017$, $p < 0.001$). There were no statistically

Table 9.1. Effects of School Supports for Teachers' Use of Evaluation for Instructional Improvement

	Main Effects	Probationary Teacher	Prior Rating at the 1st Quartile	Prior Rating at the 2nd Quartile	Prior Rating at the 3rd Quartile
Professional Development	0.017*** (0.004)	0.002 (0.015)	0.005 (0.024)	-0.011 (0.012)	0.031* (0.015)
Main Effects		X	X	X	X
Teacher Covariates	X	X	X	X	X
School Fixed Effects	X	X	X	X	X
N	167	167		115	
Adjusted R^2	0.184	0.179		0.245	
Usefulness of Principal Feedback	0.439*** (0.092)	0.886** (0.324)	-0.251 (0.322)	-0.019 (0.299)	-0.104 (0.325)
Main Effects		X	X	X	X
Teacher Covariates	X	X	X	X	X
School Covariates	X	X	X	X	X
N	256	256		173	
Adjusted R^2	0.123	0.145		0.166	
Frequency of Principal Feedback	0.000 (0.004)	0.004 (0.016)	0.012 (0.015)	0.013 (0.020)	0.012 (0.022)
Main Effects		X	X	X	X
Teacher Covariates	X	X	X	X	X
School Covariates	X	X	X	X	X
N	262	262		175	
Adjusted R^2	0.035	0.032		0.057	
Collegial Support for General Instruction	0.042*** (0.011)	0.033 (0.036)	0.004 (0.035)	0.020 (0.034)	-0.043 (0.042)
Main Effects		X	X	X	X
Teacher Covariates	X	X	X	X	X
School Fixed Effects	X	X	X	X	X
N	262	262		175	
Adjusted R^2	0.104	0.103		0.161	
Collegial Support for Evaluation Implementation	0.046*** (0.012)	0.031 (0.029)	-0.031 (0.035)	-0.021 (0.036)	0.005 (0.040)
Main Effects		X	X	X	X
Teacher Covariates	X	X	X	X	X
School Fixed Effects	X	X	X	X	X
N	262	262		175	
Adjusted R^2	0.112	0.112		0.204	

Notes. Teacher covariates include teachers' prior ratings, teaching high-stakes subjects, probationary contract, female, and White. School covariates include dummy variables for middle and high schools, and district dummy variable. We did not include other school covariates, such as demographics of students and location, because these two school districts served students with very similar socioeconomic backgrounds.
$^*p < 0.05$. $^{**}p < 0.01$. $^{***}p < 0.001$.

significant differences in the effects of professional development between probationary teachers and teachers on continuing contracts. However, professional development had a significantly larger effect for teachers with mid-high prior performance ratings than for those with high prior ratings ($\beta = 0.031, p < 0.05$).

We then examined two attributes of principal feedback: usefulness and frequency. With a one-unit change in usefulness (e.g., from "to some extent" to "to a moderate extent"), it is estimated that teachers would increase their use by 0.44 standard deviation ($p < 0.001$). More interestingly, principal feedback had a larger effect on probationary teachers than on teachers with continuing contracts. With a one-unit increase in the usefulness of principal feedback, probationary teachers would increase their use by an additional 0.89 standard deviation ($p < 0.01$). Furthermore, after controlling for employment status and other covariates, we did not observe variation in the effect of principal feedback by teachers' prior ratings. In contrast, the frequency of principal feedback did not have a significant influence on teachers' use, nor were there differential effects among different types of teachers.

Last, we assessed the effects of two types of collegial supports, for general instruction and for the implementation of this new teacher evaluation system. The results indicated that collegial supports for both general instruction ($\beta = 0.042$) and evaluation implementation ($\beta = 0.046$) were positively related to teachers' use of evaluation for improvement at the 99.9% confidence level. The effects were relatively homogenous across different types of teachers by employment status and prior performance ratings.

DISCUSSION

This chapter aims to provide descriptive evidence on teachers' use of evaluation for instructional improvement and school supports for this use. Data were collected from two rural school districts where multiple performance measures focused on students' academic progress had recently been implemented. The findings in this chapter are relevant for school leaders, policymakers, and researchers who are interested in understanding how to promote instructional improvement through building teacher capacity.

Probationary teachers who were on annual contracts, on average, were more likely to use evaluation to improve their instruction than teachers who were on continuing contracts. It may be that early-career teachers were eager to learn or that they perceived more pressure to improve under the performance accountability system. If the goal of using teacher evaluation is to not only hold early-career teachers accountable for continuous improvement, but to hold more experienced teachers accountable as well, perhaps school leaders should rethink the design of their performance evaluation and feedback systems to motivate a wider range of teachers beyond those with probationary status.

Moreover, teachers who were in the top 25% of the distribution of the prior year's evaluation ratings were significantly more likely to use information for improvement than teachers in the middle of the distribution. This strongly implies a theory of positive reinforcement; that is, teachers who were rated as high-performing were motivated to stay on top and were more likely to buy into the notion that this system could benefit their instruction. Alternatively, it could also be the case that good teachers always seek to improve regardless of how they are evaluated. A future longitudinal analysis that accounts for a time-invariant measure of teacher quality will help to further separate these two explanations.

Last, school supports, including professional development, principal feedback, and collegial supports, were found to be related to teachers' use of evaluation for improvement. This is not surprising, given that prior studies have provided similar evidence that school supports positively contribute to teacher improvement (Kraft & Papay, 2014; Sun et al., 2013). Here we underscore three additional observations. First, professional development had a stronger effect on teachers at the upper-middle range of prior ratings than on the top-performing teachers. Second, the frequency of principal feedback had little impact on teachers' reported use of evaluation for improvement, while teachers' perceived usefulness of this feedback really mattered, particularly for early-career teachers. Third, except for the above two heterogeneous effects, the school supports had relatively homogenous influences regardless of teachers' employment status and prior ratings.

The interpretation of the relationship between school supports and teachers' use of evaluation for improvement is constrained by other limitations of our data. The measure of teachers' use of evaluation for improvement and the measures of school supports both came from the same teachers' reports. This is so-called "common source bias." For example, it could be that a good teacher is more likely to seek professional development opportunities, make effective use of them, and report high satisfaction with them. At the same time, this teacher is also more likely to report the use of evaluation for instructional improvement. This issue can be addressed in future studies by collecting alternative measures from different sources, such as a third party's classroom observations, to measure teachers' use of evaluation for instructional improvement. In addition, we were unable to assess change in teachers' use over time or the long-term effect of this new teacher evaluation system, since we observed teachers' use in only one year at a relatively early stage of policy implementation. Last, we were unable to verify that using evaluation to strengthen instruction would lead to improvements in student achievement. Verifying this link will further establish the validity of this measure.

Despite these limitations, we hope this chapter can elevate the conversation about using teacher evaluation systems to support the professional improvement of all teachers. Although performance accountability through personnel management strategies is critical to understand, exploring ways to support teachers in using performance information to adjust instruction is an important activity for educational leaders and researchers to engage in. This effort can be a crucial part of broader initiatives to build school capacity to better serve students in this performance accountability era.

REFERENCES

Boyd, D., Grossman, P., Lankford, H., Loeb, S., & Wyckoff, J. (2008). *Who leaves? Teacher attrition and student achievement* (NBER working paper 14022). Cambridge, MA: National Bureau of Economic Research. Retrieved from www.nber.org/papers/w14022

Chingos, M. M., & West, M. R. (2011). Promotion and reassignment in public school districts: How do schools respond to differences in teacher effectiveness? *Economics of Education Review, 30*, 419–433.

Eisenhardt, K. M. (1989). Agency theory: An assessment and review. *The Academy of Management Review, 14*(1), 57–74.

Goe, L. (2013). Can teacher evaluation improve teaching? *Principal Leadership, 13*, 25–29. Retrieved from www.nassp.org/Content/158/PLmar13_goe.pdf

Harris, D. N., & Sass, T. R. (2011). Teacher training, teacher quality and student achievement. *Journal of Public Economics, 95*, 798–812.

Heinrich, C. J., & Marschke, G. (2010). Incentives and their dynamics in public sector performance management systems. *Journal of Policy Analysis and Management, 29*(1), 183–208.

In Search of Excellent Teaching. (2012, September 16). *New York Times*. Retrieved on December 12 2014 from www.nytimes.com/2012/09/17/opinion/in-search-of-excellent-teaching.html

Kraft, M. A., & Papay, J. P. (2014). Can professional environments in schools promote teacher development? Explaining heterogeneity in returns to teaching experience. *Educational Evaluation and Policy Analysis, 36*(4), 476–500.

Lachat, M. A., & Smith, S. (2005). Practices that support data use in urban high schools. *Journal of Education for Students Placed at Risk, 10*(3), 333–349.

Moynihan, D. P. (2008). *The dynamics of performance management: Constructing information and reform*. Washington DC: Georgetown University Press.

Papay, J. P., & Kraft, M. A. (2013). *Productivity returns to experience in the teacher labor market: Methodological challenges and new evidence on long-term career growth* (Working paper). Retrieved from scholar.harvard.edu/files/mkraft/files/papay_kraft_-_rte_may_2013_-_v2.pdf

Putnam, R. T, & Borko, H. (2000). What do new views of knowledge and thinking have to say about research on teacher learning? *Educational Researcher, 29*(1), 4–15.

Rockoff, J. E. (2004). The impact of individual teachers on student achievement: Evidence from panel data. *American Economic Review, 94*(2), 247–252.

Rockoff, J. E., Staiger, D. O., Kane, T. J., & Taylor, E. S. (2012). Information and employee evaluation: Evidence form a randomized intervention in public schools. *American Economic Review, 102*(7), 3184–3213.

Stiggins, R. J., & Bridgeford, N. J. (1985). Performance assessment for teacher development. *Educational Evaluation and Policy Analysis, 7*(1), 85–97.

Sun, M., Penuel, W. R., Frank, K. A., Gallagher, H. A., & Youngs, P. (2013). Shaping professional development to promote the diffusion of instructional expertise among teachers. *Educational Evaluation and Policy Analysis, 35(*3), 344–369.

Supovitz, J. A. (2006). *The case for district-based reform: Leading, building, and sustaining school improvement.* Cambridge, MA: Harvard Education Press.

Taylor, E. S., & Tyler, J. H. (2012). The effect of evaluation on teacher performance. *American Economic Review, 102*(7), 3628–3651.

Toch, T. (2008). Fixing teacher evaluation. *Educational Leadership, 66*(2), 32–37.

Virginia Department of Education. (2012). *Guidelines for uniform performance standards and evaluation criteria for teachers*. Richmond, VA: Author. Retrieved from www.doe.virginia.gov/teaching/regulations/2011_guidelines_uniform_performance_standards_evaluation_criteria.pdf

Wiswall, M. (2013). The dynamics of teacher quality. *Journal of Public Economics, 100*, 61–78.

CHAPTER 10

Development or Dismissal?

Exploring Principals' Use of Teacher Effectiveness Data

Timothy A. Drake, Ellen Goldring, Jason A. Grissom, Marisa Cannata, Christine M. Neumerski, Mollie Rubin, & Patrick Schuermann

As highlighted throughout this volume, state waivers from NCLB accountability sanctions and increased federal funding through Race to the Top (RTTT) grants have spurred on states throughout the country to revamp and restructure their teacher evaluation systems to include multiple measures of teacher performance, including student test score growth, teacher classroom observation scores from formalized instructional rubrics, and stakeholder feedback surveys (Kane, McCaffrey, Miller, & Staiger, 2013). Much of the discourse surrounding the implementation of these systems has focused on their use to identify and dismiss—or, in some systems, *nonrenew*—ineffective teachers.

The rhetorical link between new evaluation systems in the minds of policymakers, teachers' associations, and others makes sense in the context of parallel changes to policies and teacher employment contracts in many systems that have tied future employment to evaluation scores for larger numbers of teachers by abolishing tenure, lengthening the time frame to the tenure decision, and/or codifying the removal of teachers consistently receiving low evaluation scores over several years. The Education Commission of the States (ECS) finds that 30 states now define "ineffectiveness" with respect to teacher performance; 16 states require that the order of layoffs include a measure of teacher performance, with over half using it as the top criterion; and 25 states have revised state laws to make a connection between "unsatisfactory performance" and possible teacher dismissal, regardless of tenure or nonprobationary status (ECS, 2015). Research suggests that teacher evaluation systems can serve not only to reconstitute the teacher labor supply through the identification and dismissal of ineffective teachers (i.e., the accountability function), but also to provide valuable information to support teachers' instructional development (i.e., the developmental function) (Dee & Wyckoff, 2015; Donaldson & Papay, 2015; Taylor & Tyler, 2012).

Nonetheless, despite these policy shifts and early research evidence, we know relatively little about how data from complex, multimeasure teacher evaluation systems inform decisions about teacher renewal and dismissal in practice in schools and school systems. Cohen-Vogel (2011) finds that test scores play a limited role in teacher dismissal in Florida, especially for tenured teachers; instead, she finds that principals choose to nonrenew probationary teachers for performance before they receive tenure at the start of their 4th year because "you can simply let them go with no documentation" (p. 497). Similarly, Donaldson (2013) finds that principals did not frame dismissal decisions in terms of evaluation performance; rather, they worried primarily about the interpersonal challenges and cultural ramifications of dismissing ineffective teachers, especially if those teachers are popular.

The goal of this chapter is to investigate how teacher evaluation systems influence principals' approaches to teacher dismissal and to explore barriers principals face in using teacher effectiveness data in teacher dismissal decisions,. We also examine the changing role of the central office in supporting principals in the dismissal process. Specifically, we ask the following: How do principals use teacher effectiveness data to retain and dismiss teachers? What barriers do principals report in using these data for teacher dismissal? And how are district central offices working to overcome these barriers?

Our findings, drawn from interview and survey data from nearly 200 school and district leaders across six urban systems, highlight that teacher evaluation data are not often used for dismissal without a strong component of teacher support and development. Thus, as we set out to understand the dismissal process, we learned that this is intricately linked to using the evaluation data for support and development. In fact, these two important uses of teacher evaluation data—support/development and dismissal—are largely seen as interrelated by both principals and central office leaders.

DATA AND METHODS

As part of a larger project examining principal data use for human capital decisionmaking, we conducted semistructured interviews of central office personnel and principals in six urban school districts during the 2012–2013 school year.[1] These districts are Baltimore City Public Schools (BCPS), Denver Public Schools (DPS), Hillsborough County (Tampa) Public Schools (HCPS), Houston Independent School District (HISD), Metropolitan Nashville Public Schools (MNPS), and Shelby County (Memphis) Schools (SCS). Each of these districts has been or is currently engaged in developing new and varied measures of teacher effectiveness. Data collection proceeded in two stages. First, semistructured interviews were conducted with central office personnel in each system. Key personnel, such as the head of the human capital division and the director of professional development, were interviewed to examine the types of teacher quality and effectiveness data available to principals and system expectations for data utilization for teacher human capital decisions, including retention and dismissal. In total, we performed approximately 95 interviews with central office staff across the six systems. Second, schools were stratified by level (e.g., elementary, middle, high) and achievement level (e.g., low, high), with roughly four elementary, three middle, and three high school principals randomly selected in each system for an hour-long, semistructured interview from within each achievement stratum. In total, we performed 56 principal interviews.

Interviews with both central office personnel and principals were audio-recorded and transcribed verbatim. Transcriptions were then uploaded to qualitative software for coding. The analysis protocol, which stemmed from the original research proposal, guided development of an initial thematic coding scheme. The process was iterative in nature (Corbin & Strauss, 2008; LeCompte & Schensul, 1999); members of the research team coded a sample of central office and principal interviews, and then revised the coding scheme to address questions and concerns that emerged.

In addition to the fieldwork, we also conducted principal surveys in four of the six districts between September and November 2013. Data were collected through an online survey questionnaire.[2] After email reminders and hard-copy follow-ups to nonrespondents, a total of 764 principals responded to these surveys, representing an overall response rate of 85.2%, ranging from 79% to 92% across the six districts.

DISTRICT AND STATE CONTEXTS

Table 10.1 provides a summary of the district and state contexts with respect to collective bargaining, tenure and nonprobationary teacher contracts, teacher evaluation systems, and the relationship between teacher evaluation measures and teacher contracts at the time of this study. As evident from this table, there is important variation across districts. For example, three of the six districts are found in states where collective bargaining is illegal. In these districts we might reasonably assume that school leaders have more latitude when it comes to using teacher effectiveness measures as a means of dismissal, compared with the other three sites where collective bargaining is permissible or required. Nonetheless, policies surrounding the probationary or nonprobationary status of teachers are linked with teacher performance on the state evaluation regardless of whether the state allows collective bargaining. For example, in Nashville, Shelby County, and Denver, teachers are eligible for tenure or nonprobationary status *only after* having 2 years of demonstrated effectiveness in the evaluation system. In Hillsborough County, nonprobationary teachers are eligible for dismissal after 2 consecutive years of underperformance on their state's evaluation rating. These districts, however, are in states with different laws regarding collective bargaining, from required to permissible to illegal.

Another source of variation is the length of teacher contracts. Some systems place all teachers on yearly contracts, regardless of probationary or nonprobationary status (e.g., HISD). Others allow nonprobationary or tenured teachers multiyear contracts whose renewal is contingent upon successful classroom performance as defined by state evaluation systems (e.g., SCS). Across all systems, we see the tenuous status of probationary teachers, who either remain on probationary contracts until they demonstrate multiple years of teacher effectiveness (e.g., MNPS, SCS, DPS), or can be released at any time throughout their first few years of employment (e.g., HISD, HCPS, BCPS).

Given this variation across contexts, we organize the results section around cross-cutting themes. Where applicable, we also highlight how these various state and district policies surrounding teacher contracts and teacher evaluation might contribute to notable interdistrict differences.

RESULTS

Two major findings emerge from our study: First, principals and central office leaders use a variety of teacher effectiveness data to focus on supporting teachers throughout the school year, with dismissal as a by-product of a long support process. Second, there are a number of barriers principals face in using teacher effectiveness data for teacher dismissal, including the time it takes to gather enough documentation and complete the process; the timing of the release of data; and variation in the degree

Table 10.1. District Contexts Regarding Teacher Contracts and Evaluation

District	Collective Bargaining	Tenure/ Nonprobationary Teacher Contracts	Teacher Evaluation	Teacher Contracts & Teacher Performance
Hillsborough County Public Schools (FL)	Guaranteed right by state constitution	Probationary teachers are on yearly contracts; nonprobationary status can be granted after 3–4 years.	Teachers receive a rating based on principal observations (30%), peer observations (30%), and teacher value-added (40%). Teacher ratings include unsatisfactory, needs improvement, effective, highly effective.	Probationary teachers can be released for underperformance in the first 3–4 years at district discretion; nonprobationary teachers are released after 2 years' consecutive "unsatisfactory" rating, 2 years' "unsatisfactory" rating in 3 years, 3 years' consecutive "needs improvement," rating, or a combination of the two.
Metropolitan Nashville Public Schools (TN) Shelby County Schools (TN)	Illegal	All teachers with tenure prior to 2011 remain tenured; all other teachers are eligible for tenure after 5 years; school board grants tenure.	Teachers receive a rating based on teacher classroom observations (50%); student growth (35%); and student achievement (15%).* Teacher ratings include significantly below expectations, below expectations, at expectations, above expectations, and significantly above expectations.	Probationary teachers may receive tenure after 2 years of demonstrated effectiveness (i.e., above or significantly above expectations); tenured teachers can be released after 3 consecutive years of ratings that are below or significantly below expectations.
Baltimore City Public Schools (MD)	Permitted	Teachers receive tenure on the first day of their 4th year of teaching.	Teachers receive evaluation rating based on formal classroom observation ratings (35%); a professional expectations measure (15%); a student growth measure based on standardized test scores (35%); and a school performance measure (15%), a composite number based on factors including overall student achievement and growth (this differs from the growth measure), college preparedness (high schools only), and student and parent surveys. ** All teachers at a school receive the same score. Teacher ratings include not effective, developing, effective, and highly effective.	Untenured teachers can be nonrenewed for underperformance at any time; tenured teachers: The district must go through a formal grievance process with the union.

Denver Public Schools (CO)	Permitted	State law requires 3 consecutive years of demonstrated effectiveness for tenure.	At the time of this study, the district was piloting an evaluation system based on student growth, classroom observations, professionalism, and student outcomes. Teacher ratings include not meeting, approaching, effective, and distinguished.	Probationary teachers may receive tenure after 2 years of demonstrated effectiveness (i.e., above or significantly above expectations); tenured teachers can be released after 2 consecutive years of ratings that are below or significantly below expectations.
Houston Independent School District (TX)	Illegal	All teachers are placed on yearly contracts. Three consecutive years of effective or highly effective performance is required for nonprobationary status.	Teacher evaluation is based on instructional practice, professional expectations, and student performance. Teacher ratings include ineffective, needs improvement, effective, and highly effective.	Probationary teachers: can be released for underperformance at any time; nonprobationary teachers: the district must go through a file review process and have "cause" for dismissal; effectiveness rating and teacher observations are used as evidence.

Sources: Education Commission of the States, 2011; interviews with central offices and principals in each district.

*In Shelby County Schools, classroom observations represent 40% of the evaluation composite; the other 10% is equally divided by stakeholder feedback/student perception surveys and assessments of teacher knowledge.

**In Baltimore City, teachers in nontested grades and subjects receive the schoolwide value-added; 1st-year teachers are only rated on professional practice.

to which principals feel that the central office will uphold their recommendations. Some districts are reorganizing the work of their central offices to overcome these barriers to better support and to train principals in the dismissal process.

Using Evaluation for Teacher Support First, Dismissal Second

Across all six districts, we found in our interviews with central office leaders and principals that they often framed discussions around teachers' contracts and the use of teacher effectiveness measures within the context of teacher support first, with dismissal as a last resort. One principal commented: "Let's be honest. You can't recommend someone for dismissal if you haven't shown that you tried to help that person improve." By providing this support, teacher observation data provided principals with specific information on classroom instruction and management early in the school year, allowing them to target individualized supports to ineffective teachers.

Other measures of teachers' effectiveness—including value-added measures and overall evaluation composite scores—were used by principals and central offices to identify ineffective teachers. In half of the districts, teachers with overall evaluation scores in the "ineffective" and "needs improvement" categories were automatically given additional school-level and/or district supports. In one of the six districts, teachers with value-added scores that fell into the ineffectiveness rating were also provided additional support. In both cases, providing principals with clearly defined benchmarks, or "cut-scores," was an important strategy used by central offices to establish policies that clarified expectations around the identification of teachers who needed additional support. The other two districts without such firm policies allowed principals the flexibility to use their professional judgment to determine which teachers to support. When given autonomy, principals seemed to favor the use of observation data because of its specificity, timeliness, and transparency (Goldring et al., 2015). One principal noted that the observation process had been "extremely powerful," providing her "with a tool and a resource that . . . helps me define what I need to do to help a teacher."

Importantly, while the process of identifying ineffective teachers varied across these districts, the process of providing support was remarkably consistent across all of them. More specifically, although the names were different (e.g., plans of assistance, individual action plans, performance improvement plans, prescriptive plans of action), each of the six districts implemented a formal process whereby ineffective teachers were placed on individualized growth plans that were actively monitored by school leaders. In implementing these growth plans, all of the districts relied on observation rubrics to target specific areas in need of improvement and provide ongoing, immediate feedback to both principals and teachers on teachers' progress. One principal described the process this way:

> If you see that [a teacher] is going to need a lot of support, then you just start a structured support plan right away, targeting on a few things that you think that should be going on. And that support plan will need to be ongoing and monitored, and if you don't see huge improvements, then you need to make a decision [concerning dismissal] right away that year because you can't wait another year. So if you see some improvement . . . then that person can go on the next year and you can keep on providing that support.

In addition, these plans included provisions dictating that teachers receive more frequent classroom observations from the school leadership team, district personnel, or both. In two of the systems, outside (trained) observers were required to perform additional evaluations to reduce the potential for bias. In coordinating this work, one district also developed a centralized data system where growth plans could be uploaded and monitored in order to ensure "consistency among everyone" offering support. This system also has the advantage of creating a repository of evidence, "so at the end [of the school year] if the teacher doesn't improve, then we have all of the documents there, and we're not chasing down paperwork." Principals in four of the districts also mentioned assigning mentor teachers as part of the development process.

Across each of the districts, we found that the nonfulfillment of the requirements in the growth plans and a lack of improvement in the areas identified often became a central artifact in the documentation used to move a teacher to dismissal. Specifically, we found that this process occurred for both probationary and nonprobationary teachers. That is, while probationary teachers in these systems could be released "at will," a majority of the districts have created policies that require principals to put teachers on growth plans regardless of contract status. For example, in describing this support process, one principal commented, "You offer [ineffective teachers] every bit of help you can offer them—all of the assistance in the world, because we can't continue to train new teachers every year." Similarly, another noted,

> Of course, we give [teachers] all the supports, but then in January I'd be saying, you've had X, Y, and Z and I'm still not seeing

improvement, we have until May to make a decision, but at this point in time I'm leaning towards dismissal.

The policies and support processes highlight the important distinction districts made in trying to support rather than dismiss ineffective teachers. In fact, our survey results suggest that 76% of principals reported retaining teachers previously considered for dismissal because "the teacher had shown sufficient progress," a finding that was consistent in all four districts surveyed and the number-one factor for retaining ineffective teachers (Figure 10.1). We should also note that while value-added and evaluation composite scores were used to identify ineffective teachers to place on growth plans, these measures were generally not used by principals to document improvement. Rather, observation rubrics provided principals with concrete evidence on changes in teacher performance *within* a school year. Given the frequency (i.e., once per year) and timing (i.e., after the current school year finishes) of the release of teacher value-added, state standardized test scores, and overall teacher evaluation scores, these measures did not seem to figure prominently in our discussions with principals around the use of teacher effectiveness measures for teacher dismissal.

Figure 10.1. Dismissal and Renewal Factors

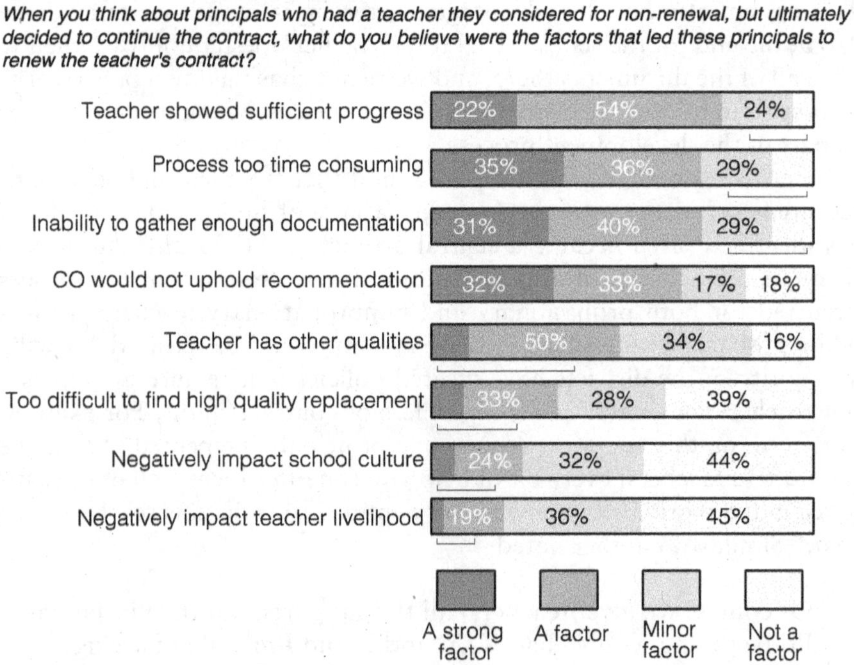

In summary, our interviews and surveys revealed that growth plans seemed to provide principals with specific, concrete guidance around the teacher support process. In the event that teachers did not comply with the plan or did not improve, principals used the documentation from the plan to recommend teachers for dismissal. In the words of one principal, this process provided her with the evidence to say, "After what I did this year I can say in my heart and soul I did everything for this teacher that I nonrenewed, and I made the complete right decision."

Importantly, this link among teacher support, performance plans, and dismissal is not without its consequences. In two of the districts, for instance, interviews with principals and central office leaders suggested that these plans of assistance have "a negative connotation" for teachers. Thus, it is important to recognize that while the overall message from the districts and principals was one of improvement over dismissal, the connection between the two through performance plans may belie that message in the minds of teachers.

Barriers to Teacher Dismissal

In our interviews with principals and central office leaders and in our survey of principals we discovered a few important barriers that inhibit the teacher dismissal process. First, principals in our sample felt that the dismissal process is very time-consuming. This is a consistent finding in the literature (Painter, 2000). For example, when asked about the reasons for renewing the contract of a teacher who had been considered for dismissal, about 71% of principals reported that the time-consuming nature of the process was a factor or a strong factor, a finding that was consistent across all four districts surveyed. Similarly, 71% of principals noted an inability to gather enough documentation to dismiss a teacher as a factor or strong factor in deciding to retain the teacher. Our interviews with principals and central office leaders seemed to reflect this finding as well. For instance, one principal said,

> If somebody I know needs to leave, you wouldn't believe the documentation process you have to have. . . . Well, I can't recommend that we get rid of this person if I don't have the documentation to recommend that he be terminated because they're going to come back to me and say you need this, you need this, you need that.

Other factors, including the difficulty in finding a high-quality replacement, other qualities that make the teacher valuable to the school, or a negative impact on the school climate or teacher's livelihood, were not considered by a majority of principals in any of the four districts surveyed to be factors in the decision to renew an ineffective teacher's contract (Figure 10.1).

Another important barrier that emerged from our interviews with central office leaders and principals in each of the systems was the timing of the release of the data. Specifically, teacher value-added and overall evaluation composite scores arrived too late for principals to make dismissal decisions. Throughout the districts, we found that decision deadlines, often occurring in the spring, take place before principals can examine growth and overall effectiveness ratings. In describing a teacher who had low test scores from the previous year, one principal noted the difficulties related to the timing of the release of data:

> Well, here we are this year. She's doing much better, much, much better. I won't have her data back. I have to decide if I was going to non-renominate her by March. So, how do I decide if I'm gonna non-renominate a teacher, who in my opinion is doing great? I won't see her scores until May 30th. So, I . . . am going off of gut that she's pulled it together because of what I'm seeing in her room.

Finally, principals feel that their recommendations will not always be supported by their central offices. Specifically, when asked about the reasons for renewing a contract for a teacher who had been considered for dismissal, about 65% of principals responded that "the central office will not uphold the recommendation for dismissal" was a factor or a strong factor in deciding to renew an ineffective teacher. Nonetheless, this finding varied across the four districts surveyed, a result that may reflect changes to the ways in which central offices are beginning to directly support principals in the dismissal process (Grissom et al., 2014). For instance, half of the districts in our study have redefined the roles of regional superintendents, principal supervisors, and/or academic support officers to directly assist principals in the work of teacher dismissal. One of the clearest examples of this is found in a district that uses a district-level leader and lawyer to meet with principals to discuss specific teachers who are being considered for dismissal. Together they examine the data and either determine that there is sufficient justification for terminating the teacher, or they coach the principal on additional things that need to be done to move the teacher to termination. One principal described the process this way:

> It starts with the classroom observations. We try to work with the teacher, bring it to their attention. . . . And from that point it

> helps to determine the way it's going to go. One, they could be in denial. Nothing's wrong with my classroom. . . . Or they may be very receptive. . . . And if it steadily digresses, I'm still documenting along the way and then I meet with someone from human resources, someone from the legal department, and my boss, the [district support officer], and we look at all the documentation. And actually, there's an outside lawyer, too, who's hired through the district, who reviews the documentation and basically sees, determines if we have enough for it to move forward for termination.

Importantly, this district views the increased number of teachers who have been dismissed as a result of the supporting evidence gained from the teacher evaluation process.

In another system, district leaders are supporting principals' development by beginning to "build out some profiles of teachers with certain data points . . . and let principals really talk about what [they] would do to support these teachers, [and] if this would be a nonrenewal in their building," given the context provided in the profiles. Similarly, another system provides principals with "very explicit data reports," which are then discussed with principals' Human Resource (HR) partners and instructional superintendents, who together look at the data. One principal in this district said, "Ultimately, it's my decision [to renew or dismiss a teacher], but they're trying to help me look at the data." In describing this process, this principal referenced a number of data elements that were examined, including student perception surveys and classroom observation scores from multiple peer and administrative observers.

In short, we found that to varying degrees, each of these systems has begun the process of redesigning professional development for principals, creating new ways to help principals develop expertise, and creating new institutional procedures and tools in order to address these barriers (Grissom et al., 2014). More broadly, we found that these changes represented a shift in the thinking of both principals and central office leaders in using data strategically to make human capital decisions (Cannata et al., 2014; Odden, 2011).

CONCLUSIONS

New teacher evaluation models and changing teacher contracts are commonly viewed as important levers in dismissing ineffective teachers. In examining these new teacher evaluation measures and teacher dismissal in six urban districts with well-developed teacher evaluation systems, we found that the evaluation process itself has provided district and school leaders with a means of delivering systematic teacher support and important opportunities to improve, while dismissal processes occur after the support processes. In particular, we found that principals rely heavily on classroom observations to support ineffective teachers and, through growth plans, gather a body of evidence that can ultimately be used as evidence for performance dismissals. In determining which teachers are placed on growth plans, most districts provide principals with specific requirements or cut scores regarding when support plans have to be provided, based on value-added measures and composite scores, while other systems leave this to principal discretion. When given autonomy, principals tend to favor the use of classroom observation data due to its timeliness, transparency, and specificity (Goldring et al., 2015).

We also found a number of barriers in the dismissal process, such as the time it takes to gather documentation and complete the dismissal process, the timing of when teacher effectiveness data become available, and varying degrees of support from the central office in upholding principal recommendations. In response, we found that districts were beginning to address these barriers by changing the ways in which they support principals with dismissal decisions. These changes center around the use of regional superintendents, principal supervisors, and/or academic support officers to better support principals in making dismissal decisions, support that might include providing principals with detailed teacher effectiveness data reports or meetings to discuss the progress of teachers being considered for dismissal.

Importantly, the mandated use of student achievement and value-added measures (VAM) of teacher effectiveness served mainly to trigger growth plans and did not seem to figure prominently in dismissal decisions themselves, for reasons that may include timing (e.g., VAM are not available when dismissal decisions need to be made); transparency and complexity (e.g., principals do not understand how VAM are calculated); and perceived validity (e.g., principals do not know how to use them for teachers in untested grades and subjects) (Goldring et al., 2015). Thus, there is a paradox in that the definition of ineffective includes reliance on value-added measures of student achievement, but the means to determine if a teacher is making progress toward becoming more effective rests principally with another data source—teacher observations.

Thus, while VAM has received a lot of policy attention in connection with human capital decisions (Harris & Herrington, 2015), more attention to teacher observation measures is needed. We found that the systems in our study that have developed strong, ongoing calibration of observation scores have increased the level of teacher trust of the data, which can lead to fewer disputes and legal actions regarding teacher dismissal. We also found that systems that allow principals to request calibration and co-observation in subjects where they lack expertise report greater use of observation data. Furthermore, districts that trained teachers on the observation rubric reported that it is a very strong form of professional development that also has the benefit of creating teacher buy-in and trust in the data, making future dismissal decisions easier to carry out.

NOTES

This research was conducted with support from the Bill and Melinda Gates Foundation. The opinions expressed in this chapter are those of the authors and do not necessarily represent the views of the sponsor.

1. Our data collection also included two charter management organizations (CMOs), though we do not utilize data from the CMOs in this analysis because of the unique contexts for personnel management. See Goldring et al. (2015) for more details about the methodology for this study.

2. The survey administration was conducted somewhat differently in two of the four systems that participated in the survey. Two of the systems were also participating in an evaluation of the Intensive Partnerships for Effective Teaching conducted by RAND/AIR. For these systems, some items were developed by RAND/AIR. These items were fielded by RAND/AIR in the spring of 2013 as part of their continued evaluation. We acknowledge their cooperation.

REFERENCES

Cannata, M., Rubin, M., Goldring, E., Grissom, J. A., Neumerski, C. M., Drake, T., & Schuermann, P. (2014, April). *Using teacher effectiveness data for information rich hiring.* Retrieved from principaldatause.org/assets/files/additionals/Data-Use-In-Hiring-2014.pdf

Cohen-Vogel, L. (2011). "Staffing to the Test:" Are today's school personnel practices evidence based? *Educational Evaluation and Policy Analysis, 33*(4), 483–505.

Corbin, J., & Strauss, A. (2008). *Basics of qualitative research: Techniques and procedures for developing grounded theory.* Washington, DC: Sage Publications.

Dee, T. S., & Wyckoff, J. (2015). Incentives, selection, and teacher performance: Evidence from IMPACT. *Journal of Policy Analysis and Management, 34*(2), 267–297.

Donaldson, M. L. (2013). Principals' approaches to cultivating teacher effectiveness: Constraints and opportunities in hiring, assigning, evaluating, and developing teachers. *Educational Administration Quarterly, 49*(5), 838–882.

Donaldson, M. L., & Papay, J. (2015). Teacher evaluation for accountability and development. In H. F. Ladd & M. Goertz (Eds.), *Handbook of research in education finance and policy* (2nd ed., pp. 174–193). New York, NY: Routledge.

Education Commission of the States. (2015). *Teacher tenure or continuing contract laws*. Retrieved from www.ecs.org/html/educationIssues/teachingQuality/teacherdb_intro.asp

Goldring, E., Grissom, J. A., Rubin, M., Neumerski, C. M., Cannata, M., Drake, T., & Schuermann, P. (2015). Make room value added: Principals' human capital decisions and the emergence of teacher observation data. *Educational Researcher, 44*(2), 96–104.

Grissom, J. A., Rubin, M., Goldring, E. B., Cannata, M., Drake, T., Neumerski, C. M., & Schuermann, P. (2014). *Central office supports for data-driven talent management decisions: Evidence from the implementation of new systems for measuring teacher effectiveness*. Retrieved from principaldatause.org/assets/files/additionals/District-Supports.pdf

Harris, D. N., & Herrington, C. D. (2015). Editors' introduction: The use of teacher value-added measures in schools: New evidence, unanswered questions, and future prospects. *Educational Researcher, 44*(2), 71–76.

Kane, T. J., McCaffrey, D. F., Miller, T., & Staiger, D. O. (2013). *Have we identified effective teachers? Validating measures of effective teaching using random assignment* (MET project research paper). Seattle, WA: Bill and Melinda Gates Foundation.

LeCompte, M. D., & Schensul, J. J. (1999). *Analyzing and interpreting ethnographic data*. Lanham, MD: Altamira Press.

Odden, A. R. (2011). *Strategic management of human capital in education: Improving instructional practice and student learning in schools*. New York, NY: Routledge.

Painter, S. R. (2000). Principals' perceptions of barriers to teacher dismissal. *Journal of Personnel Evaluation in Education, 14*(3), 253–264.

Taylor, E. S., & Tyler, J. H. (2012). The effect of evaluation on teacher performance. *The American Economic Review, 102*(7), 3628–3651.

CHAPTER 11

Implementing Student Learning Objectives and Classroom Observations in Connecticut's Teacher Evaluation System

Morgaen L. Donaldson
Casey D. Cobb

In 2012, Connecticut became one of many states to pass legislation mandating the use of multiple measures of teacher performance in its new teacher evaluation system. In this chapter, we identify challenges and opportunities that 14 Connecticut districts experienced when implementing two major components of the state model: standards-based observations and student learning objectives (SLOs). Principals found conducting classroom observations to be difficult, and educators struggled to set appropriate SLOs. Teachers reported that the new model increased the time they spent analyzing student data and that increased observations and feedback conversations were beneficial. Finally, we find that leaders focused primarily on holding teachers accountable for implementing the system without capitalizing on opportunities to improve teaching and learning.

BACKGROUND

Like most teacher evaluation systems created since Race to the Top's 2009 passage, Connecticut's System for Educator Evaluation and Development (SEED) includes standards-based classroom observations and student learning objectives (for more information, see www.connecticutseed.org/). Historically, classroom observation has been the most common component of teacher evaluation (Goe, Bell, & Little, 2008). Student learning objectives are a recent development in teacher evaluation models.

Standards-based observations are included in every new state evaluation model, and observations receive the most weight of any component (Steinberg & Donaldson, 2014). Standards-based observations have the capacity to facilitate direct, specific feedback about a teacher's instruction. The standards undergirding these measures define high-quality instruction more clearly and comprehensively than ever before. Administrators can use the rubrics introduced by these systems as the foundation for conversations about instructional improvement with teachers. Research suggests that evaluation systems relying heavily on standards-based observations can lead to instructional improvement (Taylor & Tyler, 2012) and increased student achievement (Steinberg & Sartain, in press). Moreover, standards-based evaluations are relatively strong predictors of teachers' value-added measures (Hill, Kapitula, & Umland, 2011). Kane, Taylor, Tyler, and Wooten (2011) found that a teacher's standards-based observation rating predicts student test performance over and above that teacher's value-added rating. Evaluator measurement bias and reliability remain concerns, but comprehensive training for evaluators can help mitigate these threats (Donaldson & Papay, 2015).

SLOs are "content- and grade/course-specific learning objectives that educators can validly measure to document student learning over a defined and significant period of time" (Reform Support Network, 2014, p. 5). SLOs are used in teacher evaluation models in 30 states as of March 2014 (Lacireno-Paquet, Morgan, & Mello, 2014). SLOs permit the inclusion of student performance measures in evaluations of teachers in nontested grades and subjects. Twenty-one states were using SLOs to evaluate all teachers and student support specialists as of March 2014 (Lacireno-Paquet et al., 2014).

Evidence from the private sector suggests that goal-setting can promote employee motivation and learning (Locke & Latham, 2002). When employees set "optimal" goals that are challenging and accompanied by support, they are motivated to improve their performance (Locke & Latham, 2002). Within education, scant research has investigated SLOs. Studies of SLOs in the earliest districts to adopt these measures have found that SLO ratings have small correlations with value-added estimates (Goldhaber & Walch, 2012) and that SLO quality is related to student achievement (Community Training and Assistance Center, 2004). Little research has examined the psychometric integrity of SLOs, which raises concerns about their use for high-stakes purposes.

METHODS

Connecticut's SEED required that teachers be evaluated based on student learning objectives (45% of a teacher's rating), standards-based observations of instructional practice (40%), parent or peer feedback (10%), and student feedback or whole-school measures of student performance (5%). Importantly, the law that instituted SEED also made a summative evaluation rating of "ineffective" grounds for terminating a teacher.

SEED required administrators to conduct three formal and three informal observations of teachers and student support specialists each year. Formal observations involved a brief preliminary meeting between administrator and teacher, a 30- to 45-minute structured observation, a written report, and a postobservation conference to share feedback. Administrators used a performance rubric to record their observations. Informal observations typically involved 5-minute classroom walkthroughs. Observations were stored electronically in networked databases. SEED also included SLOs, which were defined as broad instructional goals, and Indicators of Academic Growth and Development, which translated the SLOs into specific, measurable growth targets on assessments. We refer to these two types of goals as SLOs here.

The Connecticut State Department of Education (CSDE) selected 14 sites to pilot SEED in 2012–2013. The districts ranged from Bridgeport, the state's largest school district with 32 schools, 20,087 students, and 99% of students eligible for free or reduced-price lunch, to Eastford, a K–8 district with one school and 178 students, 9% of whom were eligible for reduced-price lunch. Most districts in the sample enroll a percentage of low-income students at or above the Connecticut average. Bridgeport and Windham are in the lowest decile of student achievement and highest decile of poverty, and have been the target of state intervention. Detailed information about these districts can be found at www.connecticutseed.org/?page_id=874 (Donaldson et al., 2014).

Data were collected through interviews with district leaders, principals, teachers, evaluation system trainers, district-level union leaders, and state-level union representatives. To identify an interview sample, we first purposely selected a minimum of 20% of the schools at each level within each district to maximize variation in student demographics, school size, and administrator longevity (Creswell, 2013).

Within these schools, we recruited all principals and, in some cases, assistant principals and deans of students. In all, 37 school-based leaders participated in the study. We also sampled educators who were evaluated as "teachers" under SEED, randomly selecting teachers and specialists to represent 20% of each school's faculty. We weighted these random samples to reflect the proportions of core academic teachers (i.e., teachers of mathematics, science, English language arts, and social sciences), related arts teachers (e.g., arts, physical education, and world languages), and specialists (e.g., special education teacher, school counselor) in the school. In fall 2012, 296 teachers and 67 specialists were interviewed; in winter 2013, 155 teachers and 25 specialists were interviewed; and in spring 2013, 269 teachers and 50 specialists were interviewed (see Table 11.1). We followed participants longitudinally and for the most part were successful in doing so through at least two of the rounds of interviews.

Interviews lasted 45 to 75 minutes and were audio-recorded and transcribed. We asked participants a series of questions, including how SEED differed from their prior evaluation system, how it fit with other initiatives, and how they would change SEED to better support improvements to teaching. Interview data were coded inductively and then arranged in matrices (Miles & Huberman, 1994) to facilitate the constant comparative method, which produced the findings presented here.

We conducted two rounds of surveys with teachers. The universe was defined as the population of teachers working in the schools supplying our

Table 11.1. Interview and Focus Group Sample in Phase 1 by Pilot District/Consortium

	NUMBER OF PARTICIPANTS					
District/ Consortium	Schools	District Leaders	School Leaders	Teachers	Specialists	*Total*
Bethany	1	0	2	10	2	*15*
Branford	2	2	0	11	3	*18*
Bridgeport	7	1	7	73	9	*97*
CEFS[1]	4	4	5	41	3	*57*
CREC[2]	6	1	6	31	2	*46*
Litchfield/ Region 6	4	2	5	13	8	*32*
Norwalk	3	1	3	36	5	*48*
Waterford	2	2	3	27	3	*37*
Windham	4	2	4	26	23	*59*
Windsor	2	2	2	28	9	*43*
Total	*35*	*17*	*37*	*296*	*67*	*452*

[1] Columbia-Eastford-Franklin-Sterling

[2] Capitol Region Education Council

interview sample. All teachers were invited to participate in the written or online survey. Questions included those asking teachers to report on the frequency of evaluation tasks (e.g., observations) and to compare SEED to their prior system. Response rates were 44% for the first survey (n = 684/1,555) and 26% for the second survey (n = 533/2,050). The drop-off in the response rate for the second survey was likely due to its administration after the pilot year ended. Because of the low response rates, survey data should be interpreted with some caution. Survey data were analyzed using basic descriptive statistics; we did not track individual responses over time, so we are not able to analyze these data longitudinally.

FINDINGS

Overall, we find that observations were challenging for administrators to carry out but were generally well-received by teachers. Postobservation debriefs were sporadic, however, and teachers reported a desire for more feedback from administrators. SEED's SLO component appeared to prompt teachers to spend more time analyzing student data, but also created many challenges, according to participants. Administrators generally seemed to focus on executing the components of SEED to hold teachers accountable and paid less attention to using the system to drive improvements to teaching.

Observations in a High-Stakes Context

In general, administrators and teachers expressed support for the observations. Although challenging logistically, most administrators reported completing two formal and two informal observations during the school year. By focusing their attention on classrooms, administrators prioritized their role as instructional leaders in the school.

Opportunities. Teachers reported that they had received more observations and feedback than in the years prior to SEED, which they appreciated. Half of the teachers reported that they were observed more than in previous years. Seven out of ten teachers surveyed reported having two or more informal observations, and 64% reported having at least two formal observations in that 1st year of implementation. Fifty-five percent (55%) of the respondents indicated that the value of time spent being observed under SEED was somewhat or very valuable.

Although not without its limitations, the observation rubric provided a common language for educators and evaluators to discuss practice.

Evaluators reported that it led to an increase in objectivity. One elementary principal reported telling teachers: "[G]ive yourself a grade and then tell me specifically why you would give yourself this rating, which I think really targets the discussion and focuses in on instructional practices."

Educators reported that postobservation conferences were beneficial. One principal of a large suburban high school noted that the postobservation discussions had been "really powerful in terms of having a rubric-based conversation around teaching and learning." Fifty-seven percent of teachers surveyed felt that their postobservation debriefings were somewhat or very valuable. Of those teachers who reported spending more time in postobservation conferences than previously, 69% found this experience valuable. Notably, 44% of teachers surveyed reported that observation feedback prompted them to change their practice. A teacher reported that "the best thing out of the whole process was being able to sit down numerous times with [my evaluator]—not just informally, but formally be able to sit down and say, okay, what did you see? Tell me what you saw. I want to know."

Challenges. Completion of the six required observations was one of the most challenging aspects of SEED. Across schools, evaluation loads ranged widely, from one elementary school assistant principal responsible for evaluating six teachers to another evaluator with a load of 56 teachers. One administrator noted, "I think it's a lot of observations. I mean, again, I would advocate more for having like a Kim Marshall–type of thing where you go in and do ten walk-through observations and then if you do four or five and you don't see major changes, then you do a formal with the teacher and you start making it much more—instead of having this many and this many for every single teacher."

High-poverty, low-performing schools seemed to bear a relatively greater burden. These schools were implementing multiple, simultaneous reform initiatives while serving students with the greatest needs. One urban middle school principal lamented,

> [W]e have about 5,000 behavioral referrals every year here and so to deal with behavioral referrals all the time . . . you either don't get the observations done or you're not going to address the behavioral referrals and there's only six, seven hours in a day. So it's tough, very tough.

In addition to the challenges of completing the observations, administrators and educators identified two problems with the observation rubric. First, in interviews administrators reported that they did not feel they could record things that occurred that were not part of the rubric. One principal remarked,

> There have just been occasions where I have been doing observations that I thought, okay, where does this fit in the rubric? It is not always a perfect match. Whereas in the past, because there have been so many categories and [it was] so general, we have been able to make subjective statements, anything goes. The objectivity is a tiny bit of a hindrance.

The second major issue was the difficulty in applying the rubric to student support specialists. Designed for classroom teachers, the evaluation rubrics did not work well for specialists who worked outside the classroom or with individual students. Some administrators adapted the rubrics, while others struggled to apply it in these situations.

In addition to constraints of the rubric, postobservation conferences also posed a challenge. These conferences offer an opportunity for administrator and educator to discuss what occurred during the observation and develop strategies for improvement. However, across our sample of schools, approximately 7% of teachers reported that they had not received any postobservation feedback, and an additional 21% reported that they had received feedback only once. Others had conferences weeks after the observation, mitigating the effect and relevance of the feedback.

In interviews, educators also reported that the quality and consistency of the observation varied widely. The quality of the observation experience seemed to be a function of how well-trained evaluators were to carry out the observation protocol and create meaningful written and oral feedback. One veteran high school teacher said, "Every administrator needs to be on the same page. I think that is key. I feel awful that I had an administrator that gets it and other people, especially the younger teachers, did not—where they could have been helped in their practice and in their craft, but they weren't." Some educators were disillusioned with the process and put little stock in the feedback they received. This was usually due to unhelpful or, in their view, inaccurate feedback from the evaluator.

Last, neither teachers nor administrators reported that administrators used observation results to select or develop professional development opportunities for teachers. In theory, rubric results could be used to identify professional development needs of individuals or groups and, if fine-grained enough, gauge the effects of those learning opportunities over time. Although the title of SEED emphasized teacher "development," almost no teachers reported receiving professional learning tailored to their observation results.

Student Learning Objectives in a High-Stakes Context

As discussed above, goal-setting has the potential to motivate teachers. We found that SLOs created some opportunities for motivation while also encountering several challenges.

Opportunities. Teachers reported that including SLOs in their evaluations increased their focus on student data. For example, when asked whether SEED had caused her to teach the content associated with her SLO in more depth than in prior years, one teacher observed, "I know in my case it has, as opposed to [last year] it might have been part of a unit that lasted six weeks. I see them [my students] every other day for the whole year, you know, so they can have that content down. They're going to know that standard in the Common Core . . ."

Teachers also reported spending substantially more time on setting goals and analyzing data under SEED than under their prior evaluation system. Nearly three-quarters of teachers reported spending more time on goal-setting than in previous years, with 44% reporting they spent "a lot more time" on this activity. Almost no teachers reported spending less time on this task. Fifty-three percent noted that this activity was "valuable."

Educators also reported spending more time analyzing student data within the context of SEED. Sixty-four percent of teachers surveyed said they spent more time analyzing student data than previously. Sixty-eight percent of teachers surveyed found analyzing student data valuable.

Challenges. In terms of challenges, participants reported in interviews that SLOs were not consistently rigorous across teachers. This variation appeared to be due to differences in administrators' expectations for teachers, teachers' expectations for themselves, and both groups' understanding of the SEED model as a whole.

Administrators' expectations for teachers' SLOs varied. For example, one principal observed that her expectations differed from those of her assistant principal: "In grades 3 through 5 some teachers put 100% for their goals and I let them do that whereas in K through 2, the assistant principal said she advised against that." With the extremely high goal of 100% of students reaching a benchmark, many teachers in grades 3–5 failed to achieve their goals.

Teachers corroborated this report. In a focus group, one teacher described how her experience contrasted with her colleague's: "[W]e had different supervisors and so we did get different messages and then I think we got different feedback and I think we got different structures around how to construct our SLO. I heard 'make it generic, make it easy to obtain.'" Her colleague offered a contrasting experience: "I heard aim high."

Teachers' expectations for their own SLOs also varied. Some teachers set lofty goals, while others set more modest ones. Although few teachers reported that they had deliberately set easily attainable goals, many discussed this as a possibility. First, teachers could identify a cohort that included only mid- to high-performing students who could achieve the targeted growth. One principal raised this concern: "Why wouldn't they [teachers] set them [SLOs] for the kids that they know can make improvement, and what does that mean for the kids that really need the support? That worries me."

Teachers also noted that their colleagues could game the system by modifying their SLOs at the midyear conference. One teacher said: "It's a little dangerous really to be able to modify your SLO." She explained that "a weaker educator, couldn't they just make it like 'You know what? Actually I didn't get around to teaching that. I think I'll tweak that goal.' You could really downgrade it."

In addition to expectations, the extent to which educators understood goal-setting also seemed to affect the quality of the SLOs. Principals reported that teachers lacked key data-analysis skills, which are among the skills required to set strong SLOs. Sometimes teachers' misunderstandings were quite basic. In other instances, teachers' misunderstandings seemed to be more entrenched.

In some schools, teachers were expected to adopt schoolwide SLOs established by principals. For example, a math teacher reported that she was required to focus her SLOs on the English standardized test scores and a school climate score. She reported, "I have math, and we have the same SLOs [schoolwide], so ours is editing and revising. [I am] throwing that in, you know, in my warm-ups as a word problem." She added, "The paperwork is easier, but in reality, it's not—it's not an improvement plan for the teacher, to be honest, you know?"

In interviews, educators also reported struggling to find good assessments on which to base SLOs. Assessments were identified as a particular challenge for teachers of nontested grades and subjects. One high school administrator argued:

> [The state is] saying that you have to have a goal that's related to CAPT [the state 10th-grade assessment]. And you teach fashion or you teach PE or you teach whatever, and because you teach tenth-graders, you have to have a CAPT-related goal, [which] feels really punitive to those teachers and arbitrary. And I understand we have to be accountable for moving the scores. But the reality is for a

> teacher's evaluation to be based on something they have so little control over is not logical.

Educators argued for "building-based assessments"—assessments that are developed locally by teachers for use in their own schools—but these were not uniformly available.

DISCUSSION

The implementation of Connecticut's pilot initiative raised important questions. In this state, 85% of a teacher's summative rating is based on his or her observational rating (40%) and his or her performance on student growth measures, or SLOs (45%). These weights are relatively similar to those of the other 45 states that have adopted new teacher evaluation systems in the past 5 years (Steinberg & Donaldson, 2014). As such, the challenges and opportunities that surfaced here may be instructive for other settings as states and districts strive to modify their systems to fully realize their potential.

Overall, we find that both observations and SLOs have promise. Of the two, observations were executed with relatively more fidelity and were perceived by teachers as more beneficial. Observations were generally well received by teachers, who reported wanting more observations and feedback to inform their instruction. As with evaluation systems prior to Race to the Top, the major challenges related to observation were administrator time and capacity (see Kimball & Milanowski, 2009). In fact, these challenges may be greater now than in the past, since many states require more teachers to be evaluated more frequently.

SLOs, too, have promise as an evaluation component. However, our data suggest that implementing SLOs requires substantial district, school, and educator capacity. Setting valid and appropriate SLOs remains a challenge. Many of the criticisms of value-added models are relevant in the context of SLOs. A major problem includes a lack of psychometric integrity of many of the indicators used within SLOs. Further, student growth, even if measured well, is often difficult to attribute to individual teachers. Measurement issues aside, there is still the expectation that there should be some way to capture student growth and tie it to the goals of teachers.

Moreover, goal-setting motivates teachers to the extent that it supports their autonomy and competence (Deci & Flaste, 1995). In the cases in which goals were mandated, goal-setting offered teachers little autonomy, in an effort to promote schoolwide coherence. Goal-setting also likely had little effect on their sense of competence because the goal was distant from their instructional priorities and their notion of success as an instructor of their particular content or grade. Given all of these challenges to SLOs, how can we maximize their potential without falling prey to their downsides?

Our research highlights several areas for future research. Studies should investigate the implementation of observations and SLOs after a system has been fully established. After 3 or 5 years of implementation, do these findings still obtain? Our study also suggests that future research should investigate which principals, under what conditions, are able to carry out evaluations in ways that produce desired results. We know that principals matter in teacher evaluation, but much less about the factors that affect their capacity to use teacher evaluation to hold teachers accountable and improve their practice.

SLOs are also worthy of further research. Most recent research has focused on value-added models, standards-based observational instruments, and, to a lesser extent, student surveys. Despite the fact that 30 states incorporate SLOs in their evaluation systems and 21 states use nothing but these measures as their student performance component, scant research has investigated them (Lacireno-Paquet et al., 2014). As noted above, there has been almost no research on the psychometric properties of these measures and few studies on their effects on teachers' practice or student achievement. If SLOs remain in use, it will be important to devote more attention to them.

REFERENCES

Community Training and Assistance Center. (2004). *Catalyst for change. Pay for performance in Denver: Final report.* Boston, MA: Author. Retrieved from www.ctacusa.com/wp-content/uploads/2013/11/CatalystForChange.pdf

Creswell, J. (2013). *Qualitative inquiry and research design.* Thousand Oaks, CA: Sage.

Deci, E., & Flaste, R. (1995). *Why we do what we do: Understanding self-motivation.* New York, NY: Penguin.

Donaldson, M. L., Cobb, C., LeChasseur, K., Gabriel, R., Gonzales, R., Woulfin, S., & Makuch, A. (2014). *An evaluation of the pilot implementation of Connecticut's System for Educator Evaluation and Development.* Storrs, CT: University of Connecticut Center for Education Policy Analysis.

Donaldson, M. L., & Papay, J. (2015). Teacher evaluation for accountability and development. In H. F. Ladd & M. Goertz (Eds.), *Handbook of research in education finance and policy* (2nd ed., pp. 174–193). New York, NY: Routledge.

Goe, L., Bell, C., & Little, O. (2008). *Approaches to evaluating teacher effectiveness: A research synthesis.* Washington, DC: National Comprehensive

Center for Teacher Quality. Retrieved from www.tqsource.org/publications/EvaluatingTeachEffectiveness.pdf

Goldhaber, D., & Walch, J. (2012). Strategic pay reform: A student outcomes-based evaluation of Denver's ProComp teacher pay initiative. *Economics of Education Review, 31*(6), 1067–1083.

Hill, H. C., Kapitula, L., & Umland, K. (2011). A validity argument approach to evaluating teacher value-added scores. *American Educational Research Journal, 48*(3), 794–831.

Kane, T. J., Taylor, E. S., Tyler, J. H., & Wooten, A. L. (2011). Identifying effective classroom practices using student achievement data. *Journal of Human Resources, 46*(3), 587–613.

Kimball, S., & Milanowski, A. (2009). Examining teacher evaluation validity and leadership decision making within a standards-based evaluation system. *Educational Administration Quarterly, 45*(1), 34–70.

Lacireno-Paquet, N., Morgan, C., & Mello, D. (2014). *How states use student learning objectives in teacher evaluation systems: A review of state websites* (REL 2014–013). Washington, DC: U.S. Department of Education, Institute of Education Sciences, National Center for Education Evaluation and Regional Assistance, Regional Educational Laboratory Northeast & Islands. Retrieved from ies.ed.gov/ncee/edlabs

Locke, E. A., & Latham, G. P. (2002). Building a practically useful theory of goal setting and work motivation: A 35 year odyssey. *American Psychologist, 57,* 705–717.

Miles, M., & Huberman, A. M. (1994). *An expanded sourcebook: Qualitative data analysis*. Thousand Oaks, CA: Sage.

Reform Support Network. (2014). *A toolkit for implementing high-quality student learning objectives 2.0.* Washington, DC: U.S. Department of Education. Retrieved from www2.ed.gov/about/inits/ed/implementation-support-unit/tech-assist/toolkit-implementing-learning-objectives-2-0.pdf

Steinberg, M., & Donaldson, M. (2014). *The new educational accountability: Understanding the landscape of teacher evaluation in the post-NCLB era* (Working paper). Storrs, CT: University of Connecticut Center for Education Policy Analysis.

Steinberg, M., & Sartain, L. (in press). Does teacher evaluation improve school performance? Experimental evidence from Chicago's Excellence in Teaching Project. *Education Finance and Policy.*

Taylor, E. S., & Tyler, J. H. (2012). The effect of evaluation on teacher performance. *American Economic Review, 102*(7), 3628–3651.

CHAPTER 12

Using Multiple Measures for Developmental Teacher Evaluation

Gary T. Henry
J. Edward Guthrie

Growing numbers of state and local education agencies have overhauled their teacher evaluation systems to include student test score growth along with measures of teachers' performance from other sources such as classroom observations and student surveys. Some research based on simulations suggests that evaluating teachers based on information about teachers' contributions to their students' test score growth and using these ratings to remove the most ineffective teachers could raise overall test scores in following years (Goldhaber & Hansen, 2010; Hanushek, 2009; Winters & Cowen, 2013). Other studies have shed light on the predictive validity of different ways to combine information from multiple sources to rate teachers for evaluation purposes, with value-added measures as the target criterion being predicted (Mihaly, McCaffrey, Staiger, & Lockwood, 2013). Apart from these applications of value-added for summative evaluation purposes, the inclusion of value-added among multiple measures of teacher performance in evaluations can offer formative benefits to develop teachers' instructional practices and improve student outcomes. Indeed, a study of an observation-based evaluation program shows that rigorous, external observations along with feedback from the observers can improve teachers' value-added scores (Taylor & Tyler, 2012), suggesting the potential for evaluation to improve student outcomes not only through selective retention decisions but through the development of existing teachers. In this chapter, we describe a system that can be used to marshal data from multiple sources to leverage value-added to support the development of teachers and teacher effectiveness.

BACKGROUND

A challenge for teacher evaluation is to obtain performance measures that more accurately reflect schools' and teachers' contribution to student learning than raw test scores or proficiency percentages, which are biased by the systematic sorting of students and teachers with different abilities into schools and classrooms (Tekwe et al., 2004). The most popular and empirically justified measures of teachers' contributions to student test score growth come from value-added models, which estimate how a teacher's students performed in comparison to similar students on the same test in that year. Value-added models were developed to decompose the variance in student test scores and thus isolate the influence of various schooling inputs on student achievement (Todd & Wolpin, 2003). Teachers' value-added (TVA) scores serve as micro-impact estimates of teachers' effectiveness, bypassing direct measurement of the teaching and learning process to focus on one important educational output: student achievement. To address concerns that TVA scores, like raw achievement or proficiency measures, are biased by the sorting of students across teachers, in one prior study TVA scores under natural nonrandom assignment were shown to reliably predict teachers' contributions to student achievement when teachers and students were then randomly assigned (Kane, McCaffrey, Miller, & Staiger, 2013), thereby empirically neutralizing one of the most significant criticisms of their use in teacher evaluations.

Teaching is a complex and multidimensional process, and instruments designed to assess teachers' instructional quality are correspondingly multifaceted. In the Taylor and Tyler (2012) study, the observations were based on the Danielson Framework for Teaching (2011), which includes 22 components of teaching within 4 domains; the Measures of Effective Teaching (MET) project used the 12-dimensional Classroom Assessment Scoring System (CLASS) observation rubric along with the 7-scale Tripod student survey to add direct measures of teachers instructional practices into the teacher evaluation process (Mihaly et al., 2013). For each of these dimensions, teachers can directly translate raters' evaluations of their performance into actions to improve in these areas, since the dimensions measure practices, or inputs. The connection between ratings and actions is not as clear for teacher value-added scores. While TVA provides less biased feedback on outcomes to teachers and administrators than raw test scores or proficiency percentages, they alone offer no direction to teachers in how to improve instruction, nor guidance to principals in what skills to help teachers develop. Instead, measures that capture one or more dimensions of teachers' instructional practice are required if value-added evaluations are to be used for developmental purposes. Moreover, these measures of specific instructional practices should be empirically associated with gains in student learning (TVA scores) if teachers are to be given evidence-based guidance about what to do to improve their scores and their students' achievement.

However, to date, few studies have attempted to link measures of practice to teachers' value-added scores for the purpose of identifying practices most likely to increase student achievement. Where research has examined relationships between value-added and other sources of data, it has done so to assess either the ability of raters to discriminate between levels of teacher effectiveness (Jacob & Lefgren, 2005, 2008) or the power of subjective measures to predict future value-added (Ferguson, 2012; Mihaly et al., 2013). Both approaches, though they find significant correlations between subjective teacher ratings and TVA, compare measures in terms of how well they reflect an implicitly unidimensional concept of teaching quality. Harris, Ingle, and Rutledge (2014) go further, examining correlations between teachers' value-added and ratings from their principals on several characteristics and abilities. While this study offered a more robust conceptualization of teacher quality, as dimensions of instruction are considered independent rather than as parallel measures of a common latent variable, the aim of their study is also to inform summative teacher evaluation policy rather than formative practice.

If teachers are to be evaluated on the basis of their TVA scores, it is incumbent upon principals or other administrators to be able to provide them with advice about how to improve those scores. In this chapter, we identify measures of instructional practices from a study of the statewide teacher evaluation system in North Carolina that are systematically associated with improvements in teachers' TVA scores and lay out a system that could be implemented elsewhere to provide teachers with empirically grounded feedback about instructional practices most likely to improve their TVA scores. We begin with a short description of the North Carolina Educator Evaluation System.

NORTH CAROLINA'S TEACHER EVALUATION SYSTEM

The North Carolina Educator Evaluation System (NCEES) relies on six standards (Public Schools of North Carolina, 2013) for evaluating teachers. Five of the standards are rated by the teacher's principal relying on their classroom observations and other evidence: (1) teachers demonstrate leadership, (2) teachers establish a respectful environment for a diverse population of students, (3) teachers know the content they teach, (4) teachers facilitate learning for their students, and (5) teachers reflect on their practice. Within each of these standards, principals rate teacher performance as Not Demonstrated, Developing, Proficient, Accomplished, or Distinguished, with associated numerical values from 1 to 5. Standard 6, "teachers contributed to the academic success of students," is not assessed directly by principals but is based on the teachers' contribution to their students' achievement scores gains as estimated through a proprietary value-added model, the Educator Value-Added Assessment System (EVAAS), trademarked by the SAS Institute. In this chapter, the five principal ratings are considered to be inputs into the evaluation process and measures of teachers' practices and performance, and the EVAAS scores serve as the TVA scores and as such are both predictors (prior-year scores) and target criteria (future scores).

Other sources of data measuring teachers' classroom practices include Tripod student surveys (Ferguson, 2012) and the CLASS classroom observation instrument (Pianta & Hamre, 2009). The CLASS instrument includes ratings on 12 dimensions of instruction within three domains: Emotional Support, Instructional Support, and Classroom Organization. The Tripod survey is designed around seven alliterative abilities of effective teachers: Captivate, Confer, Consolidate, Clarify, Care, Challenge, and Control. As Schweig (2014) demonstrates, multilevel exploratory factor analysis (MEFA) is necessary to identify the empirical measurement model of student surveys. We identify five latent factors of classroom dynamics at the elementary and secondary levels. These factors, along with the principal rating standards and CLASS domains and dimensions, are listed in Table 12.1.

Concurrent correlations between measures of teachers' instructional practices or performance and TVA are also displayed in Table 12.1. These correlations are in the range of those in studies of the construct validity of value-added (Harris et al., 2014; Jacob & Lefgren, 2008). Each of the five principal ratings, as well as the composite, correlates with TVA at around 0.20, with the highest correlation observed for the standard reflecting teachers' ability to promote student learning at 0.22. Among the dimensions of teacher practice measured by student surveys, academic press (labeled "higher-order instruction" at the secondary level) and classroom management most strongly correlate with value-added, with academic press correlating at 0.31 and 0.28 at the elementary and secondary levels, respectively, and the corresponding correlations for classroom management 0.39 and 0.29. At the domain level, CLASS observation ratings of teachers' Emotional Support (0.25), Instructional Support (0.23), and Classroom Organization (0.18) are

Table 12.1. Correlations Between Teacher Effectiveness and Student Achievement

	Correlation	p-value
Principal Ratings		
Standard 1 (Leadership)	0.200	.00
Standard 2 (Classroom Environment)	0.191	.00
Standard 3 (Content Knowledge)	0.219	.00
Standard 4 (Facilitates Learning)	0.220	.00
Standard 5 (Reflection)	0.192	.00
Composite Rating	0.213	.00
Student Survey (Tripod Elementary)		
Positive Learning Atmosphere	0.173	.00
Sage on the Stage	–0.178	.07
Academic Press	0.308	.00
Collaborative Environment	0.231	.00
Classroom Management	0.394	.00
Student Survey (Tripod Secondary)		
Academic Support	0.265	.00
Higher-Order Instruction	0.277	.00
Busywork	–0.228	.00
Classroom Management	0.291	.00
Student-Led Environment	0.151	.00
Classroom Observation (CLASS)		
Domains		
Emotional Support	0.254	.03
Instructional Support	0.230	.04
Classroom Organization	0.183	.11
Dimensions		
Positive Climate	0.308	.01
Negative Climate	–0.321	.00
Teacher Sensitivity	0.112	.33
Regard for Student Perspectives	0.212	.06
Behavior Management	0.195	.09
Productivity	0.010	.93
Instructional Learning Formats	0.197	.09
Content Understanding	0.284	.01
Analysis and Problem Solving	0.156	.18
Quality Feedback	0.161	.16
Instructional Dialogue	0.134	.24
Student Engagement	0.178	.12

each positively and significantly correlated with value-added. Among the subdimensions that make up the domains, the two climate variables, Positive Climate (0.31) and Negative Climate (–0.32), demonstrate the strongest associations, followed by Content Understanding (0.28) and Regard for Student Perspectives (0.21).

While the correlations suggest construct validity, they do not in and of themselves solve the main problem with using other measures of teachers' practices and performance for developmental evaluation: providing advice about the specific practices that teachers can use to improve their TVA scores, especially for teachers whose TVA scores are low. In a recent qualitative study on the implementation of value-added in evaluation (Goldring et al., 2015), teachers, principals, and district administrators raised the issue of a lack of direction from value-added scores alone in explaining why such scores are discounted in favor of observational data in teacher development. Yet relying on observations alone does not address the problem that teachers with low TVA scores need principals and mentors to offer concrete recommendations about the behaviors and practices that are most likely to lead them to improve their TVA scores in the following year.

MEASURES ASSOCIATED WITH IMPROVING TEACHERS' VALUE-ADDED SCORES

In a prior study (Henry, Guthrie, Barrett, & Marks, 2015), we took a first step in identifying focal measures for teachers' development by associating observational measures with change in value-added scores in consecutive years. We used this approach to identify two types of focal measures for teachers' development: (1) measures of practices that are associated with year-to-year growth in TVA scores and (2) measures of practices associated with teachers' capacity to improve in following years. Both types of measures are identified using regressions that control for teachers' prior (lagged) TVA scores and thus suggest specific ways that teachers may improve their future TVA scores. The model for (1) takes the prior year's TVA scores as capturing the effect of teachers' prior practices on prior student outcomes. By controlling for this prior value when regressing current TVA scores on current measures of practice, we seek to identify those practices most associated with *gains* in TVA. This approach is meaningfully distinct from simple concurrent correlations between observed practices and value-added because whereas correlations may identify strong associations between TVA scores and practices that may be largely static or intrinsic to teachers, our model isolates practices related to teachers' change in value-added and thus can be inferred to be malleable. As shown in Table 12.2, Panel A, we find that principals' ratings of teachers' facilitation of student learning (Principal rating), students' ratings for collaborative instructional formats[1] (Tripod elementary), higher-order instruction[2] (Tripod secondary), classroom management[3] (Tripod elementary and secondary), and positive classroom climate (CLASS) are associated with growth in value-added performance—that is, higher concurrent TVA scores than would be expected on the basis of the teachers' prior TVA scores.

In this analysis, two measures from the Tripod survey, Busywork and Student-Led Environment, were negatively related to current TVA scores after controlling for prior scores. The Busywork factor is distinguished by classrooms rated as productive but nonengaging or collaborative by students, and Student-Led Environment describes classrooms that are engaging and collaborative, but neither productive nor challenging. We take

Table 12.2. Measures Associated with Improving Teachers' Value-Added Scores

	Source	β
Panel A: Effective and Ineffective Practices		
Effective Practices		
Facilitating Student Learning	Principal Ratings	0.09
Collaborative Environment	Student Survey–Elementary	0.22
Classroom Management	Student Survey–Elementary	0.17
Higher-Order Instruction	Student Survey–Secondary	0.14
Classroom Management	Student Survey–Secondary	0.12
Positive Climate	Classroom Observation	0.29
Ineffective Practices		
Busywork	Student Survey–Secondary	-0.15
Student-Led Environment	Student Survey–Secondary	-0.20
Panel B: Teachers' Capacity to Improve		
Reflection on Practice	Principal Ratings	0.02
Collaborative Environment	Student Survey–Elementary	0.17
Higher-Order Instruction	Student Survey–Secondary	0.20
Classroom Management	Student Survey–Secondary	0.18

Note. Betas represent standardized regression coefficients from models in which value-added is regressed on two lagged values of value-added and significant measures identified through backward stepwise regression by data source. For Effective and Ineffective Practices, the target criterion (DV) is value-added from the concurrent year of the observational measures. For Capacity to Improve, the target criterion (DV) is value-added from the year following the observational measure.

this result to indicate that teachers whose classrooms are marked by either of these dynamics regress from their prior years' performance as measured by value-added.

The second set of measures (Table 12.2, Panel B) again control for teachers' prior value-added but this time seek to identify practices from the previous year that signaled their capacity for the growth demonstrated in the current year. These practices, though perhaps less important from a developmental standpoint, may help teachers and principals identify growth potential and more meaningfully interpret value-added scores. For instance, a teacher at a given level of value-added performance who has a high rating on a measure associated with future improvement may reasonably believe that his or her performance will improve the following year. Principals' ratings of teachers' reflection on their practice, students' ratings of collaborative environments (Tripod elementary), higher-order instruction (Tripod secondary), and classroom management (Tripod secondary) were identified as measures of teachers' capacity to improve their TVA scores and are systematically associated with gains in future value-added scores after controlling for current TVA scores.

The measures that we have identified for improving TVA scores are associations, not causal effect estimates of the practices, though we discuss below how causality could be empirically tested as more data become available. The measures found to be correlated with value-added growth have several advantages for principals providing advice about how teachers can develop and improve their TVA. First, these practices have been found to have systematic empirical relationships with changes in the TVA scores. Second, these are measures of malleable practices that may be influenced by support and interventions. The measures found to be significant in this study represent a limited number of measures that allow principals and other administrators to focus their advice and support on specific practices. Third, because all teachers being evaluated can have these measures, teachers with lower values on one or more of these positive measures (or high values on the Busywork or Student-Led Environment measures) can be guided to improve those specific practices. Use of these measures in teachers' evaluation can expand the number of teachers for whom empirically validated measures can be included, since classroom observations, principal ratings, student surveys, and teacher surveys do not require test scores for calculating values for individual teachers. They may make the process of teacher evaluation using quantitative indictors fairer because most if not all teachers will have direct measures of their performance. They may allow us to refine and target the measurement processes to reduce the costs and burden of data collection.

FROM MULTIPLE MEASURES TO A SYSTEM OF TEACHER EVALUATION MEASURES

Based on these benefits that can accrue from the empirical identification of measures that relate to increases in teachers' TVA scores, it is reasonable to envision a system of teacher evaluation measures that allows school leaders to marshal information in ways that support teacher development. Rather than assuming that the same measures will be related to TVA scores in other states or districts, we describe a process whereby measures that are associated with higher future TVA scores than would be expected by prior TVA scores within the district or state can be identified and put to use in the teacher development process. The following steps are part of a process for using measures of teacher effectiveness to provide feedback and develop instructional quality:

1. Identify measures of intrinsically valuable practices.
2. Identify measures of practices empirically related to TVA scores by calculating correlations between measures of teacher practices from ratings, surveys, and direct observation and TVA scores at the state or district levels.
3. Identify measures of practices empirically related to improvements in TVA scores by estimating two regressions: (1) to identify practices that increase teachers' capacity using concurrent measures of practice and TVA scores to predict future TVA scores and (2) to identify practices associated with higher TVA scores than would be predicted by their prior scores at the state or district levels.
4. Group teachers into quintiles of performance at the highest level of data collection (state or district) for the three groups of measures: TVA scores (when available), measures associated with higher TVA scores and gains in TVA, and measures of intrinsically valuable practices.
5. For teachers with TVA scores, identify those in the lowest quintile(s) of their TVA scores, and for teachers without those scores, identify those in the lowest quintiles of measures associated with gains in TVA.
6. Determine the lowest scores on the practices identified in Steps 1–3 for each teacher in the lowest quintile(s) of TVA scores and for teachers without TVA scores.
7. Focus teachers in the lowest quintile(s) of practices deemed to have intrinsic importance (Step 1) to improve in these areas.

8. Focus low-value-added teachers or teachers without TVA scores on improving practices associated with increases in TVA scores in Step 3 to improve these practices.
9. Support teachers with professional development for the focal areas identified in Steps 7 and 8 with activities that may include paired mentorship with teachers identified as highest-performing in these areas of weakness or formal training.
10. Reanalyze relationships between measures periodically (Steps 2–3) to allow for changes in associations as standards, assessments, demographics, and policy contexts change.

The process as outlined above offers several potential benefits. First, it focuses teacher development efforts on both intrinsically valuable measures of teachers' practices and specific measures that are linked to improvements in TVA scores. The process is inclusive and uses the practices associated with increased TVA practices for both teachers with TVA scores and those for whom the TVA scores are not available. This procedure assumes that the practices associated with gains in TVA scores will be effective for teachers with low scores on those measures who do not have TVA scores. The process can be customized for states or districts based on the data that they choose to collect and the specific associations within their jurisdictions. It seems likely that over time, when specific practice measures are the focus of developmental activities, the variance in those measures may decrease and the associations with TVA scores may be attenuated, thus reducing the utility of continuing to focus on them. Periodically repeating the analysis with the possibility of identifying other focal variables will help avoid diminishing returns if the practices change substantially. In addition, if teachers' contributions to other student outcome measures, such as grit or motivation, become available in the future, the system could be expanded to consider those as well.

Of course, there are important assumptions and limitations of the process. One important assumption is that the associations between practice measures and TVA scores, as well as practice measures and changes in TVA scores, identify practices that, if adopted by teachers, will make them more effective. We argue that we should consider this the best working hypothesis that we have about how to help teachers improve their students' learning, and that this hypothesis fills an important gap between value-added evaluation theory and practice reported by teachers, principals, and district leaders (Goldring et al., 2015). This working hypothesis could be tested over time as states accumulate more years of data and can establish causal claims for teachers investing in practices in terms of improving their value-added scores.

CONCLUSION

In this chapter, we have identified several practices that explain or predict changes in teachers' value-added scores based on the analysis of scores and measures of teachers' behaviors and practices from North Carolina. For example, the practices that explain teacher improvement in TVA scores include principal ratings of facilitating student learning and student ratings of collaborative, challenging, and well-managed classrooms. Rather than being overwhelmed with data from multiple sources, if educational administrators are aware of and focus on a limited number of practices such as these during performance reviews with teachers, they can focus on a manageable number of areas for improvement. Further, the system we have presented, if the data are made available, will allow administrators and teachers to pinpoint practices that each teacher can improve. This could fill a need identified by teachers and principals and make the information available efficiently actionable.

We are not arguing that the only practices that teachers should focus on improving are those identified as predicting gains in their value-added scores. We recognize that some practices have intrinsic importance, for example, higher-order instruction or academic support, and should be encouraged and promoted among teachers. However, in a system where everything is a priority, nothing is a priority. In addition, it is unfair to make judgments about teachers' performance on a measure for which educational leaders cannot provide an evidence-based recommendation about how the teacher who scores low on the measure can improve. Rather than just advising a teacher to improve on measures on which she or he scores low, the system described here provides the first level of evidence-based practices by identifying practices associated with gains in a performance measure that is itself silent on how gains can be produced.

However, the specific practices identified with gains were identified through associations with increasing teachers' improving their contributions to student learning. We do not have causal estimates of the effects of implementing developmental teacher evaluation. However, the practices selected for principals and teachers—for example, using higher-order instructional practices, academic press and academic support—do explain and predict higher teacher value-added scores. This process can be embedded in an evaluation process and data shared with teachers and administrators that, if they choose to use it, provide the best supported practices that can help them improve the academic performance of their students. In light of the fact that teacher evaluation policies are being enacted with little empirical support for their efficacy, it seems prudent for educational policymakers to consider this evidence-based approach to developmental teacher evaluation. Research has begun to show that teacher evaluation can increase students' learning when it includes meaningful feedback to teachers (Taylor & Tyler, 2012). Merely reporting value-added scores to teachers and principals without explaining how it connects to their everyday practice does not constitute meaningful feedback, yet this is currently the extent to which value-added measures have been incorporated into evaluation systems.

This system could be—and, we believe, should be—rigorously empirically evaluated as an intervention. However, states and districts may wish to adopt this as an evidence-based practice that allows them to implement a teacher evaluation system that promotes teacher development rather than solely rating or ranking teachers.

NOTES

1. Items loading strongest on Collaborative Environment relate to teachers encouraging students to share thoughts and ideas, explain their thinking, and make choices.

2. Items loading strongest on Higher-Order Thinking relate to teachers pushing students to explain their answers as well as thinking and prioritizing critical reasoning over memorization.

3. Items loading strongest on Classroom Management measure the extent to which student behavior is a problem or interferes with productivity.

REFERENCES

Danielson, C. (2011). *Enhancing professional practice: A framework for teaching* (2nd ed.). Alexandria, VA: Association for Supervision and Curriculum Development.

Ferguson, R. F. (2012). Can student surveys measure teaching? *Phi Delta Kappan, 94*(3), 24–28.

Goldhaber, D., & Hansen, M. (2010). Using performance on the job to inform teacher tenure decisions. *American Economic Review, 100*(2), 250–255.

Goldring, E., Grissom, J. A., Rubin, M., Neumerski, C. M., Cannata, M., Drake, T., & Schuermann, P. (2015). Make room value added: Principals' human capital decisions and the emergence of teacher observation data. *Educational Researcher, 44*(2), 96–104.

Hanushek, E. A. (2009). Teacher deselection. In D. Goldhaber & J. Hannaway (Eds.), *Creating a new teaching profession* (pp. 165–180). Washington, DC: Urban Institute Press.

Harris, D. N., Ingle, W. K., & Rutledge, S. A. (2014). How teacher evaluation methods matter for accountability: A comparative analysis of teacher effectiveness ratings by principals and teacher value-added measures. *American Educational Research Journal*, *51*(1), 73–112.

Henry, G. T., Guthrie, J. E., Barrett, N., & Marks, J. T. (2015). Multiple measures for developmental teacher evaluation: Constructs and processes. Working paper. Nashville, TN: Vanderbilt University.

Jacob, B. A., & Lefgren, L. (2005). *Principals as agents: Subjective performance measurement in education* (NBER working paper 11463). Cambridge, MA: National Bureau of Economic Research. Retrieved from www.nber.org/papers/w11463

Jacob, B. A., & Lefgren, L. (2008). Can principals identify effective teachers? Evidence on subjective performance evaluation in education. *Journal of Labor Economics*, *26*(1), 101–136.

Kane, T. J., McCaffrey, D. F., Miller, T., & Staiger, D. O. (2013). *Have we identified effective teachers? Validating measures of effective teaching using random assignment* (MET project research paper). Seattle, WA: Bill and Melinda Gates Foundation.

Mihaly, K., McCaffrey, D. F., Staiger, D. O., & Lockwood, J. R. (2013). *A composite estimator of effective teaching* (Research Brief). Cambridge, MA: Harvard University Center for Education Policy Research.

Pianta, R. C., & Hamre, B. K. (2009). Conceptualization, measurement, and improvement of classroom processes: Standardized observation can leverage capacity. *Educational Researcher*, *38*(2), 109–119.

Public Schools of North Carolina. (2013). North Carolina Professional Teaching Standards. Downloaded from www.ncpublicschools.org/docs/effectiveness-model/ncees/standards/prof-teach-standards.pdf

Schweig, J. (2014). Cross-level measurement invariance in school and classroom environment surveys: Implications for policy and practice. *Educational Evaluation and Policy Analysis*, *36*(3), 259–280.

Taylor, E. S., & Tyler, J. H. (2012). The effect of evaluation on teacher performance. *The American Economic Review*, *102*(7), 3628–3651.

Tekwe, C. D., Carter, R. L., Ma, C.-X., Algina, J., Lucas, M. E., Roth, J., . . . Resnick, M. B. (2004). An empirical comparison of statistical models for value-added assessment of school performance. *Journal of Educational and Behavioral Statistics*, *29*(1), 11–36.

Todd, P. E., & Wolpin, K. I. (2003). On the specification and estimation of the production function for cognitive achievement. *The Economic Journal*, *113*(485), F3–F33.

Winters, M. A., & Cowen, J. M. (2013). Would a value-added system of retention improve the distribution of teacher quality? A simulation of alternative policies. *Journal of Policy Analysis and Management*, *32*(3), 634–654.

CHAPTER 13

Teacher Evaluation in Michigan

Venessa A. Keesler
Carla Howe

In this chapter, we describe the implementation of a new educator evaluation system in Michigan. Michigan applied for Race to the Top (RTTT) funds in 2009 and 2010 but did not receive them. The state then applied for and received a waiver to No Child Left Behind (NCLB). When the U.S. Department of Education offered waivers to key components of NCLB, they did so by requiring states to develop strategies to address three principles—career- and college-ready standards and assessments, differentiated accountability and supports, and educator evaluations. Our experience in Michigan highlights some of the steps taken and challenges faced by those states that are attempting to implement educator evaluations statewide without the RTTT funds to assist. It also highlights internal challenges states face—balancing federal education requirements with the role of the state in determining education policy, and figuring out how to implement federal and state mandates in a local-control state.

A note about the authors: Venessa A. Keesler is currently the deputy superintendent for accountability services at the Michigan Department of Education (MDE). She assisted with the writing of Michigan's second RTTT application and then took a full-time position as the director of evaluation, strategic research, and accountability. Carla Howe is a senior advisor at Applied Engineering Management Corporation but served as the educator evaluation consultant for MDE during much of the time frame covered by this article. We were two of the chief architects of Michigan's educator evaluation policy and approach.

RECENT HISTORY OF EDUCATOR EVALUATIONS IN MICHIGAN

In the years since NCLB was enacted in 2002, very few state assessment results have shown evidence of closing achievement gaps between defined subgroups of students (i.e., White, Black, Hispanic/Latino, Asian/Pacific Islander, Students with Disabilities, Low Income, English Language Learner), which was a main goal of the legislation. Researchers, educators, and policymakers turned their focus to teacher evaluation in the late 2000s. If NCLB's focus on status measures of student achievement wasn't enough to close the achievement gap and ensure student learning, perhaps the method by which teachers were evaluated was falling short? Studies indicated that virtually all teachers were rated satisfactory or better during annual evaluations based on classroom observations, even though student achievement varied considerably within and across districts (Weisberg, Sexton, Mulhern, & Keeling, 2009). In addition, research began to emerge indicating that a teacher's effect on students is additive and cumulative, so that if students have several highly effective teachers in a row, they will show greater gains in achievement; unfortunately, the opposite is also true. Students who experience two to three unsatisfactory teachers in a row can show serious, long-term deficits (Rivkin, Hanushek, & Kain, 2005; Sanders & Rivers, 1996).

The renewed focus on teacher evaluation at the policy level meant that difficult work was to follow: How can a teacher be determined to be effective? What does effectiveness mean? How can teacher quality be ensured?

With these questions and concerns came the impetus for new educator evaluation systems across states that relied on more than one observation per school year and an accompanying checklist—and certainly more than a status measure. Policymakers and researchers increasingly began to focus on the use of multiple measures in teacher evaluation, following the belief that a rigorous evaluation system recognizes "student achievement, acknowledges good practice, supports teacher goals, shapes performance, motivates to improve on weaknesses, and removes the rare bad teacher from the profession" (Peterson & Peterson, 2006, p. 1).

RACE TO THE TOP AND EDUCATOR EVALUATIONS IN MICHIGAN

Because RTTT required states to develop and implement educator evaluation systems that included student growth as a significant component and that required *all* educators to be evaluated, many states—Michigan included—passed laws to make applications more competitive. The original legislation passed in 2010 required that all educators be evaluated annually, and that student growth be included as a "significant" part, but did not define significant. Districts were also required to report the results of these evaluations using one of four effectiveness labels (highly effective, effective, minimally effective, ineffective) into the state's personnel database, the Registry of Educational Personnel.

The original 2010 legislation provided a lot of flexibility to districts. After this law passed, districts were to work to develop an evaluation system at the local level, and MDE played a role by gathering and providing support materials to facilitate this development at the local level. The entire landscape for educator evaluation changed, however, in July 2011, when a new version of the legislation passed. The July 2011 legislation required districts to adopt and implement new evaluation systems by September 2011 for all teachers and school administrators. Some of the main requirements of the 2011 legislation, known as HB 4627 (2011), included the following:

- Evaluate the teacher's or school administrator's job performance at least annually, with timely and constructive feedback.
- Establish clear approaches to measuring student growth and provide teachers and school administrators with relevant data on student growth.
- Evaluate a teacher's or school administrator's job performance using multiple rating categories (i.e., highly effective, effective, minimally effective, ineffective) that take into account data on student growth as a significant factor.
- Use the evaluations, at a minimum, to inform decisions regarding each of the following:
    - » The effectiveness of teachers and school administrators, ensuring that they are given ample opportunities for improvement.
    - » Promotion, retention, and development of teachers and school administrators, including providing relevant coaching, instructional support, or professional development.
    - » Whether to grant tenure or full certification, or both, to teachers and school administrators using rigorous standards and streamlined, transparent, and fair procedures.
    - » Removing ineffective tenured and untenured teachers and school administrators after they have had ample opportunities to improve, and ensuring that these decisions are made using rigorous standards and streamlined, transparent, and fair procedures.

- Use 3 years' worth of student growth and assessment data for a teacher if available. If 3 years' worth of data are not available, all available data are to be used.
- Include a midyear progress report for a teacher who is in the 1st year of a probationary period or who has received a rating of minimally effective or ineffective in the most recent year-end evaluation.
- Include observations, including a review of the teacher's lesson plan and the state standard being used in the lesson and a review of the student engagement in the lesson. A given observation does not need to cover an entire class period, but multiple observations are required unless a teacher has received the rating of effective or highly effective in his or her two most recent year-end evaluations.
- Include student growth measures "in significant part" in the first 2 years (but the July 2011 legislation gave no guidance as to what significance meant).[1]

The legislation also indicated that by the 2013–2014 school year, a statewide system would be in place that included growth measures. The growth measures were to make up 25% of a teacher's annual evaluation in 2013–2014, 40% in 2014–2015, and 50% in 2015–2016.

The checklist of requirements made light of the challenging work that would be necessary at the district level in order to have fair, reliable, and valid measures. Districts did not necessarily have personnel skilled in metrics, growth, or evaluation system development to implement this work with fidelity.

In addition to the myriad requirements listed above, a notable component was the addition of the Governor's Council for Educator Effectiveness, later to be renamed the Michigan Council for Educator Effectiveness (MCEE). This council, as named in the law, was to develop the educator evaluation system for statewide implementation beginning in 2013–2014. This council consisted of members who were appointed by the Governor (Deborah Ball, University of Michigan; Mark Reckase, Michigan State University; Nick Sheltrown, National Heritage Academies) and the House and Senate Majority Leaders (David Vensel, Principal, Jefferson High School; Jennifer Hammond, Principal, Grand Blanc High School, respectively). It is important to note that the Michigan Department of Education was represented with the only nonvoting member (Joseph Martineau, Bureau of Assessment and Accountability), to be appointed by the Superintendent of Public Instruction.

The MCEE was tasked with many responsibilities, including making recommendations no later than April 30, 2012, regarding a student growth and assessment tool that (1) was a value-added model, (2) measured growth in core areas and other areas, (3) complied with laws for students with disabilities, (4) had a pre- and posttest, and (5) could be used with students of varying ability levels.

In addition to identifying a student growth and assessment tool, the MCEE was expected to also develop a state evaluation tool for administrators that would be based on data on attendance rates, graduation rates, professional contributions, training, progress reports, school improvement plan progress, peer input, and pupil/parent feedback. They were to recommend changes for obtaining a professional teaching certification, and a process for evaluating and approving local educator evaluation tools. By April 30, 2012, the MCEE produced an interim progress report that concluded that a pilot study was imperative and that rushing to develop a system "would be reckless, both fiscally, and technically." The pilot study was to be conducted during the 2012–2013 school year in 12 school districts. Teacher observation tools and administrator evaluation tools would be piloted in order to provide information on validity, and to gather feedback from principals and teachers. The council would also pilot a student growth model, including a value-added model.

The MCEE released its final report in July 2013. This report was a comprehensive document, addressing everything from student assessment and growth data to observation models to how to combine components into a final evaluation rating. It also included recommendations regarding a system for obtaining a waiver from the state system. It can be found at www.mcede.org.

During the next stage of the process, the state legislature took up consideration of the MCEE's recommendations and explored options for funding them. This began 2 years of negotiations, bill-drafting, budget-making, discussions, testimony, presentations, advocacy, and lobbying by many key players in Michigan's education system: the governor, the legislature, the State Board of Education, the Michigan Department of Education, all of the various stakeholder groups (principals, superintendents, state teachers' unions), academic researchers, and various for-profit companies. Note that Michigan's NCLB waiver required it to have an evaluation system in place that used state assessment data.

The MCEE report was used as the starting point to form both possible legislation and a budget strategy. One challenge is that implementing the system recommended by the MCEE in total would have been costly in terms of both state and local spending. The other is that it recommended a complicated system that led many legislative debates to become bogged down in details.

VALUE-ADDED MODELS IN A STATEWIDE POLICY CONTEXT

With Michigan's 2011 version of the law, a relatively obscure research methodology, the value-added model, suddenly was thrust into the spotlight at a statewide level. In Michigan, the new law mandated student growth data that "was a value added model" for all teachers of all subjects and grades, including an alternate assessment. This was a quantum leap from the way VAMs had previously been used—primarily in research settings, except in a few states like Tennessee that had been producing value-added models for teachers for a number of years.

For the authors (and our colleagues around the country), who have experience in both the research and the state agency worlds, this was a potentially troubling development. VAMs work very well when complete testing data are available on a student, when there are enough students per teacher, and when data on demographic variables are available. This is rarely the reality in a statewide testing context. Students have varied assessment histories—some have been included in state testing their whole lives; others have moved in and out; others have bounced between general, modified, and alternate assessments; others have been living here but have not been tested for a variety of reasons. Demographic data are imperfect in even the cleanest state administrative data systems. And perhaps most significantly, many states (Michigan included) only test in a limited number of subjects: reading, mathematics, science, and social studies. In addition, state testing in science and social studies typically occurs only once per grade span, not once per grade (i.e., one test in elementary school, one in middle school, and one in high school).

Additionally, VAMs suffer from the fact that they are a relatively complex statistical tool and very unfamiliar and intimidating to the general public—and moreover, to the teachers to whom that growth is meant to be attributed.

Beyond these technical challenges, there are issues and concerns with incorporating measures of growth and achievement into an evaluation, even if those scores are linked to individual students through roster verification. One of the main challenges of utilizing a growth score or a value-added score within an evaluation is that students are not randomly assigned to teachers (Rothstein, 2009). This challenge leads directly to the next challenge: Often with any of these models, there is a leap to causal inference (Betebenner, 2009) where none can truly be made due to the lack of randomization.

Finally, value-added models are very complex and can require proprietary software like that developed by SAS for states such as Tennessee and North Carolina. Betebenner (2009) contends that value-added measures can be problematic because they do not truly give educators what they are most interested in (i.e., information about the growth of individual students), but rather an estimate of the value a teacher added to the students that he or she instructed.

EDUCATOR EVALUATIONS CURRENTLY IN USE IN MICHIGAN

The MCEE's recommendations largely were not implemented. MDE was able to get a small modification to the bill stating that districts are required to use state-provided student assessment data where available (to meet U.S. Department of Education's requirements for Elementary and Secondary Education Act [ESEA] Flexibility), but the statute is very similar to the 2011 law. The key things that Michigan's current law requires include the following:

1. Annual evaluations for teachers and administrators.
2. Clear approaches to measuring student growth and providing relevant data to teachers and administrators.
3. Use of multiple rating categories that take growth as a significant factor, and that use state assessment data beginning in 2014–2015 where available. As an interesting side note, 2014–2015 is also a year of transition for Michigan with regard to student assessment as we switch from our former MEAP assessment to our new M-STEP assessment, due to the full implementation of the Common Core State Standards in Michigan and the need to accurately assess those standards. Therefore, state-provided measures of growth will not be available for 2014–2015, as 2 years of data from a stable assessment system are needed to provide valid growth measures to districts.
4. Fifty percent (50%) of the evaluation will be based on student growth and assessment data beginning in 2015–2016, but the legislature did not enact legislation requiring the use of a specific student growth and assessment tool after reviewing recommendations contained in the MCEE report. In the interim, we are advising districts to use state assessment data where available, local assessment data, and student learning objective data to produce growth data for evaluation.
5. Classroom observations that include a review of the lesson plan and the state standard being used, but they do not have to be for the full class period.
6. Performance evaluations for administrators.

Note that the MCEE recommended four observation tools and that these are now in use in many districts, but again, the legislature has not enacted legislation requiring the use of a specific observation tool. In the meantime, districts are encouraged to use one of the four observation tools recommended by the MCEE. But in the absence of legislation, it is not clear which observation tools may ultimately be required, if any. This also creates a challenging situation for MDE, as we struggle to develop systematic supports when we do not have the authority to say which observation tools can and cannot be used, nor any knowledge about which ones may be required in the future.

SUPPORTING DISTRICTS IN THE MIDST OF UNCERTAINTY: MDE'S RESPONSE

When the U.S. Department of Education, under Arne Duncan's leadership, made the decision to include the requirement for educator evaluations in Race to the Top and ESEA Flexibility, it had both positive and negative consequences. On the positive side, there is now wide-scale implementation of educator evaluations in many states. States are using assessment data in these evaluations, they are requiring observations, and more teachers are being evaluated than ever before. However, the rapid escalation of this policy has led to it being much more of a compliance exercise (i.e., something states must do to receive ESEA Flexibility approval or RTTT dollars) rather than what educator evaluations should be: realistic, embedded, high-quality evaluations that lead to individualized improvement plans.

In our opinion, it is not possible to implement educator evaluations for every teacher in a state within a period of 2 to 3 years and have them be uniformly meaningful. To give some sense of the scale, Michigan has nearly 100,000 teachers and an additional 25,000 administrators, spread across nearly 900 districts and 3,400 schools. Complicating matters even further is the fact that evaluation science is still evolving; researchers are still producing information on how and when to use VAMs.

In Michigan, we have consistently evaluated *every* teacher and administrator in *every* district and school in Michigan for the last 3 years (2011–2012 through 2013–2014). This is a dramatic step forward, given that previously evaluation mostly focused on new teachers or on those who were known to have performance issues. At the same time, there is little to no consistency in evaluation systems across districts, and the MDE currently lacks sufficient authority to strongly enforce a consistent system. So what can a state agency do in this context?

From the state agency perspective, our key goal is to figure out how to support our districts in developing and implementing local evaluation systems that are fair, unbiased, and high-quality, and that result in improved instructional practice as well as improved leadership. We have several challenges, including a lack of coherence among state policies and a lack of staff and resources at MDE. In the midst of this, we have done the following:

- Created and provided technical assistance with regard to aspects of the law; on observation systems recommended by the MCEE; and on using state-provided assessment data.
- Created guidance with regard to using student learning objectives; we know that the state assessment system will never produce enough state data to provide meaningful information for every teacher in every grade and school subject. There is, in our opinion, an open debate on whether a state assessment system should even try, given the costs associated with statewide testing and the difficulty in conceptualizing standardized tests in physical education or the arts. Regardless, even if it were possible and desirable, we are not currently funded to develop this sort of system. Local districts need support in understanding how to help educators set and measure student learning objectives, and how that process provides the student growth data that they need for their evaluations.
- Kept professional development as a central feature of the conversation; the point of educator evaluations is to improve instructional practice. Therefore, every evaluation should lead to specific and targeted supports for teachers and administrators in the form of ongoing, job-embedded professional learning. MDE supports this through professional learning standards, as well as through advocating for professional learning supports in any educator evaluation bill.
- Continue to develop and implement interim assessments that provide pre- and posttest data in an online environment for use in evaluations.

The MDE is also developing proposed legislation that focuses on the most important components of an evaluation system. These include observations, student learning objectives, and more realistic timelines for the level and inclusion of state-provided student growth.

The needed legislation should specify the number of observations, and also specify the training required of personnel conducting observations.

To improve practice and focus on instruction, teachers need actual information—gathered in a fair and unbiased manner—on their pedagogy and practice. Observers need to know what they are observing, and they need adequate support to carry out observations.

Student learning objectives (SLOs) are widely used in evaluating student growth in nontested grades and subject areas. SLOs provide a method for instructionally relevant goal-setting and evaluation of growth. SLOs are also growth data that teachers can understand and see, in a time frame that matters for their practice. By the time the state returns growth data to schools and teachers, those students are gone from the school. State growth data provide an objective benchmark, but it is not data that will change practice in a real-time manner. Therefore, MDE believes that SLOs should be required in the legislation, along with training for principals and teachers to ensure high-quality implementation. For many states, basing 50% of the evaluation on student growth data was a key component of legislative requirements, including in Michigan. However, after 4 years of implementation, we caution restraint on this. The state-provided assessment measures are simply not ready yet. A state needs to administer an assessment for at least 2 years (preferably more) to get data that meet the face validity test. Moreover, developing, piloting, field-testing, and implementing new assessments is challenging. Add to that the contentious environment around the Common Core State Standards, Next Generation Science Standards, and consortia-based assessments like Smarter Balanced and PARCC, and the result is an extremely unstable and challenging environment in which standards are shifting, new assessments are being created and brought online, and practitioners in the field—those who will be evaluated by those assessments—are confused and uncertain how to proceed.

In the midst of this confusion is a deep distrust of assessment data, fear over how they will be used, and administrators who do not fully understand how to use them. Layer on the technical challenges associated with VAMs, and this creates a situation where requiring a certain percentage of student growth data to come from state assessments is inadvisable at best, and destructive at its worst. The MDE believes we should still require local districts to use state assessment data where available. But we should avoid specifying exact percentages and usage for another 3 to 5 years while the assessment systems come fully online, teachers and principals adapt to the new standards and assessments, and technical roster systems can be created to ensure appropriate attribution of scores.

Debates around educator evaluations sometimes fail to recognize that teaching is a craft and that we need an army of teachers to do this work. Again, in Michigan, there are nearly 100,000 teachers. All of them need realistic evaluations and meaningful feedback that leads to appropriate and targeted professional development. Conducting educator evaluations without requiring and supporting an appropriate and high-quality professional development system becomes merely an exercise in pushing data between local districts and the state.

ROLE OF RESEARCH IN RECENT CHANGES

Education research has been a motivating force in much of this work at the state and federal levels. Research findings on the importance of teachers to student learning and on the fact that much of the variance in student learning is at the teacher level, not the school level, quantified what many of us knew anecdotally—teachers matter, and they matter a great deal. The research community also brought us the use of value-added models; by using them in research studies, and being able to show policymakers how they help diagnose student learning and attribute it to teachers, policymakers became interested in them as a tool to bring a level of quantitative rigor to evaluation systems. Certainly U.S. Department of Education policy on the use of student growth was influenced by research as well. By the same token, research has helped move policymakers *away* from value-added modeling. For example, researchers often dealt with missing data through listwise deletion, imputation, or other established practices that translate poorly to policy and high-stakes large-scale implementation. It is hard to explain to teachers that when complete data were not available on all their students, the VAM simply imputed it. So as these tools of the research trade were mandated to become part of statewide policy and accountability, the challenges of using them in that manner were highlighted—often by the research community! In Michigan, we have been struggling to get a stable, legislated, agreed-upon system, which could then be studied to determine its effectiveness. In the interim, we have formed some general partnerships to support this policy.

The other challenge is the level and type of data collected by the state. Many research partners are interested in observation data, or the scores for each component of the final evaluation, but at the state level, we only collect the final evaluation rating for each teacher. It is not even clear to MDE that there is a specific benefit to collecting all of that finer-grained data and storing it at the state level. This becomes a data-collection mandate that is time-consuming and costly to locals and to the state. A preferred solution would be to strategically partner with researchers to study representative samples of the evaluations.

MDE (and states around the nation) have drawn heavily on the research of the Measures of Effective Teaching project, funded by the Gates Foundation, as well as the body of evidence on student learning objectives. But the question that policymakers ask with regard to any policy is, "What works?" So for MDE, we need to know what is considered best practice in terms of the components of an evaluation (i.e., growth data, observation data, professional practice), and then we need to know how it is working in Michigan. More importantly, we need to know how evaluation results are being used to inform improvement in educators—what is changing about instruction or leadership because of these evaluations? Are we able to remediate and support teachers more specifically?

We also need to know where the evaluation system is working in Michigan and where it is not. What is the fidelity of implementation around the evaluation system? What is the rigor of the results? What specific steps are districts taking after the evaluation to use the results to drive change? We are not yet producing state-provided growth or value-added scores, but when we do, there will be a body of evidence we need around that—do these scores align with practice in the classroom? With the observation findings?

One overriding question for states is whether an "effective" label actually means that a teacher is effective. And how is implementation supporting a uniform definition?

VALIDITY OF USE

When teachers' evaluation results are used for multiple decisions, from tenure, to merit pay, to placement, to retention (Gallagher, 2012), all of which are high-stakes for the teacher (Danielson, 2008), ensuring the validity of the system is necessary. In addition to the many high-stakes decisions that might be made based on evaluation results, there is a growth component or purpose in the results of the evaluation as well—that is, to determine targeted professional development for teachers in areas of demonstrated weakness or needed growth. As Danielson (2008) noted, teaching is difficult and never perfect, making the need for an evaluation system that promotes professional growth necessary to promote change in teachers' practices.

Ensuring that the instrument used to quantify teachers' effectiveness is valid based on their many practices is critical for all stakeholders with a vested interest in the education of students. From policymakers to principals, understanding the validity of the instrument by which teachers are being evaluated will assist in making informed decisions that impact educators and students (Howe, 2014). A valid instrument allows stakeholders to trust the results rendered from the instrument to support educators in improving instruction, attending specialized professional development, and ultimately increasing student achievement.

NOTE

1. In the first year of implementation, statewide survey results indicated that 59% of districts interpreted "significant" to mean somewhere between 11% and 40%.

REFERENCES

Betebenner, D. (2009). Norm- and criterion-referenced student growth. *Educational Measurement: Issues and Practice, 28,* 42–51.

Danielson, C. (2008). *The handbook for enhancing professional practice: Using the framework for teaching in your school.* Alexandria, VA: Association for Supervision and Curriculum Development.

Gallagher, C. (2012). *Presenting findings from measures of teacher effectiveness: Key reporting considerations for states and districts.* San Francisco, CA: WestEd.

House Bill 4627 of 2011, 96th Michigan State Legislature, Regular Session. (2011).

Howe, C. (2014). *Validity of the educator evaluation instrument in the state of West Virginia* (Unpublished doctoral dissertation). Wayne State University, Detroit, MI. Retrieved from digitalcommons.wayne.edu/oa_dissertations/987

Peterson, K. D., & Peterson, C. A. (2006). *Effective teacher evaluation: A guide for principals.* Thousand Oaks, CA: Corwin Press.

Rivkin, S. G., Hanushek, E. A., & Kain. J. F. (2005). Teachers, schools, and academic achievement. *Econometrica 73*(2), 417–458.

Rothstein, J. (2009). Student sorting and bias in value-added estimation: Selection on observables and unobservables. *Education Finance and Policy, 4*(4), 537–571.

Sanders, W. L., & Rivers, J. C. (1996). *Cumulative and residual effects of teachers on future student academic achievement.* Knoxville, TN: University of Tennessee Value-Added Research and Assessment Center.

Weisberg, D., Sexton, S., Mulhern, J., & Keeling, D. (2009). *The widget effect: Our national failure to acknowledge and act on differences in teacher effectiveness.* New York, NY: The New Teacher Project. Retrieved from www2.ed.gov/nclb/methods/teachers/hqtflexibility.html

CHAPTER 14

Multiple Measures in Teacher Evaluation

Lessons Learned and Guidelines for Practice

Peter Youngs
Jason A. Grissom

In an example of rapid policy diffusion, most states and many school districts have implemented evaluation systems incorporating multiple measures of teacher performance in recent years, particularly since the introduction of Race to the Top. These measures include classroom observation instruments, teacher value-added models (VAMs), student surveys, and teacher portfolios. Along with this increased policy focus on holding teachers accountable for their performance, questions have been raised about whether these measures are being used to support teacher development, their psychometric properties, and challenges teachers and administrators face in enacting them. In this concluding chapter, we first discuss ways in which new approaches to teacher evaluation can promote teacher growth and/or inform human capital decisions. We then draw on the chapters featured in this volume as well as other recent scholarship to examine evidence related to the reliability and validity of these new evaluation approaches and to identify guidelines for their use at district, school, and preparation program levels. We conclude by addressing issues that states and districts must consider in implementing multiple measures of performance in teacher evaluation.

USES OF TEACHER EVALUATION MEASURES

Several chapters in this volume and other recent research specify two main purposes of teacher evaluation: helping teachers improve their instruction and informing human capital decisions in schools and districts (Kennedy, 2010; Papay, 2012). In terms of developing teachers, classroom observation instruments, student surveys, and teacher portfolios can all potentially promote constructive changes in instruction when they are based on empirical evidence regarding effective teaching and when they help teachers identify areas in need of improvement. For example, Pianta and Hamre (this volume) provide empirical support for the three domains of the Classroom Assessment Scoring System (CLASS)—emotional support, classroom organization, and instructional support—by demonstrating relationships between teachers' CLASS observation ratings and their students' test score growth (see also Bill and Melinda Gates Foundation, 2012). There is also evidence that teachers' ratings on content-specific observation tools, such as the Protocol for Language Arts Observations (PLATO) and the Mathematical Quality of Instruction (MQI) instrument, are associated with student achievement gains (Grossman, Loeb, Cohen, & Wyckoff, 2013; Hill, Kapitula, & Umland, 2011). Similar to CLASS, PLATO and the MQI focus on specific domains and thus can help teachers determine areas of their practice that need to be strengthened.

Much like the observation instruments discussed above, student surveys, such as the Survey of Teacher Practice (STeP) and the Tripod student survey, can be used to provide feedback to teachers in areas such as academic press, learning environment, and classroom management. A growing number of studies have reported correlations between teachers' ratings on STeP and Tripod and their VAM scores in mathematics and reading (e.g., Balch, this volume; Bill and Melinda Gates Foundation, 2010; Henry & Guthrie, this volume). In addition, teacher portfolios, such as edTPA and the National Board for Professional Teaching Standards (NBPTS) assessments, are based in part on research on associations between student learning and teachers' use of formative student assessment, their provision of feedback to students, and their knowledge of content-specific pedagogy (Black & Wiliam, 1998; Hattie & Timperley, 2007; Hill, Rowan, & Ball, 2005; Youngs & Whittaker, this volume). The use of such portfolios can help teachers determine which aspects of their planning, instruction, and assessment practices are in need of improvement.

Along with their potential to support teacher development, teacher evaluation measures can also be used to inform human capital decisions in schools and districts. In particular, data from teacher VAMs, classroom observation instruments, and student surveys can be used to make distinctions among teachers with regard to their performance. Goldhaber (2015) argues that teacher VAMs can thus potentially affect workforce quality by altering the supply of potential candidates as well as those who are actually selected to teach; increasing the effectiveness of practicing teachers; and influencing decisions related to retention, tenure, and promotion. Similarly, Odden (2011) explicates ways that classroom observation instruments and teacher portfolios can be used in making decisions related to teacher promotion, compensation, and dismissal. In addition, policy discussion around the 2014 California state court ruling in *Vergara v. California* has placed renewed emphasis on the role of teacher evaluation data in making human capital decisions. In this ruling, California's laws with regard to awarding tenure after 18 months of teaching and the role of seniority in making teacher personnel decisions were deemed unconstitutional.

However, for data from new teacher evaluation measures to be useful in informing decisions concerning teacher advancement, pay, and dismissal, two conditions must be met. First, it is necessary to establish evidence of their reliability and validity with regard to these particular uses. Second, it is necessary for teachers and administrators to feel confident that these new measures provide accurate, stable ratings of teacher performance. The next four sections describe research on the psychometric properties of new evaluation approaches and provide guidelines for their use by district administrators and principals.

VALUE-ADDED MODELS

Reliability and Validity

Despite their widespread use for differentiating teacher performance and informing personnel decisions, VAMs are imperfect measures of teacher contributions to student achievement because they are potentially both biased and unreliable. For example, nonrandom assignment of students to teachers presents an important threat to their accuracy (Cohen & Goldhaber, this volume). If some teachers are consistently assigned to students who are easier or harder to teach, bias could arise even after adjustments are made for observable student characteristics that can affect achievement, such as prior achievement, socioeconomic status, and English language proficiency. The degree of bias in value-added scores due to nonrandom student assignment is an unsettled issue among researchers (see, e.g., Chetty, Friedman, & Rockoff, 2014; Corcoran & Goldhaber, 2013; Goldhaber & Chaplin, 2015; Kane, McCaffrey, Miller, & Staiger, 2013; Rothstein, 2010).

Another issue concerning VAMs is that estimated teacher effects on student achievement often vary from one school year to the next (Cohen

& Goldhaber, this volume). Several empirical studies have reported intertemporal correlations in the range of .2 to .5 (Aaronson, Barrow, & Sander, 2007; Goldhaber & Hansen, 2013; McCaffrey, Sass, Lockwood, & Mihaly, 2009), variation that is similar to that observed for output-based measures of performance in other professions characterized by complex labor (Brookings Brown Center Task Group on Teacher Quality, 2010). The magnitude of the sampling error (i.e., the error associated with the assignment of students to teachers) decreases as the number of students and/or classes informing the VAM measure increases, suggesting that calculating VAM scores over a longer time horizon can improve them (Goldhaber & Hansen, 2013; McCaffrey et al., 2009). Still, low-to-moderate reliabilities mean that many teachers identified by VAMs as relatively high-performing in one year will be identified as relatively low-performing the next year for reasons related to the statistical properties of the measure rather than variation in underlying performance (Corcoran, this volume).

A third issue involving VAMs is the extent to which principals find teacher VAM data to be useful. In a study of several urban districts, Goldring and colleagues (2015) reported that principals identified several concerns with regard to using VAMs in teacher evaluation and focused much more on classroom observation data than VAMs in making high-stakes decisions concerning teachers in their schools. Principals discounted value-added information because of issues concerning its transparency, lack of specificity, and the long time lag before scores were returned to them. In a different study that utilized data from Miami-Dade County Public Schools, Grissom, Loeb, and Doss (this volume) examined whether teachers' VAM scores were associated with principals' decisions with regard to retaining teachers. The authors found that principals placed high priority on several teacher performance dimensions that were not correlated with teachers' value-added estimates; these included motivating students to learn, helping them develop strong interpersonal skills, and building relationships with parents/community (Grissom et al., this volume).

Challenges

Inconsistent signals from VAM scores regarding teacher performance over time can undermine teachers' confidence in the evaluation process and the information it provides and, as a result, the potential for teacher evaluation to motivate teachers to improve their practice. Instability and bias in VAM scores can also weaken their usefulness for principals and district administrators seeking to use them for human capital decisions. In most states and districts, it is possible to generate individual VAM scores for fewer than 30% of teachers because many subjects are not part of state testing programs and some subjects are only tested in a few grades. In response, many states and districts include schoolwide or grade-level VAM scores in reading and/or mathematics in the overall evaluation of teachers in nontested subjects and grades. Such implementation choices likely further undercut teachers' confidence in evaluation outcomes because they necessarily make some teachers' evaluation scores a function in part of the performance of students they did not teach in the subject tested, if at all.

Other implementation choices can have similar undermining effects. For example, some districts and states have required school leaders to equate (or approximate) teachers' observation ratings with their VAM scores. That is, raters are expected to give low observation scores to teachers with low VAM scores, presumably under the implicit assumption that VAM scores measure "true" teacher performance and thus a high observation score for teachers whose VAM scores are low is necessarily incorrect. These sorts of requirements seem misguided, however, given that these instruments are designed to measure different aspects of teacher performance and that both are likely to be imperfect measures of those underlying facets (Cohen & Goldhaber, this volume; Grissom et al., this volume).

There may be particular measurement challenges for some categories of teachers. For example, Jones (this volume) discusses several challenges that districts are likely to encounter in using VAMs with special education teachers. First, there may be questions about their reliability in light of the degree to which special educators' responsibilities can differ across schools. Second, some students with disabilities (SWDs) may perform very poorly on state assessments and/or need extensive accommodations that can threaten the validity of their scores. Third, a given special educator's VAM score is likely to be unstable due to having small numbers of students and/or coordinating their instruction with general educators. Policymakers generally have not been attuned to these issues, resulting in reduced accuracy of value-added measures for this important group of teachers and an increase in the likelihood that they are unfairly disadvantaged in their evaluations.

Guidelines for Practice

Districts can potentially address issues related to bias and reliability with regard to VAMs by ensuring that students are more equitably (or even randomly) assigned to teachers and by using at least 2 years of VAM data in calculating a teacher's evaluation rating. Principals should not be required to equate teachers' observation ratings with their VAM scores, and given both the potentially limited information provided by VAM scores and the importance that school leaders place on teachers' outside-class behavior, it is necessary to supplement VAM information with other measures of performance. Moreover, it is important to distinguish between the use of VAMs in making personnel decisions and their use for research/diagnosis at the district level; despite potential issues related to bias and reliability, VAM data in the aggregate can be useful to districts in identifying needs at particular schools and making resource allocation decisions.

CLASSROOM OBSERVATION INSTRUMENTS

Reliability and Validity

As Cohen and Goldhaber (this volume) note, classroom observation instruments confront a potential source of error—the observer—that is not applicable when teacher VAMs are calculated, and generalizability studies indicate that observers are the greatest source of error when using observation tools (Ho & Kane, 2013; Mashburn, Downer, Rivers, Brackett, & Martinez, 2014). To reduce observer effects, it is necessary to demonstrate that a given observation instrument has met a high standard of reliability (Cohen & Goldhaber, this volume; Pianta & Hamre, this volume). High reliability is a function of the processes used to select and train observers as well as how demanding it is for them to assess various aspects of instruction. These demands vary. For example, it is often straightforward to rate whether a teacher communicates the objectives of a lesson or the degree of student misbehavior during a lesson. In contrast, it may be more challenging to assess teachers' responses to students' interpretations of texts or the quality of the connections they make between mathematics content and students' cultural experiences.

Another source of error involves whether observations of the same teacher are likely to be stable over time (Cohen & Goldhaber, this volume; Pianta & Hamre, this volume). If the ratings of a given teacher vary substantially across observations, they are unlikely to represent fundamental aspects of their instruction, and they can undermine observers' and participants' confidence in the evaluation system. Alternatively, when ratings are at least fairly consistent from one observation cycle to the next, they are more likely to represent core teaching skills and serve as a catalyst for teachers and principals to focus on instructional improvement (Pianta & Hamre, this volume). Drawing on data from the Measures of Effective Teaching (MET) project, Polikoff (2015) reports year-to-year correlations from .45 to .55 for three of the four observation instruments featured in the study (the fourth had significantly lower stability). While these correlations are generally greater than those for VAMs, they are still lower than what may be necessary for use in high-stakes personnel decisions (Cohen & Goldhaber, this volume).

A classroom observation instrument may over- or underestimate a teacher's actual level of instructional quality for several reasons (Cohen & Goldhaber, this volume). For example, it is unclear from research how teachers' ratings are affected by the timing of observations (e.g., across the school day, across the school year) or whether the observations are associated with high or low stakes. It is unknown if student characteristics such as academic ability, special needs, or English language learner status can make it easier or harder for a teacher to engage in the instructional practices measured by a given instrument. It is uncertain whether some curricula may facilitate or limit use of practices valued by a particular observation tool. In addition, it is unknown how well generic observation instruments, such as CLASS and the Framework for Teaching (FFT), reveal detailed information about teachers' enactment of content-specific pedagogy (Youngs & Whittaker, this volume).

Challenges

Race to the Top and No Child Left Behind waivers have led many districts to scale up their use of classroom observation instruments in short periods of time, which can pose difficulties in terms of identifying observers, training and calibrating them, and ensuring high implementation standards (Pianta & Hamre, this volume). In their study of several Connecticut districts, Donaldson and Cobb (this volume) identified challenges that principals, district administrators, and teachers faced in enacting observation processes. They reported that it was difficult for principals to complete six observations of each teacher and each instructional specialist in their schools on annual basis; this was particularly onerous in high-poverty schools. In addition, many school leaders struggled to apply the observation rubric to specialists who worked with individual students and/or outside of classrooms. Further, the authors found a wide variation in the quality and frequency of postobservation conferences and that classroom observations only infrequently led to meaningful professional learning opportunities for teachers.

Jones (this volume) delineates three key aspects of special educators' professional responsibilities that have important implications for classroom observations. First, in special education, instruction is typically planned for and provided to individual students. Second, learning objectives in special education are often unique and distinct from those in general education. Third, special educators' instructional practices and work roles often differ from those of general educators. In terms of classroom observation instruments, there have been few empirical studies of the utility of tools such as CLASS or PLATO for special educators. Similar kinds of considerations may well apply for other teachers not teaching in traditional classrooms.

Guidelines for Practice

To address potential bias associated with classroom observers, it is necessary to use a well-designed system for training observers, recalibrating them over time, and ensuring that two independent observers would assign the same ratings to the same lessons and quality of practice (Cohen & Goldhaber, this volume; Pianta & Hamre, this volume). Some school districts are implementing systems in which teachers are observed by different kinds of raters (e.g., principal, specially trained peer) throughout the year to help guard against an individual rater's potential biases and to allow the district to compare patterns across raters to diagnose when an individual rater may need to be retrained or recalibrated (Goldring et al., 2014). More simply, Pianta and Hamre (this volume) argue that it is also important to standardize rules and procedures regarding the qualifications of observers, the number and length of observations, and when during the school day they should occur. Given the demands on principals' time, it may be necessary to require more classroom observations (e.g., three to five per year) of early-career teachers and low-performing teachers than of experienced teachers who are performing well. Finally, districts may need to supplement generic observation instruments with content-specific ones, such as PLATO, MQI, and instruments designed for use with special educators, in order to support teachers' development of content-specific instructional practices (Youngs & Whittaker, this volume).

STUDENT SURVEYS

Reliability and Validity

Compared to teacher VAMs and classroom observation instruments, there has been much less research on the psychometric properties of student surveys. Balch (this volume) presents a validation framework for the development of student surveys and then describes validity evidence for the Survey of Teacher Practice (STeP). This evidence is promising. In particular, pilot data from almost 13,000 middle and high school students in seven Georgia districts show that teachers' STeP scores were highly correlated with their students' reports of academic engagement and self-efficacy, and surveys showed some correlation with VAM scores. Combined with strong face validity of survey items, these results suggest that student surveys can provide useful measures of teacher practices as experienced by their direct recipients.

Other student survey tools have shown evidence of similarly positive properties. For example, the MET study reported that the reliability of the Tripod student survey data for middle school teachers—calculated in this instance as the correlation across different sections of the same class taught by the same teacher—was quite high (in the range of .80 and above). The MET study also reported stable ratings for individual teachers when the Tripod surveys were administered on two occasions during the same school year (i.e., in December and March); these correlations ranged from .70 to .85 for elementary and middle school teachers when correcting for measurement error (Bill and Melinda Gates Foundation, 2010). Year-to-year stability of Tripod scores in the MET study was similar to the stability of teacher observations (Polikoff, 2015).

Challenges

A primary challenge associated with student surveys to measure teacher performance is that what we know about their properties comes from just a few studies. It will be important to consider issues of reliability and bias when STeP, Tripod, and other student surveys are implemented more widely with elementary and secondary students. Similar to classroom observations, it is unclear if student characteristics, certain curricula, and/or the timing of student surveys are likely to affect students' ratings of their teachers. Districts that scale up their use of student surveys over short periods of time may face challenges with regard to administering them in uniform ways and providing useful feedback to teachers and principals. In addition, there are questions about how or whether surveys should be administered to young children (e.g., children in grades K–2) and to students with disabilities. Teacher buy-in to the validity and usefulness of student surveys is also an ongoing threat to their implementation and potential to affect practice.

Guidelines for Practice

In considering the use of student surveys as part of evaluating teachers, districts need to ensure that evidence has been established regarding their reliability and validity, which typically is only available for established survey providers. Working with teachers to adapt established student surveys to the local context can be useful for generating teacher buy-in (Balch, this volume). Districts also need to develop uniform procedures for administering student surveys to most groups of students while possibly modifying these procedures for early elementary students and SWDs. Districts or survey providers might also implement cleaning procedures that identify mischievous responders (Balch, this volume). Finally, districts need to collect data over time to assess whether students' ratings of their teachers seem to be affected by the timing of the surveys, particular curricula, or student characteristics so that they can make appropriate adjustments to procedures or scores.

OTHER MEASURES

The discussion of reliability, validity, and challenges to implementation thus far is not meant to be exhaustive, and these issues no doubt apply to other measures of teacher effectiveness as well, though we have even less research upon which to draw. Take edTPA, for example, the subject of the Youngs and Whittaker chapter in this volume. Nearly all of what we know about its reliability and validity comes from a 2012–2013 field test (Pecheone, Shear, Whittaker, & Darling-Hammond, 2013), though the findings there generally support the soundness of the instrument's properties. It is yet unclear whether candidates' scores on edTPA predict their ratings on observation instruments or their impact on student achievement as 1st- and 2nd-year teachers (Youngs & Whittaker, this volume). As use of edTPA for hiring and supporting novice teachers grows, it will be important for researchers to continue to evaluate it and for policymakers and school districts to make implementation and interpretation adjustments in response. Similar guidelines could be stated for other new teacher performance instruments that are likely to come online as states and districts continue to invest in multiple-measures-based systems.

IMPLEMENTING MULTIPLE-MEASURES SYSTEMS

Teachers' work is complex. They are not only responsible for teaching rigorous academic content in ways that promote learning and engagement among diverse learners; they must also support students' social and affective development and manage students' behavior. In addition, teachers must plan units and lessons, often in more than one subject, and they need to formatively and summatively assess student learning. Further, they are responsible for developing relationships with parents and contributing to school operations. The measures of teacher performance featured in this book all address key aspects of teachers' work, but any single measure is inherently limited, making it necessary for school districts to use multiple measures in evaluating and providing feedback to teachers.

But how should these measures be used together? State and district policymakers want to combine metrics to produce a summative measure of a teacher's performance. For summative evaluation, they need to know how much weight should be afforded different components—should value added be worth 35%? Fifty percent? Fifteen?—and how they can be summed together to produce a "true" measure of a teacher's job performance. These questions are not statistical ones but are instead based on policy and political calculations and professional judgments. Researchers certainly can provide some guidance and can assess the trade-offs of some decisions over others, but how much of a teacher's evaluation score should come from classroom observations relative to student test score growth or student surveys are as much questions about what the designers of the evaluation system value as they are about statistics and measurement.

As a general rule, however, in combining measures, designers of evaluation systems should aim to give higher weight to measures with good reliability and validity properties and lower weight to measures whose properties are more suspect. Long-run value-added scores for an experienced teacher who has taught many groups of students in a tested subject may provide a useful signal about that teacher's effects on student achievement. In contrast, the school's overall value-added, calculated from the potentially small set of subjects or grade levels administering standardized end-of-year tests, is ill-suited to the job of capturing the performance of a teacher of an untested subject. In the former case, devoting a significant share of a teacher's evaluation to value-added may be justifiable. In the latter, assigning any weight to the available value-added measure suggests comfort with treating teachers potentially arbitrarily and capriciously.

Concerns about the reliability and validity of value-added measures for many teachers are leading some states and districts to reduce the role of those measures in teacher evaluation particularly in favor of scores from observations. Widespread use of rigorous rubric-based instruments likely is helping to allay fears that principals' observations are simple checks on a checklist that produce satisfactory scores for everyone. As chapters in this volume underscore, however, use of a rigorous instrument is not sufficient for obtaining valid information from observations. Generic instruments, such as CLASS or FFT, may be limited in the extent to which teachers and principals can address content-specific instruction as part of the evaluation process, which may be particularly important in some subjects. Questions remain about the validity of common observation instruments for measuring teacher performance for some populations, such as special education students. Perhaps more important, observers themselves are substantial sources of error. Rigorous systems for training observers to understand and implement rubric-based observations are absent in many places, as is systematic attention to observer calibration and recalibration to ensure fidelity to the instrument. Failure to adequately train observers, to monitor their implementation of observation protocols, and to periodically calibrate their scores undermines the potential of observation systems to help drive teacher improvement by degrading the quality—and thus the usefulness—of the information collected and by reducing teachers' confidence that their observation scores reflect what they in fact do in the classroom.

Indeed, investing in building and maintaining teacher confidence in the evaluation system is key. Statistical noise in VAM scores, particularly in systems that calculate those scores from just 1 or 2 years of student data, ensures that many teachers will receive scores in consecutive years that will suggest swings in their performance that are inconsistent with the teachers' perceptions of the work they did. A teacher whose scores oscillate from the 75th percentile to the 25th to the 65th over a few years due simply to random variation will soon learn to disregard value-added as disconnected from their actual effort, particularly if—as in many systems—value-added itself is never explained well and districts and principals are not providing consistent messages about how to interpret their results. In a sense, value-added scores' statistical noise is self-undermining with regard to teacher confidence, and this feature, perhaps together with policymakers' tendency to overinterpret the scores as a performance measure, may well help explain their falling favorability ratings. We wish to highlight that working to ensure accuracy, specificity, and integrity in teacher observation ratings, in the feedback provided about them via student surveys, and the like is necessary for ensuring teacher confidence in other sources of information about teacher performance.

Even when multiple measures are of the highest quality, teachers will sometimes perform well on one measure and poorly on another (or well on one part of a given measure, but poorly on another part of the same measure). This situation arises because different measures are designed to capture different aspects of teachers' performance. There are two considerations to note. First, districts need reporting systems in place to help teachers make sense of these seemingly inconsistent messages so that they can be used for improvement (and, as above, so that they do not undermine confidence in the evaluation system). Second, some disagreement among measures should be expected because teacher performance is multidimensional (Grissom et al., this volume). Many policymakers have a sense that different performance measures should be highly correlated with one another, but they need not be. Institutional features in evaluation systems aimed at increasing those correlations, such as some states' policy of holding principals accountable for how close their teacher evaluation scores align with the teachers' value-added, serve to distort the information the evaluation system provides.

We conclude with two additional observations. First, some of the concerns raised throughout this book regarding the reliability and validity of evaluation measures become much less serious when the purpose of teacher evaluation is formative—that is, when evaluation data are conceived of primarily as guideposts for supporting teacher development. Tying evaluations to high-stakes decisions such as compensation and contract renewal brings the reliability and validity of performance measures to the forefront. Given the current state of the properties of many of the measures we have discussed, taking multiple-measures teacher evaluation seriously for all teachers but using it primarily as a vehicle for identifying areas for targeting teacher professional development and other support opportunities is advisable. Second, we argue that it is important to distinguish between the use of teacher education data for human resource decisions and the use of such data for research/diagnosis purposes, especially at the district level. Despite the fact that VAMs, classroom observations, and student surveys face a number of challenges, data from these measures can be useful to districts in making decisions regarding allocation of resources among schools and how to focus on particular needs in individual schools.

REFERENCES

Aaronson, D., Barrow, L., & Sander, W. (2007). Teachers and student achievement in the Chicago public high schools. *Journal of Labor Economics, 25*, 95–135.

Bill and Melinda Gates Foundation. (2010). *Learning about teaching: Initial findings from the Measures of Effective Teaching Project* (MET project research paper). Seattle, WA: Author.

Bill and Melinda Gates Foundation. (2012). *Gathering feedback for teaching: Combining high-quality observations with student surveys and achievement gains* (MET project research paper). Seattle, WA: Author.

Black, P., & Wiliam, D. (1998). Assessment and classroom learning. *Assessment in Education, 5*(1), 7–72.

Brookings Brown Center Task Group on Teacher Quality. (2010). *Evaluating teachers: The important role of value-added.* Washington, DC: The Brookings Institution.

Chetty, R., Friedman, J. N., & Rockoff, J. E. (2014). Measuring the impacts of teachers I: Evaluating bias in teacher value-added estimates. *American Economic Review, 104*(9), 2593–2632.

Corcoran, S. P., & Goldlhaber, D. (2013). Value-added and its uses: Where you stand depends on where you sit. *Education Finance and Policy, 8*(3), 418–434.

Goldhaber, D. (2015). Exploring the potential of value-added performance measures to affect the quality of the teacher workforce. *Educational Researcher, 44*(2), 87–95.

Goldhaber, D., & Chaplin, D. (2015). Assessing the "Rothstein Falsification Test": Does it really show teacher value-added models are biased? *Journal of Research on Educational Effectiveness, 8*(1), 8–34.

Goldhaber, D., & Hansen, M. (2013). Is it just a bad class? Assessing the long-term stability of estimated teacher performance. *Economica, 80*(319), 589–612.

Goldring, E., Grissom, J. A., Rubin, M., Neumerski, C. M., Cannata, M., Drake, T., & Schuermann, P. (2015). Make room value-added: Principals' human capital decisions and the emergence of teacher observation data. *Educational Researcher, 44*(2), 96–104.

Goldring, E., Neumerski, C. M., Cannata, M., Drake, T. A., Grissom, J. A., Rubin, R., & Schuermann, P. (2014). *Principals' use of teacher effectiveness data for talent management decisions.* Retrieved from principaldatause.org/assets/files/reports/Summary-Report-201405.pdf

Grossman, P., Loeb, S., Cohen, J., & Wyckoff, J. (2013). Measure for measure: The relationship between measures of instructional practice in middle school English language arts and teachers' value-added scores. *American Journal of Education, 119*(3), 445–470.

Hattie, J., & Timperley, H. (2007). The power of feedback. *Review of Educational Research, 77*(1), 81–112.

Hill, H. C., Kapitula, L., & Umland, K. (2011). A validity argument approach to evaluating teacher value-added scores. *American Educational Research Journal, 48*(3), 794–831.

Hill, H. C., Rowan, B., & Ball, D. L. (2005). Effects of teachers' mathematical knowledge for teaching on student achievement. *American Educational Research Journal, 42*(2), 371–406.

Ho, A., & Kane, T. (2013). *The reliability of classroom observations by school personnel* (MET project research paper). Seattle, WA: Bill and Melinda Gates Foundation.

Kane, T. J., McCaffrey, D. F., Miller, T., & Staiger, D. O. (2013). *Have we identified effective teachers? Validating measures of effective teaching using random assignment.* Seattle, WA: Bill and Melinda Gates Foundation.

Kennedy, M. (Ed.). (2010). *Teacher assessment and teacher quality: A handbook.* San Francisco, CA: Jossey-Bass.

Mashburn, A. J., Downer, J. T., Rivers, S. E., Brackett, M. A., & Martinez, A. (2014). Improving the power of an efficacy study of a social and emotional learning program: Application of generalizability theory to the measurement of classroom-level outcomes. *Prevention Science, 15*(2), 146–155.

McCaffrey, D. F., Sass, T. R., Lockwood, J. R., & Mihaly, R. (2009). The intertemporal variability of teacher effect estimates. *Education Finance and Policy, 4*(4), 572–606.

Odden, A. R. (2011). *Strategic management of human capital: Improving instructional practice and student learning in schools.* New York, NY: Routledge.

Papay, J. P. (2012). Refocusing the debate: Assessing the purposes and tools of teacher evaluation. *Harvard Educational Review, 82*(1), 123–141.

Pecheone, R. L., Shear, B., Whittaker, A., & Darling-Hammond, L. (2013). *2013 edTPA field test: Summary report.* Stanford, CA: Stanford Center for Assessment, Learning, and Equity.

Polikoff, M. S. (2015). The stability of observational and student survey measures of teaching effectiveness. *American Journal of Education, 121*(2), 183–212.

Rothstein, J. (2010). Teacher quality in educational production: Tracking, decay, and student achievement. *Quarterly Journal of Economics, 125*(1), 175–214.

About the Contributors

Ryan Balch is the CEO of My Student Survey, a company that supports districts and states in the administration and development of student surveys of teacher practice. He completed his PhD at Vanderbilt University, where his dissertation focused on the development and validation of student surveys. Previously, Ryan was the director of teacher, principal, and school evaluation for the Baltimore City Schools from 2012 to 2014. During this time, he oversaw the creation and implementation of the district's new systems of evaluation. Ryan also worked as a science teacher and department chair for 6 years at Riverwood High School in Georgia.

Marisa Cannata is research assistant professor in the Department of Leadership, Policy, and Organizations at Peabody College of Education and Human Development, Vanderbilt University, and director of the National Center on Scaling Up Effective Schools. Her research interests include continuous improvement research, reform implementation and scale, charter schools, and teacher hiring and career decisions.

Casey D. Cobb is associate dean and professor of educational leadership at the Neag School of Education at the University of Connecticut. He is the current editor of *Educational Administration Quarterly* and a member of the executive committee of the University Council for Educational Administration. Dr. Cobb is coauthor of *Fundamentals of Statistical Reasoning in Education* and *Leading Dynamic Schools: How to Create and Implement Ethical Policies*. He is a National Education Policy Center Fellow, and he holds an AB from Harvard University and a PhD from Arizona State University.

Julie Cohen is an assistant professor of curriculum, instruction, and special education at the University of Virginia. She received her doctorate in curriculum and teacher education at Stanford University. Her dissertation research, funded by the National Academy of Education and the Spencer Foundation, focused on features of high-quality teaching across elementary content areas. Her research interests include the conceptualization and measurement of teaching quality, the ways in which accountability systems shape teaching practice, and the development of effective instructional practices in preservice teacher education and professional development. Recent publications have appeared in *Educational Researcher* and the *American Journal of Education.*

Sean P. Corcoran is an associate professor of educational economics at New York University's Steinhardt School of Culture, Education, and Human Development, and an affiliated faculty member of NYU's Institute for Education and Social Policy. Among other things, his research focuses on human capital in the teaching profession, the economics of school choice, and school finance. His published papers have examined long-run trends in teacher quality, the impact of income inequality on the level and equity of education funding in the United States, the properties of teacher value-added measures, and the high school choices of middle school students in New York City.

Morgaen L. Donaldson is an associate professor of educational leadership and director of the Center for Education Policy Analysis at the Neag School of Education, University of Connecticut. She studies policies and practices related to educator quality, educator evaluation, teacher leadership, and teachers' unions and has published on these topics in a range of scholarly and practitioner outlets. She holds an AB from Princeton University and an MA and EdD from the Harvard Graduate School of Education.

Christopher Doss is a graduate student at the Stanford University Graduate School of Education. He is pursuing a doctorate in the economics of education. His research focuses on policies that affect students and teachers in the early childhood level, as well as the K–12 level. Previously, he was a high school physics and chemistry teacher. Christopher holds a master's degree in education from the Harvard Graduate School of Education and a bachelor's degree in chemistry from Brown University.

Timothy A. Drake is a PhD candidate in K–12 education leadership and policy at Vanderbilt University. His research interests include school leadership, data-driven decisionmaking, and teacher evaluation policy. Tim will begin working as an assistant professor of education leadership at North Carolina State University in January 2016.

Dan Goldhaber is the director of the Center for Education Data & Research (CEDR) at the University of Washington Bothell and the director of the Center for Analysis of Longitudinal Data in Education Research (CALDER) at the American Institutes for Research (AIR). His significant research on various aspects of teacher quality, the teacher labor market, education policy, and postsecondary education outcomes has been published in a number of peer-reviewed journals. Dr. Goldhaber serves on several advisory boards and works closely with education stakeholders on the national, state, and district level to help translate research into effective and improved practice.

Ellen Goldring is Patricia and Rodes Hart Chair of Education Policy and Leadership and Chair, Department of Leadership, Policy and Organizations, at Vanderbilt University's Peabody College of Education and Human Development. Her research interests focus on the intersection of education policy and school improvement, with particular emphases on school organization and education leadership.

Jason A. Grissom is associate professor of public policy and education at Vanderbilt University's Peabody College of Education and Human Development. His research focuses primarily on school and district leadership. Recent work examines how school leaders evaluate teachers and use different measures of teacher effectiveness to make talent management decisions in their schools, including how they hire, assign, support, and retain teachers. He also studies school leader evaluation and leadership turnover. His research has been funded by the Institute of Education Sciences, the Bill and Melinda Gates Foundation, and the Wallace Foundation. He holds a master's degree and PhD from Stanford University.

J. Edward Guthrie is a doctoral candidate in K–12 education leadership and policy at the Peabody College of Education and Human Development, Vanderbilt University, and a research assistant with the Education Policy Initiative at Carolina (EPIC). His research interests include teacher quality, value-added modeling, and school turnaround.

Bridget K. Hamre is an associate research professor and associate director of the University of Virginia's Center for Advanced Study of Teaching and Learning (CASTL). Dr. Hamre's areas of expertise include student–teacher relationships and classroom processes that promote positive academic and social development for young children, and she has authored numerous peer-reviewed manuscripts on these topics. This work documents the ways in which early teacher–child relationships and teachers' social and instructional interactions with children support children's development and learning and may help close the achievement gap for students at risk of school failure.

Gary T. Henry holds a Patricia and Rodes Hart Chair and serves as professor of public policy and education at Vanderbilt University. His current research interests are education policy, school reform, evaluation, teacher preparation, and teacher policy.

Carla Howe is a senior advisor at Applied Engineering Management Corporation and provides support for education stakeholders with an emphasis on the effective implementation and use of information and reporting systems for educational decisionmaking. Her work at state education agencies in Michigan and West Virginia spanned a multitude of areas, including educator evaluations, accountability, data governance, and reporting. She earned her PhD in educational evaluation and research from Wayne State University in Detroit, Michigan, with a focus on instrument validity.

Nathan D. Jones is an assistant professor in special education in the School of Education at Boston University, and he previously worked as a research scientist in the Understanding Teaching Quality Center at Educational Testing Service. In his research, Dr. Jones focuses on issues related to teacher quality, namely the development and study of measures of effective teaching practice and the assessment of quality special education instruction. He is currently leading a 4-year Institute of Education Sciences study on special education teacher evaluation and is co-principal investigator on a 3-year W.T. Grant study examining the training of administrators as raters in a consequential teacher evaluation system.

Venessa A. Keesler is deputy superintendent of accountability services at the Michigan Department of Education (MDE). The Accountability Services division includes offices and programs that oversee standards and assessments, teacher certification, business operations, systems integration, public and governmental affairs, strategic research, and accountability. Venessa previously served as director of the Office of Evaluation, Strategic Research, and Accountability at the MDE and as a classroom teacher in Massachusetts, teaching 7th-grade social studies. Venessa holds a bachelor's degree in sociology from Harvard University and a PhD in measurement and quantitative methods from Michigan State University.

Jihyun Kim is a doctoral student in educational policy at Michigan State University. Before joining this program, she worked as a regular homeroom teacher for 5th- and 6th-grade students in an elementary school in Seoul, Korea. She received her bachelor's degree in elementary education and master's degree in elementary school administration from Seoul National University of Education in Korea. Her research interests include teacher quality, teachers' social networks, policy implementation, principals' leadership, and comparative research using qualitative and quantitative research methods.

Susanna Loeb is the Barnett Family Professor of Education at Stanford University, faculty director of the Center for Education Policy Analysis, and a codirector of Policy Analysis for California Education. She specializes in education policy, looking particularly at policies and practices to support teachers and school leaders. Her work spans early education, K–12, and higher education. Loeb holds a doctorate in economics and a master's in public policy from the University of Michigan, and a bachelor's in political science and civil engineering from Stanford University.

R. Brock Mutcheson is a PhD candidate in educational research and evaluation and a graduate research assistant in the Office of Assessment and Evaluation at Virginia Tech. His research interests focus on using quantitative research methods to understand issues related to K–12 educational policy. Currently, Brock is studying the impacts of teacher evaluation policies and investigating the psychometric properties of teacher evaluation instruments. He holds an MA in educational leadership and a BS in education, and he has worked as a public school teacher and administrator.

Christine M. Neumerski is a research associate in the Department of Leadership, Policy and Organizations at Vanderbilt University's Peabody College of Education and Human Development. Her research interests focus on improving instruction in high-poverty urban schools, instructional leadership, and school reform. She holds a PhD from the University of Michigan.

Robert C. Pianta is dean of the Curry School of Education at the University of Virginia and founding director of the Curry School's Center for Advanced Study of Teaching and Learning. Pianta's research interests focus on teacher–student interactions and relationships and on the improvement of teachers' contributions to students' learning and development. Pianta is the creator of an observational assessment of teacher–student interactions known as the Classroom Assessment Scoring System or CLASS, with versions for use with infants through 12th-grade students, all of which have been shown to capture features of teacher–student interactions that contribute to learning and development.

Mollie Rubin is a research associate in the Department of Leadership, Policy and Organizations at Vanderbilt University's Peabody College of Education and Human Development. Her research interests are rooted in sociology and the study of public education, the study of social problems, and inequality. Her work is focused upon school improvement, particularly the role of institutional and organizational contexts in which reform efforts occur. More generally, her research explores how policies aimed at improving teaching, school leadership, and school effectiveness shape the practice, effectiveness, and identity of teachers and school leaders.

Patrick Schuermann is a research assistant professor at Vanderbilt University's Peabody College, where he directs several leadership development projects, including a master's program for independent school leaders. His research interests include education leadership, the intersection of technology and professional development, and the design and delivery of learning resources.

Min Sun is an assistant professor in the College of Education at the University of Washington, Seattle. She specializes in using quantitative methods to understand the impact of federal, state, and district policies on preparing, recruiting, distributing, evaluating, and incentivizing teachers and principals and policy effects on teaching and learning outcomes. She also studies spillover mechanisms and effects among teachers. In addition, her research interests include understanding the impacts of policy interventions in schools and the heterogeneous effects of these interventions across subgroups of schools, teachers, and students.

Andrea Whittaker is director of teacher performance assessment at the Stanford Center for Assessment, Learning, and Equity (SCALE), where she manages design, development, and implementation support for edTPA, a national partnership among 35+ states, the American Association of Colleges of Teacher Education, and Stanford University. For 15 years prior to her Stanford position, Andrea was a professor of education at San José State University, where she served as faculty and department chair for elementary education. Since the early 1990s, she has participated in numerous state, national, and international initiatives related to policy, assessment, and best practices in teaching and learning.

Peter Youngs is an associate professor in the Department of Curriculum, Instruction, and Special Education in the Curry School of Education at the University of Virginia. His research interests focus on education policy effects on teaching and learning in the core academic subjects, including policy related to teacher preparation and professional development and its effects on teachers' instructional practices, commitment to teaching, and retention in the teaching profession. His research has been funded by the Carnegie Corporation of New York, the National Science Foundation, and the William T. Grant Foundation. He holds a master's degree and PhD from the University of Wisconsin.

Index